Communication for Constructive Workplace Conflict

Communication for Constructive Workplace Conflict

Jessica Katz Jameson

WILEY Blackwell

Published by John Wiley & Sons, Inc., Hoboken, New Jersey.
Published simultaneously in Canada.

For general information on our other products and services or for technical support, please
contact our Customer Care Department within the United States at (800) 762-2974, outside the
United States at (317) 572-3993 or fax (317) 572-4002.

Wiley also publishes its books in a variety of electronic formats. Some content that appears in
print may not be available in electronic formats. For more information about Wiley products,
visit our web site at www.wiley.com.

Library of Congress Cataloging-in-Publication Data:

Name: Jameson, Jessica Katz, author.
Title: Communication for constructive workplace conflict / Jessica Katz
   Jameson.
Description: First Edition. | Hoboken : Wiley, [2023] | Includes index.
Identifiers: LCCN 2023002883 (print) | LCCN 2023002884 (ebook) | ISBN
   9781119671565 (paperback) | ISBN 9781119671695 (adobe pdf) | ISBN
   9781119671657 (epub)
Subjects: LCSH: Conflict management. | Interpersonal conflict–Prevention.
   | Communication in organizations. | Organizational behavior.
Classification: LCC HM1126 .J356 2023 (print) | LCC HM1126 (ebook) | DDC
   303.6/9–dc23/eng/20230126
LC record available at https://lccn.loc.gov/2023002883
LC ebook record available at https://lccn.loc.gov/2023002884

Cover Design: Wiley
Cover Images: © Robert Wilson/Fotolia; skynesher/Getty Images

Set in 9.5/12.5pt STIXTwoText by Straive, Pondicherry, India
Printed and bound by CPI Group (UK) Ltd, Croydon, CR0 4YY

C005083_130423

Contents

List of Boxes

List of Tables

List of Figures

Preface

Conflict is everywhere, all the time. This statement is obvious, but people may not fully appreciate the point. When someone says, "I don't want to cause conflict," what they really mean is that they do not wish to bring the conflict out in the open. The conflict, or the state of incompatible beliefs or goals, is already there. But the word "conflict" is associated with fighting, war, death, destruction, loss, and overall discomfort. As a result, people often choose not to directly engage in conflict and, ironically, increase their level of discomfort by prolonging and escalating the situation. People ruminate about it in the shower or when trying to sleep. They talk to family, friends, and coworkers. They blog about it or share their stories on social media sites looking for others who will validate their complaints, concerns, or feelings. What people don't realize when they say, "I don't want to cause conflict," is that they are denying both themselves and others the possibility of solving a problem, transforming an uncomfortable situation, and/or improving a relationship.

On the other hand, people do routinely communicate their needs and collaboratively generate solutions. But when the interaction goes smoothly, it is not characterized as conflict. As a result, people may not realize that the same communication tools used in those situations can be applied to moments in which they are confronted by seemingly incompatible goals. The purpose of this book is to broaden the conversation about conflict to consider how people can overcome the sense of fear and futility it engenders. People, whether in leadership positions or line staff employees, can communicate in ways that help build workplace conflict environments that are supportive of constructive conflict, that is, environments that are inviting and productive rather than adversarial and uncomfortable.

This book is the product of over 20 years of research on conflict management in organizational settings. Over the years I have conducted research using a variety of methodological approaches, sometimes working with undergraduate and graduate students in controlled environments, but more often in the field, where

I have interviewed employees and observed communication in corporate jobs, healthcare organizations, nonprofit organizations, and state and county government. Most of my research has been applied, resulting in insights and implications from and for the various audiences I have worked with. Yet even though the types of people, professions, and organizations I have worked with are diverse in every meaning of the word (i.e., age, ability, sex, education, ethnicity, race, religion, social class, profession, rank, sexual orientation), some aspects of conflict and its management are remarkably consistent, and these have become the themes of this book. Over the years, I have taught numerous courses in conflict management, given many conference presentations, facilitated organizational retreats, conducted conflict management workshops, and served as a mediator for our university and state employee mediation program. These experiences have provided additional insights while serving to confirm the interactional patterns, dynamics, and conclusions found in more formal research studies.

Many books offer prescriptive conflict management advice for organizational leaders and members. My work with people in different organizational environments has revealed the many obstacles to putting those ideas into practice. When confronted with conflict in the workplace, many employees become paralyzed by what seems like a no-win situation. Fear of the hierarchy, perceptions of powerlessness, and organizational politics prevent people from speaking up, sometimes with severe consequences. Financial scandals destroy organizations and economies, planes crash, patients die, governments shut down. Yes, these are the most extreme cases; yet on the more modest side, failure to proactively engage in conflict results in tense workplace climates, relational deterioration, fatigue, absenteeism, and low morale. These environments have very real economic and health costs for organizations and their employees.

This book will not argue that every instance of conflict should be directly confronted; the old adage to "choose your battles" still applies. However, this book *will* demonstrate that the consequences of not taking on conflict directly can be serious for individuals, groups, and organizations. More importantly, I will illustrate that conflicts do not have to be "battles," and, in fact, it is the prominence of this metaphor that is one of the biggest barriers to effectively managing conflict. Although other books provide examples of effective conflict management, often with the help of third-party intervention, those books do not convey how conflict participants overcome the obstacles to engaging conflict in the first place. Identifying strategies to overcome those obstacles is a gap this book seeks to fill. *Communication for Constructive Workplace Conflict* starts from the perspective that organizational members socially construct an environment that is either more supportive of conflict or, alternatively, discourages organizational members from engaging in conflict and seeking third-party assistance. The introductory chapter will provide the theoretical framework for the book, outlining social construction theory broadly and then more specifically describing the communication as constitutive of organization (CCO) theoretical perspective (Brummans, 2013). The book then provides a specific framework for communication to illustrate how everyday communication can create a workplace environment that is supportive of constructive organizational conflict management.

The acronym LEARN stands for Listen, Engage, Acknowledge, Rapport (building), and Nurture (see Figure P.1). Listening may sound obvious, but it may be the hardest part of communication, especially in conflict situations. When people have a need, and they believe they know the best way to meet that need, they often find it difficult to really listen to other perspectives or alternatives. As I write this book, we are in the midst of the COVID-19 pandemic. While this is not a workplace conflict, per se, it has certainly created a public conversation about how best

Figure P.1 LEARN framework for creating a constructive communication environment.

to meet what appear to be competing needs of public health and economic sustainability. The discussion of when and how to re-open businesses, schools, and public spaces is critically important, and, as we have seen, private citizens and public figures do not always seem open to listening to other perspectives and views, which escalates the conflict and complicates the decision-making and public policy process. As a mediator, I have seen firsthand how conflicts that started out adversarial and seemingly intractable, or highly resistant to resolution, turn into collaborative conversations once parties actually listen to the other person's underlying concerns and interests and better understand the other's perspective. When an environment is created that supports listening, it opens the door for creative brainstorming and problem solving that can lead to solutions that meet all parties' needs. This is certainly not a new idea, but common interpersonal and social conflicts demonstrate the challenges of listening. Unit One of this text addresses listening in detail, focusing first on the obstacles to listening (Chapter 2) and then presenting practical tools for practicing active and non-evaluative listening that can help individuals gain clarity on their own interests as well as better understanding the interests of others (Chapter 3). The remainder of the LEARN framework is best summarized with an anecdote from a nontraditional work setting: a Hollywood film set (described in Box P.1).

Box P.1 Earning Public Support

An assistant director (AD) was on a television set in downtown Los Angeles. They were shooting a scene for the television series "The Mentalist"[1] along the busy Hollywood Boulevard, which they were unable to shut down in the middle of the day. It is the AD's responsibility to make sure the conditions are exactly the way the director wants the scene to look, which in this case meant keeping the large crowd of tourists (interspersed with paid extras) under control. The AD started by introducing himself, "Hey guys, my name is Larry Katz, and I'm the assistant director for the TV show we are filming. We are going to be shooting in a minute, and I'm happy to have you stay here and even be in the scene, but we need everyone to be quiet to make this work, okay?" Once he had the crowd's attention he spoke to a few people individually while the camera and other crew were setting up the scene. "So where are you from? ... Detroit? ... Cool, how long have you been in LA?" When the

---

[1] For readers who may be interested, the actual scene shot was from Season One, Episode 19, "A Dozen Red Roses," (2009). https://www.metacritic.com/tv/the-mentalist/season-1/episode-19-a-dozen-red-roses.

director was ready, Larry returned to speaking to the whole group to regain their attention. "Okay, I need everyone to be quiet now . . ." Not only was the crowd quiet when he needed them to be quiet, tourists were helping him out by telling newcomers on the scene what was going on and when they needed to be quiet.

This brief anecdote is useful because it vividly demonstrates the process of proactively preparing for conflict and constructive conflict management. Larry accomplished several goals in the way he approached the situation:

1) He *engaged* the group whose help he needed immediately by directly speaking to the group of tourists, introducing himself and establishing his credibility as assistant director.
2) He *acknowledged* their interest in seeing a television show in production, and possibly being in the show, while also stating his own interest in completing the scene.
3) He built *rapport* with the group by offering an explanation about what was happening and why quiet was needed; this communication treated others as equals.
4) He *nurtured* the relationship by asking questions to maintain a level of engagement with individual members of the group, even at times when he did not immediately need something from the group.

In short, Larry communicated in ways that earned the respect of those whose cooperation he needed. In a nice coincidence, the four points above spell EARN, which, when combined with Listening, complete the LEARN acronym. It is also interesting to note that, unlike many workplace conflicts, there was no long-term relationship between Larry and this group of tourists, and some might argue he did not need to go to all the trouble of using such a constructive approach. Yet this communication acknowledged that a state of conflict existed: Larry and the tourists had potentially incompatible needs for the use of that space on Hollywood Boulevard. Through engaging the crowd, acknowledging his own needs as well as theirs, building rapport, and nurturing relationships, he generated goodwill from the crowd (as shown by the way they helped him do his job). As a bonus, he likely created goodwill toward the television show. I would be willing to bet that a large percentage of those tourists went home and told all their friends they might appear in a scene, and probably could not wait to get all their friends together to watch *The Mentalist*. While most people may not get to work under such "exotic" circumstances, this story is a great reminder of the role that people play as emissaries for their organizations and even industries. The extra effort Larry put in on the front end likely gained dividends on the back end for him and for his organization.

Unit Two of this text addresses the *engage* part of the LEARN framework. Many years of research on conflict styles have demonstrated two overarching dimensions to how people respond to conflict: they may actively engage using styles such as competing or collaborating, or they may use more disengaged and passive styles of avoiding or accommodating (Thomas & Kilmann, 1974; Putnam & Wilson, 1982; Rahim, 1983, 2011). Chapter 4 reviews common conflict styles models, while also describing the tendency to be more passive in the workplace due to power discrepancies, whether due to hierarchical role, one's interpersonal networks, or membership in privileged versus marginalized identity groups. While it is acknowledged that conflict styles have their basis in cultural norms (Oetzel & Ting-Toomey, 2003) and avoidance is sometimes the best strategy, studies of intercultural and inter-group conflict are included to provide implications for constructive conflict management that are sensitive to cultural differences. Chapter 5 continues to focus on the *engage* aspect of the framework by focusing on the importance of employee voice. The concept of organizational dissent is defined as communication that occurs when an organizational member disagrees with an action, activity, or policy of an organization or organizational leader (Kassing, 2011). This chapter illustrates the potential benefits of organizational dissent and communication strategies that help overcome the fear of speaking up in situations where power is a key concern.

Unit Three offers the recommendation to *acknowledge* others in conflict. An underlying source of conflict is often rooted in a lack of recognition of others, and, sadly, this is often connected to implicit bias and assumptions about what others are able to contribute based on characteristics such as ability, sex, class, race, and other demographic or social identity characteristics. Chapter 6 presents theories of identity in conflict transformation along with research demonstrating how face-saving communication supports collaborative conflict management. A case study of doctor and nurse conflict illustrates how power and identity are often underlying sources of conflict and provides specific examples of how acknowledging another's position, expertise, and/or needs during a conflict produces more productive communication that protects and sustains working relationships. Chapter 7 brings focus to the importance of acknowledging individual contributions in group and team settings. Acknowledgment is especially important as research supports the ease with which minority voices often go unrecognized or silenced in team communication. This chapter draws from a case study of nonprofit board meetings to illustrate how the lack of acknowledgment is an impediment to deliberation and problem solving and, conversely, how confirming communication and acknowledgment help lead groups to constructive conflict management and productive decision making.

Unit Four covers the way that building *rapport* with others makes it easier to address conflict directly when it arises. Chapter 8 specifically attends to building relationships and trust, including how we express emotion (Gayle & Preiss, 1998), provide social support (Boren, 2014), and incorporate relational needs into conflict management. This chapter demonstrates the long-term benefits of building rapport that establishes trust and either prevents future conflict or facilitates constructive conflict management. Chapter 9 focuses on rapport in terms of the importance of accepting one's own responsibility and role in conflict situations, which has been found in countless studies to be a major factor in moving conflict from adversarial to collaborative. This chapter also reviews the concepts of attribution error and implicit bias as obstacles to taking responsibility. Finally, the chapter describes implications of research on organizational apology (Bisel & Messersmith, 2012), forgiveness, and restorative justice (i.e., Paul & Putnam, 2017; Paul & Riforgiate, 2015), all of which emphasize nonjudgment, growth, and transformation.

Unit Five addresses the final part of the LEARN framework, *nurturing* relationships. Like building rapport, this is a long-term communication strategy that emphasizes a network perspective, reminding us of the importance of connections we have to others, both inside and external to our specific workplace. COVID-19, which has physically separated us and reduced the routine interactions of bumping into colleagues in the hallway, at the coffee station, or at the water cooler, has forced us to be more intentional in activating our networks to get our jobs done (or, for many people who are unable to work, to get basic needs met). It is much easier to call on someone for assistance when we already have a strong relationship in place. The same is true when conflict erupts: we will find it easier to directly and constructively address the problem if we have a good relationship with the other party. Chapter 10 emphasizes the organization's role in nurturing relationships by designing conflict management systems that adopt an interest-based orientation to conflict management (Ury, Brett, & Goldberg, 1988). Focusing on the interests of organizational members rather than who has the power in a relationship, for example, is more likely to foster goodwill and prosocial communication (that is, communication for the good of the group) that leads to constructive conversations. Chapter 11 specifically examines the role of online dispute resolution, virtual communication tools, and social media in conflict and collaboration. Managing conflict online has become more and more relevant as workplaces are more likely to be global and increasingly reliant on remote work. While social media use can have a negative effect on conflict by separating and polarizing those with disparate views (often referred to as filter bubbles or echo chambers), this chapter includes specific examples of organizations that are using social media and other forms of virtual communication to promote dialogue and participatory environments.

Chapter 12 concludes the book by synthesizing the preceding chapters to reinforce the LEARN framework in the context of developing communication networks that promote collaboration and productive conflict management. This chapter demonstrates the value of creating and supporting an organizational infrastructure that connects internal organizational members and external constituents. In so doing, the LEARN framework becomes a way of being that creates expectations for communication and interaction that build a constructive environment.

References

Bisel, R. S., & Messersmith, A. L. (2012). Organizational and supervisory apology effectiveness: Apology giving in work settings. *Business Communication Quarterly*, *75*(4): 425–448.

Boren, J. P. (2014). The relationships between co-rumination, social support, stress, and burnout among working adults. *Management Communication Quarterly*, *28*(3): 3–25. https://doi.org/10.1177/0893318913509283.

Brummans, B. H. J. M. (2013). What is an organization? Or: is James Taylor a Buddhist? In D. Robichaud & F. Cooren (Eds.), *Materiality, agency, and discourse* (pp. 66–89). New York: Routledge.

Gayle, B. M., & Preiss, R. W. (1998). Assessing emotionality in organizational conflicts. *Management Communication Quarterly*, *12*, 280–302.

Kassing, J. W. (2011). *Dissent in organizations*. Malden, MA: Polity Press.

Oetzel, J. G., & Ting-Toomey, S. (2003). Face concerns in interpersonal conflict: A cross-cultural empirical test of the face negotiation theory. *Communication Research*, *30*(6), 599–624. http://dx.doi.org/10.1177/0093650203257841.

Paul, G. D., & Putnam, L. L. (2017). Moral foundations of forgiving in the workplace. *Western Journal of Communication*, *81*(1): 43–63. https://doi.org/10.1080/10570314.2016.1229499.

Paul, G. D., & Riforgiate, S. E. (2015). "Putting on a happy face," "getting back to work," and "letting it go": Traditional and restorative justice understandings of emotions at work. *Electronic Journal of Communication*, *25*: 1–2.

Putnam, L. L., & Wilson, C. E. (1982). Communicative strategies in organizational conflicts: Reliability and validity of a measurement scale. *Annals of the International Communication Association*, *6*(1): 629–652. https://doi.org/10.1080/23808985.1982.11678515.

Rahim, M. A. (1983). A measure of styles of handling interpersonal conflict. *Academy of Management Journal*, *26*: 368–376.

Rahim, M. A. (2011). *Managing conflict in organizations* (4th ed.). Westport, CT: Quorum Books.

Thomas, K. W., & Kilmann, R. H. (1974). *Thomas–Kilmann Conflict Mode Instrument*. Tuxedo, NY: Xicom.

Ury, W. L., Brett, J. M., & Goldberg, S. B. (1988). *Getting disputes resolved*. San Francisco, CA: Jossey-Bass.

Acknowledgments

When the timeline for a project like this spans eight years, there are a lot of people who must be acknowledged. I'm going to go in chronological order in an effort not to miss anyone. I want to thank Dr. Ken Zagacki, mentor, colleague, and friend, who was also my Department Head and inspired me to document my research on conflict management in a book. In those early days Dr. Matt Cronin introduced me to a publishing contact who provided helpful feedback and advice and procured a first round of reviewers whose insights were critical to the book that evolved. Several former grad students, some of whom now bear the PhD title (or are on their way) helped with various stages of this project; these include Dr. Eli Typhina, Dr. Chris Kampe, Dr. Byungsoo Kim, and my "dream team": Dustin Harris, Chandler Marr, and Nolan Speicher, who gave me the support needed to keep the project alive when I became Department Head in Fall 2019. I also need to thank the many, many undergraduate and graduate students who have taken my courses in conflict management over the years, and a recent group that read early chapters and provided feedback. A special shout-out to Kayla Pack Watson for teaching me an important lesson that made its way into the book and to Gracie Gray for making an extra effort to give me feedback. My colleagues have been patient when I disappeared for brief periods of time to get some writing done and many have also listened to me when I needed an ear. Sometimes my colleagues have even given me the opportunity to practice my conflict management skills (smile). I'm also grateful to Sheri Schwab, our current Vice Provost for Institutional Equity and Diversity (OIED) at NC State. Early in my career she suggested I participate in mediation training and join a new group of mediators to help with faculty and staff conflict. This experience enabled me to learn how to be a mediator and provided the inspiration for several of the cases described in this book. I'm also grateful to several current and past members of the OIED who have taught me a lot about microaggressions and creating inclusive environments, including Melvin (Jai) Jackson, Stephanie Helms Pickett, Melissa Edwards Smith, and Adrienne Davis. Most of my family members have provided instrumental or social support for this project. My brother, Larry Katz, is a prominent part of the development of the LEARN framework, and I would never have known his story if our mother, Adrienne Katz, was not bragging on him (as mothers do). My father, Bill Katz, has also been my #1 fan and cheerleader, and inspired my interest in mediation and negotiation with stories from his years as an employee relations director. I am very grateful to my mother and NC State colleague, professor emerita Dr. Susan Katz for her willingness to read the book and use her technical writing skills in the service of copyeditor. My son, Peyton, husband, Brian Jameson, and mother-in-law, Terry Jameson, sacrificed spending time with me, listened to me worry about whether I would ever get the project completed, and provided the love and support needed to nurture a creative, productive home environment. A final big thank you to the entire team at Wiley for their patience, time, and encouragement.

1

Theoretical Framework – The Social Construction of Conflict

We now accept the fact that learning is a lifelong process of keeping abreast of change. And the most pressing task is to teach people how to learn.

Peter Drucker (1909–2005, management and leadership author)

It is fitting that the acronym for the communication for constructive workplace conflict framework is LEARN. It is often in those conflicts in which parties are open to learning something new, for example about another person's life experience, background, or values, that conflict is managed in the most collaborative and constructive manner. This is at least partially because every time someone learns something new – about another person or social identity group, experiences they have never had, or other worldviews – this new information has the potential to become part of how they see, understand, and talk about the world in which we live. This is a simplified version of a theoretical framework called the social construction of reality (Berger & Luckman, 1966; Searle, 1995).

This book is based on the assumptions of the social construction of reality: that it is through interaction and communication with others that humans build a set of norms, expectations, and understandings that then guide continued behavior and worldviews. Importantly, while this worldview and the rules that guide our behavior are somewhat stable, they also can (and in most cases do) change over time. Examples include change in what is considered "professional" attire in the workplace (what used to be suits and ties for men and dresses or skirts for women is, at least in the United States, no longer the norm). Expectations about where work is performed have also changed. We used to assume that workplace communication consisted of face-to-face interaction that took place among people co-located in the same physical space; yet given trends such as globalization, use of contractors, and telework, what we think of as organizational communication looks much different today.

Communication for Constructive Workplace Conflict, First Edition. Jessica Katz Jameson.
© 2023 John Wiley & Sons, Inc. Published 2023 by John Wiley & Sons, Inc.

In this introductory chapter, I discuss how the social construction of reality underlies organizational communication in general and how we talk about and manage conflict specifically. I begin by describing the organizational communication perspective of *communication as constitutive of organization* (Ashcraft, Kuhn, & Cooren, 2009; Kuhn, 2012) and then draw from political science theory to demonstrate the role of conflict processes in changing organizational and societal expectations using the *social conflict helix* (Rummel, 1976). Looking at social conflict is relevant to a book on workplace conflict because it brings to the forefront the role of power – who is perceived to have more, and who is perceived to have less – which creates underlying assumptions and implicit biases that must be identified and understood to make any progress toward constructive conflict management. Before delving into the theoretical framework, this chapter begins with a set of definitions of the key terms to be used throughout this textbook.

Defining Conflict and Constructive Conflict Management

The meaning of the word *conflict* is broad and thus ambiguous and open to interpretation. When I use the term *conflict*, I am referring to the variety of situations in which one or more interdependent parties perceive incompatible goals or perceive that another party is trying to obstruct their goal achievement (Wilmot & Hocker, 2010). The term *goals* refers to both tangible goals, such as task completion, and implicit goals, such as how we present ourselves to others (identity goals) and how we negotiate our roles in different relationships (relational goals). As others have noted, conflict is by definition an emotional process (Jones, 2000) and, since expressing negative emotion can have negative consequences in the workplace, conflict often remains hidden from those who are in a position to do something to manage it (Kolb & Bartunek, 1992). For example, if an employee believes they are being overlooked for a promotion, they might experience anger. Rather than directing anger toward a supervisor, the employee may decide they cannot afford to lose their job or harm the relationship. Yet if the conflict remains hidden, nothing can be done to address the employee's concerns. Over time, this employee is likely to feel increased frustration which may result in poor performance as well as a variety of negative personal outcomes such as stress, burnout, and poor health. These outcomes are bad for the employee and the organization, which is why all organizational members should be motivated to build environments for constructive conflict management in the workplace.

The term *conflict management* is also a conscious choice over the term *conflict resolution*. The latter is an artifact of the dominant *rights-based* approach to conflict, which presumes that there is an objective solution to a conflict based on some rule or standard that will indicate who is right or wrong. My research, and that of many others, reveals that rights-based processes may resolve a specific issue in contention but do not resolve the entire conflict. Furthermore, there are many conflicts that do not have a right or wrong answer, and thus rights-based approaches fail to bring parties to a resolution. The term conflict management thus reflects the reality that underlying conflicts, especially those based on different assumptions, values, and worldviews, must continue to be managed. I also rely heavily on the term conflict transformation. *Conflict transformation* suggests a situation in which underlying *interests* (including task, identity, and relational goals) have been addressed, greater understanding has occurred, and the situation is changed to one in which the conflict no longer exists (or at least is deemed less important than the relationship). When conflict is authentically engaged with an emphasis on interests and when parties are open to learning, transformation is much more likely than in situations where conflict is avoided and remains hidden or in which one party uses rights or power to force a certain outcome. Transformation is often discussed in this book as the ultimate goal of constructive conflict management, although it is not always possible, practical, or achievable.

My definition of *workplace* comes from my identity as a scholar of organizational communication, a sub-discipline of the field of communication. *Organization* is difficult to define clearly because it can denote both the *process* of organizing to achieve a common goal and the *entity* that is created through the process of organizing (Nicotera, 2020). If we focus on the organization as entity, an organization might include a social club, advocacy group, or little league sports team. The contexts I have studied have primarily been places where people organize for work, such as businesses, universities, hospitals, or nonprofit organizations, and therefore this book focuses on the workplace as a sub-category of organizations.

Organizational communication is often defined as the interaction of interdependent parties to achieve a common goal. As many scholars have noted, the very essence of organizing is rife with tension, as organizational members have individual as well as common goals, and those goals are often in conflict (Mumby, 2013). When one considers the definition of conflict provided above – a situation in which one or more interdependent parties perceive incompatible goals or perceive that another party is trying to obstruct their goal achievement – it may appear obvious that organizations are, by their very nature, places where conflict is omnipresent.

This book therefore examines workplace conflict at all levels of the organization. *Dyadic conflict* occurs between two people, such as coworkers or between a supervisor and their direct report. *Group conflict* often occurs within a unit or a work team. *Inter-group conflict* may occur between two units or teams, but inter-group conflict might also describe contract disputes between workers and management, or conflict that occurs between members of different demographically based identity groups, whether stemming from differences in age, race, ethnicity, ability, or sexual orientation. Throughout this book there will be discussions of workplace diversity and multiple ways scholars have written about it, including intercultural conflict (such as Oetzel & Ting-Toomey, 2003), social identity conflict (such as Tajfel, 1982), and the effect of diversity on workplace conflict (see Ayub & Jehn, 2014). The highest level of conflict takes place at the *organizational level* when organizations or industries are in conflict, such as conflict between hospitals and insurance companies or manufacturing companies and conservationists. While I firmly believe that the insights of the LEARN framework can be applied to other contexts (i.e., intimate relationships, family conflict, nation-states), I cannot make direct claims or provide cases that illustrate these contexts since my research has been limited to the workplace.

Finally, it is necessary to define the various parties that may be involved in workplace conflict. I often refer to conflict participants as *parties*. In describing conflicts that involve a *third party* – an individual who becomes involved to help manage or transform the conflict, I will often use the term *disputant* to distinguish the parties in conflict from the third party. In some workplace conflicts, one party has raised the conflict or even filed a formal grievance against another party. In such cases I will refer to that party as a *grievant* and refer to those they are in conflict with as the *respondent(s)*. While this language has a more rights-based or legal orientation, it is a good example of how the language we use to describe phenomena such as conflict limits how we understand and experience it. The way that organizations talk about conflict is directly related to whether organizational members perceive they can directly address it. For example, in an organization where coworkers repeatedly tell others not to "rock the boat," a message is sent that raising conflict will lead to trouble, and an environment of conflict avoidance is likely to be created. The case in Box 1.1 summarizes a study of newspaper coverage of a city-wide conflict to demonstrate the language that city officials and journalists use to describe conflict and how it is managed. While it may be argued that this is not a workplace conflict, this case illustrates how media reporting influences the social construction of reality and how many people understand conflict and the options available for its management.

Box 1.1 The Social Construction of Conflict in City Government

Following the terrorist attacks of September 11, 2001, New York City faced the worst budget crisis in its history. Questions about how city officials would balance public needs for education, transportation, and critical social services (e.g., police, fire, and waste disposal) dominated the news. Unlike news coverage of international or national policy that may be perceived as having limited impact on the lives of ordinary citizens, these stories had direct consequences for citizens of New York City and the surrounding areas. Public policy decisions, such as city budgets, must be responsive to multiple stakeholders and thus create situations that are inherently conflictual. This provided an appropriate subject for an investigation of how newspaper journalists report on the process of conflict management, such as who participates, what communication venues are used, and how various interests are represented. This study brought conflict theory into conversation with theories of media and democracy to examine the role of journalism in the social construction of conflict.

In our analysis of newspaper coverage of this conflict (Jameson & Entman, 2004), Robert Entman and I examined whether attention was given to interests-, rights-, and power-based orientations to conflict (Ury, Brett, & Goldberg, 1988). Historically, organizations have been most likely to operate from rights- and power-based orientations. A rights-based orientation frames conflict as a dispute to be won or lost by the party with the better case or argument, consistent with a legal view of conflict. A power-based orientation is also adversarial, suggesting that conflicts are won or lost according to who has more power resources, rather than the better argument. An interest-based orientation offers a more collaborative response to conflict by examining the deeper needs or concerns underlying conflict issues and exploring creative ways to dovetail interests to the satisfaction of all parties. Importantly, interests are different from positions, which are one's stated desire or preferred outcome of a conflict (Fisher, Ury, & Patton, 1991). By clarifying the participants' interests instead of concentrating on the positions they take, interest-based techniques can transform disputes, yielding outcomes satisfactory to all and establishing trust that can enhance future interactions and negotiations.

Our thesis was that news coverage would be more likely to focus on a limited number of participants (primarily politicians and policy decision-makers) and emphasize positions over interests. This was based on journalistic norms that frame stories in terms of key players and polarized positions. Such framing supports the social construction of conflict as adversarial and further reinforces the belief that participation is futile because only those with power can impact conflict outcomes. Reporting only the positions of politicians and key figures actually distances the issues from the public, whereas coverage of diverse citizens and their interests might enable readers to see the direct impact of the crisis on their lives and conclude that their participation matters.

We examined coverage of the budget crisis from January 1, 2002, to January 15, 2003, in the city's four leading newspapers of general circulation, *New York Daily News*, *New York Post*, *New York Times*, and *Newsday*. The analysis served two purposes: to explore the metaphors used in news of conflict over the budget, and to assess the extent to which interest-based methods (as opposed to rights- or power-based methods) are embedded in news stories. We found the most common conflict metaphor used across the four papers included *war* or *fight* language in describing the budget conflicts. This was found 61 times, more than twice that of any other conflict metaphor and almost as many as all others combined. Examples of this metaphor include references to the "budget battle," found in all four papers, "going to war with Albany" (*Post*), a proposal being "dead on arrival" (*Daily News*), "wrangling over budget cuts" (*NY Times*), and "taking a whack" at the car lobby (*Newsday*).

A second metaphor across the board was conflict as a game. The most common reference described that a proposal was either on or off "the table," with the *Times* using this metaphor 10 times in our sample. The *Post* referred to having "cards to play," and "playing the Albany game." The *Daily News* said that City Hall "couldn't play this one any closer to the vest," while *Newsday* quoted the Mayor as saying the city council may want to "play hardball." The game metaphor, while more neutral than the war metaphor, still suggests that conflict consists of adversarial teams and that there will be winners and losers. While in politics this is often true, the language obscures the possibility of constructive conflict management. Other metaphors found in all four papers, although less often, included conflict as something broken that needed to be fixed ("fiscal mess," "hammer out" an agreement) or conflict as a legal case. The legal metaphor reinforces the idea that conflict is adversarial and the goal is to present a winning argument.

The majority of references to conflict management strategies were power-based. This is consistent with our expectation in a society where the dominant conflict metaphor is war and where journalistic norms emphasize the adversarial nature of conflict. Conflict management described as a matter of politics is expected, but what is noteworthy is the lack of reference to opportunities citizens may have had to participate in the political decision-making process. In fact, in the sample of stories we analyzed, only one paper described

Bloomberg's attempts at "open government." *Newsday* ran a transcript of Mayor Bloomberg's State of the City Address in which he described the open office he created in City Hall:

> In the bullpen [note use of the sports metaphor], there are no walls, no barriers to communication … anyone can get up and talk to anyone at any time, and that includes me. We are already extending this emphasis on communication and teamwork to other levels of government. (Janison, 2002)

If this case study is typical, media reporting of conflict undermines the public's ability to imagine more collaborative options for conflict management, not only in politics but perhaps also in other spheres of society. It reinforces the sense that public participation is not worth the effort because individuals cannot make a difference anyway. This further promotes a view of conflict as adversarial, combative, and futile, and impedes the ability to envision constructive ways of managing conflict.

The media analysis included one more finding especially germane to this point, and that is the relative paucity of media coverage of impacts of the budget conflict on everyday citizens. When journalists cover positions, they explain what each party wants: the mayor favors increased property taxes or the police chief argues to cut education spending (for example). But this does not get at the underlying interests. Reporting the interests would tell readers why people support their positions, such as increasing taxes in order to pay for public transportation or decreasing education spending to increase public safety. This is the information an individual needs in order to arrive at an informed position on the policy him- or herself and to understand the reasons why others might oppose that position. By elucidating the interests that lay beneath positions, media coverage could provide clarity on the issues and encourage participation in a public dialogue that leaves more people feeling satisfaction rather than alienation.

Yet our content analysis revealed that the four papers offered 389 statements of policy stands as opposed to 103 mentions of impacts. In other words, *positions* were discussed nearly four times as often as *interests*. The impacts receiving the most attention included the lessening of educational quality, negative consequences for the New York City economy, and difficulties for poor people resulting from the budget cuts. Given that the sample here consisted of 140 newspaper stories, the average story offered less than one mention of an impact (103 impacts/140 stories = 0.74 impacts per story), compared with about 2.5 positions per story. Thus, most stories barely mentioned interests, while providing considerably more attention to policy positions. This study suggests that the dominant media approach to describing the processes of democratic politics focuses on the game – who's ahead, who's behind, what strategies and maneuvers each side is trying. Moreover, as Cappella and Jamieson (1997) suggest, a self-perpetuating spiral of cynicism operates when this conflict script dominates the news. It is no wonder that surveys of citizen attitudes show large majorities distrust government and politicians and, by extension, are skeptical about the possibilities of managing society's conflicts in ways that are fair and effective (cf. Ansolabehere & Iyengar 1995; Patterson 1993). It is no surprise that many Americans internalize this attitude and conclude that engaging in conflict, whether in politics or in the workplace, is a no-win situation.

For Reflection and Discussion:

1) How does the way we read about conflict influence our perceptions of conflict, how we feel about the prospect of conflict, and how we respond to conflict?
2) Describe other ways that we see conflict in the media, whether in the news or in fictional representations such as television dramas and movies. How does this influence how we feel about conflict and how it is or can be managed?

Source: Jameson, J. K., & Entman, R. M. (2004) / SAGE Publications.

The Social Construction of Organization

The communication as constitutive of organization (CCO) perspective has been well articulated by others such as Ashcraft, Kuhn, and Cooren (2009), Kuhn (2012), and Putnam and Nicotera (2009). Since the organization provides the focal context for this book's treatment of conflict and its management, a brief overview of the assumptions of the CCO approach is informative. CCO transcends the question of whether organizational structure influences behavior or behavior influences structure by proposing that the organization does not exist without communication. In other words, organizational members create rules and processes through communication, and those rules and processes enable and constrain certain behaviors. As organizational members follow the rules or appropriate them in ways that work best for them, structures are simultaneously reinforced and subtly changed (McPhee, Poole, & Iverson, 2014). While CCO downplays the fact that organizations have seemingly concrete structures such as departments, it emphasizes that all formalized policies, rules, and organizational charts are constructed through the interaction and decision making of individuals. In everyday communication, these various policies and rules only have influence to the extent that they are invoked in a given interaction. Most employees have experienced moments in which such documents are distorted, obscured, or ignored in pursuit of individual interests. Organizational members continually negotiate the behaviors that are considered acceptable through ongoing interaction, socialization, and institutionalization (Ashforth & Anand, 2003). These norms, enacted alongside the rules, constitute the organization and its culture, which then enables and constrains future interaction. It is through this ongoing process of communication that organizational members reinforce, resist, enact, and transform the organization.

Included in the constitution, or construction, of organization are norms for the interpretation of conflict when it arises and the options organizational members perceive to be available for managing it. Importantly, there are typically differences in the formal structures of organizational conflict management made available (such as grievance procedures) and employee perceptions of what is safe and, therefore, a realistic course of action (Jameson, 2001). This finding is consistent with Kirby and Krone's (2002) research on work–life policy, which concluded that employee interactions – what coworkers tell each other about the policy – had greater influence on action than the formal organizational documents. There is also a significant literature on dispute system design (Lipsky, Seeber, & Fincher, 2003; Ury, Brett, & Goldberg, 1988) that offers advice for developing grievance procedures that provide due process: the belief that the organization will treat individual employees in a fair and impartial manner should they perceive unjust behavior from another organizational member (this will be discussed in more detail in Chapter 10). Yet, as employees talk to each other about their experiences with employee relations or share stories of what has happened to those who have filed grievances, a narrative, or common perspective, is socially constructed that may warn employees not to use the grievance procedure if they want to preserve their reputation and keep their job.

People hear stories about organizational conflict both within their organizations and from other sources. In too many cases, colleagues warn each other that complaining about the boss will result in an undesirable work schedule. A friend tells a story about someone in their organization who was fired after filing a grievance. The media reports stories of whistleblowers who become ostracized by peers with permanent damage to their reputation. As these stories proliferate they construct a common understanding that conflict is best avoided (of course, the opposite may also be true, and some organizations may have very positive stories about how conflict is managed). Thus, the CCO perspective emphasizes the continuous interdependence among how people talk, what they talk about, and the expectations that become understood as the organizational culture (Kuhn, 2012). In terms of organizational conflict management, this point cannot be overstated. Organizational leaders often point to grievance procedures, union formation, or alternative dispute resolution options as evidence of organizational justice, yet in many cases employees' experiences with organizational conflict bear little resemblance to these tools or processes. The CCO perspective provides a foundation for understanding how organizational members socially construct the institutional culture or climate that then influences and constrains behavior (Ashcraft, Kuhn, & Cooren, 2009). This perspective reminds us of the influence our language choices have on our environment and experience, as cultural; communication scholars Tenzin Dorjee and Stella Ting-Toomey recently wrote "language and labels matter as it has the transformational power to either uplift the people from the abyss of despair or push them further down to anxiety and chaos" (2020, p. 258).

The overarching premise of this book is that the LEARN framework – Listen, Engage, Acknowledge, Rapport (building), and Nurture relationships – is a useful guide for the kind of communication that constitutes an organization that is primed for constructive conflict management and transformation. The next section further explains how societal expectations are socially constructed and specifically focuses on the role of conflict in the process, providing more evidence of the importance of engaging in constructive conflict management to create change.

The Social Construction of Conflict

In 1976 Richard Rummel described what he called the conflict helix of social systems. He defines conflict as a social process that involves a constant balancing of power and continuous change. The helix represents a structure of expectations within a social system: norms that reduce uncertainty and create expectations for communication and other organizational behavior. Rummel posits five phases of social conflict (see Figure 1.1). In the latent phase, conflict is under the surface as differences in values, opinions, perspectives, beliefs, and attitudes always exist. A triggering event moves conflict from the latent phase to the manifest phase of initiation. Once the conflict is out in the open, decisions must be made about whether and how to respond. There is uncertainty here because the potential results of engaging the conflict are unknown. Given a decision to exercise voice and attempt to have one's interests heard, phase three is entered, balancing of power. This phase includes status quo testing, manifestation of power, and either accommodation (one party acquiesces to the other) or competing (one or both parties engage in coercion). Phase three is largely the subject of this book. As described above, the LEARN framework provides guidance for the use of cooperative power

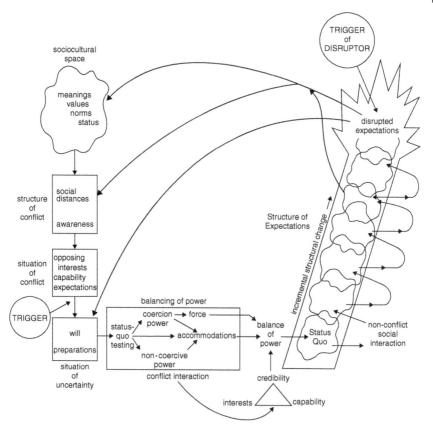

Figure 1.1 The process of conflict. *Source:* Reproduced from Rummel, R. J. (1976) / John Wiley & Sons.

(Listen, Engage, and Acknowledge) as well as recommendations for ongoing communication (Rapport (building) and Nurture) that set the stage for ongoing constructive conflict communication that reduces the need for coercive power balancing. Phase four is the balance of power that results from the interaction of phase three: either a return to the status quo or a change to the system. Phase five occurs when there is a new disruption: an internal or external event that disrupts the current balance and begins a new cycle of initiation. Rummel's helical structure, which is illustrated as a ladder, reminds us that the system is not starting over, *per se*. Even when the balancing of power returns the system to the status quo, there is incremental movement that comes just from the fact that the conflict was initiated. Thus the helix demonstrates that it is important to find ways to constructively engage, rather than avoid, conflict in order to negotiate the structure of expectations and create new norms for communication and interaction.

There is one important caveat to this book's emphasis on constructive conflict management (*non-coercive conflict management* in Rummel's words). There are times when power is so out of balance that the more powerful are either unwilling to listen or unable to fully hear and acknowledge the concerns and interests of others. In these situations, those with less power are marginalized in society (or the workplace), which means they are feeling, in the least, ignored and, at worst, persecuted. As Rummel's model shows, over time there will likely be a triggering act after which the status quo is no longer acceptable. See Box 1.2 for an application of Rummel's model to a social conflict.

Box 1.2   Racial Conflict in the United States

The summer of 2020 was a stark reminder of what happens when conflict is not directly engaged. While Black and Brown people in the United States have suffered from systems of inequity and institutional racism since the founding of our country, it took the tragic death of George Floyd to put this conflict back on top of social, political, and organizational agendas. Using Rummel's model of the social conflict helix, we can say that, as a society, we were in a latent stage of inter-racial conflict with varying levels of awareness ranging from those who experience racism as a daily feature of life to those in complete denial or ignorance of its existence. The video recording of the police officers holding George Floyd down and stepping on his neck until he could no longer breathe were seen across the country and made it impossible to ignore this reality – this event was a triggering event that moved the whole country into a balancing-of-power phase, as seen by the protests that took place across the country. These protests varied in their form and used more or less coercive power, in Rummel's words, depending on the goals of different participants and how much force was used in resistance to the protests. Many organizations and institutions responded to Floyd's death and the protests that followed. Responses ranged from senior executives, celebrities, and politicians speaking out against racism and inequality to organizational leaders taking a close look at their diversity and inclusion practices to consider how their recruitment and other policies might reinforce systemic inequities. Even as I complete my writing in Fall of 2022, it is too soon to say whether we will have real, transformative change or whether we will return to the status quo, but the key point here is to demonstrate that we need to engage in productive conflict communication in order to bring about change.

For Reflection and Discussion:

1) Discuss how values, beliefs, and attitudes, social interactions, and the balancing of power among individuals and institutions (such as law enforcement, education, and media) illustrate examples of Rummel's conflict phases: latent conflict, triggering event, manifest conflict, balancing of power, and a revised structure of expectations.

2) What is the relationship between the social environment (racism, in this example) and conflict that occurs in the workplace? What are some examples of individual and organizational actions or behaviors that would construct a workplace environment that demonstrates a commitment to anti-racism and organizational justice for all organizational members?

A workplace example might help apply Rummel's (1976) conflict helix to the organizational environment more clearly. The following story is a compilation of conflict experiences from my own mediation sessions, student stories, and examples from research participants over the past 20 years. Imagine someone in a position of power is verbally aggressive with employees. Depending on the organizational culture and norms that have been constructed, this behavior may be considered more or less acceptable. (Law and medicine, for example, are professions with norms in which employees may accept aggressive communication as a natural symptom of a high-stress profession; yet the same behavior may not be acceptable elsewhere.) In one workplace, several employees experienced aggressive communication from a manager, but they only talked about their dissatisfaction to their peers, a process that is referred to as lateral dissent (Kassing, 2011; see Chapter 5). This illustrates Rummel's *latent* conflict phase: differences in expectations existed, but the conflict had not become manifest – it was not directly confronted.

One day, this manager issued a written warning to an employee in response to what was considered an excessive absence rate. The warning became a *triggering event* that caused the employee to file a grievance with employee relations, moving the conflict into the manifest phase. The grievant claimed that the absences were a result of verbal abuse, which made her sick to the point she could not go to work. The employee relations manager suggested that the grievant and respondent participate in mediation, a collaborative, interest-based approach in which the parties try to negotiate an agreement about how to work together with the help and guidance of a mediator. Mediation thus initiates phase three, the *balancing of power*. In mediation, the grievant described her perceptions of her manager's communication style and how it had affected her. The respondent explained that his anger was never directed at the employee, it was a by-product of frustration and a personal communication pattern that would be difficult to change. As the mediator facilitated brainstorming of how the parties could improve their communication moving forward, the manager agreed to be more aware of his communication style and suggested that the employee "call him out" when she felt he was behaving aggressively. The employee agreed that she better understood the underlying source of the manager's frustration, and agreed to try to let him know when she thought he was communicating inappropriately. If the parties are able to implement this agreement successfully, it could create system-wide change if the manager successfully alters his communication style with all employees. Rummel would call this a new *balance of power* (phase four). This example illustrates the cycle of conflict and how every conflict interaction impacts the environment and future approaches to conflict management.

Of course, this example also illustrates that other outcomes of balancing power are possible. Rather than recommending mediation, the employee relations department might have considered the manager's communication an unacceptable risk. Fearing claims of a hostile environment, employee relations might have completed an investigation, presented a warning to the supervisor, or recommended termination. These activities would have sent a widespread message about appropriate and expected behavior throughout the organization. Alternatively, if the grievant had decided to leave the organization, the supervisor's behavior might have returned to the status quo, sending a very different message to employees about the organizational culture and expectations and reinforcing the idea that dissent is futile. These examples again demonstrate how conflict communication constitutes the organization, in ways either that lead to conflict avoidance or that support constructive conflict management.

The theories presented above, communication as constitutive of organization and the social conflict helix, demonstrate the interdependent relationship between human communication and the social construction of organizations. Through individual conflict experiences at work and storytelling, organizational members develop a shared narrative that both prescribes and constrains conflict behavior. The examples presented in this chapter are intended as both a cautionary tale and a reason for hope: if organizational members are actively constituting their organization through the way they communicate, then organizational members can create cultures of constructive conflict management.

Chapter Summary

The theories and empirical data reported in this chapter describe processes of human interaction and communication that socially construct the definition of conflict, the experience of conflict, and the pathways seen as available for conflict management. At a broad level, communication is constitutive of organization (Ashcraft, Kuhn, & Cooren, 2009). Organizations exist through coordinated social interaction and the constant negotiation among organizational members and the written artifacts they construct, such as rules and policies. Our understanding of conflict and how it can or should be managed also comes from examples we see and read about, often through mediated channels such as newspaper and television reporting. As demonstrated in Box 1.1, the stories we hear and read often send the message that engaging in conflict with more powerful others – be they managers, business owners, or government agencies – is futile. Yet it is also clear that if we choose to remain silent in matters of conflict, our needs will continue to be unmet while frustration and other negative outcomes will increase.

Rummel's (1976) model of social conflict illustrates the way a dyadic conflict between an employee and manager can challenge organizational members' existing structure of expectations, which can result in a return to the status quo or a change in the balance of power. Yet the very act of initiating conflict contributes to movement along the conflict helix and changes the nature of the organization and future expectations, even if in incremental ways. These theories are intended to underscore the point that we can communicate in ways that help create a constructive culture of conflict management. When we are open to Listening, Engaging, Acknowledging, Rapport-building, and Nurturing relationships, and if workplaces can create these norms, it becomes easier to address conflict situations directly, creating the potential for collaborative and constructive conflict management that leads to better outcomes for individuals and the organizations of which they are a part.

Activity: Identifying Typical Responses to Workplace Conflicts

Step 1: Make a brief list of different types of conflict you have seen in a workplace. The conflict could be between two employees, an employee and a supervisor, or even two groups of employees (as examples).

Step 2: Talk to a partner, with each of you sharing a different kind of conflict and discussing how you have seen it managed: What did the parties do (or not do)? How did their actions make the conflict better or worse? Discuss the impact of these conflicts on the workplace.

References

Ansolabehere, S., & Iyengar, S. (1995). *Going negative: How political advertisements shrink and polarize the electorate*. New York: Free Press.

Ashcraft, K., Kuhn, T., & Cooren, F. (2009). Constitutional amendments: "Materializing" organizational communication. *The Academy of Management Annals. 3*: 1–64. https://doi.org/10.1080/19416520903047186.

Ashforth, B. E., & Anand, V. (2003). The normalization of corruption in organizations. *Research in Organizational Behavior, 25*(1): 1–52.

Ayub, N., & Jehn, K. (2014). When diversity helps performance: Effects of diversity on conflict and performance in workgroups. *International Journal of Conflict Management, 25*(2): 189–212. https://doi.org/10.1108/IJCMA-04-2013-0023.

Berger, P., & Luckman, T. L. (1966). *The social construction of knowledge: A treatise on the sociology of knowledge*. Garden City, NY: Doubleday.

Cappella, J. N., & Jamieson, K. H. (1997). *Spiral of cynicism: The press and the public good*. New York: Oxford University Press.

Dorjee, T., & Ting-Toomey, S. (2020). Understanding intergroup conflict complexity: An application of the socioecological framework and the integrative identity negotiation theory. *Negotiation and Conflict Management Research, 13*(3): 244–262. https://doi.org/10.1111/ncmr.12190.

Fisher, R., Ury, W., & Patton, B. (1991). *Getting to yes: Negotiating agreement without giving in* (2nd ed.). New York: Penguin Books.

Jameson, J. K. (2001). Employee perceptions of the availability and use of interests-, rights-, and power-based conflict management strategies. *Conflict Resolution Quarterly, 19*(2): 163–196.

Jameson, J. K., & Entman, R. M. (2004). Journalism in the democratic management of policy conflict: Narrating the New York budget crisis after 9/11. *The Harvard International Journal of Press/Politics, 9*(2): 38–59.

Janison, D. (2002, January 30). Few ripples seen in city address. *Newsday*.

Jones, T. S. (2000). Emotional communication in conflict: Essence and impact. In W. Eadie & P. Nelson (Eds.), *The Language of Conflict and Resolution* (pp. 81–104). Thousand Oaks, CA: Sage.

Kassing, J. W. (2011). *Dissent in organizations*. Malden, MA: Polity Press.

Kirby, E., & Krone, K. (2002). "The policy exists but you can't really use it": Communication and the structuration of work-family policies. *Journal of Applied Communication Research, 30*(1): 50–77. https://doi.org/10.1080/00909880216577.

Kolb, D. M., & Bartunek, J. M. (1992). *Hidden conflict in organizations: Uncovering behind-the-scenes disputes*. Thousand Oaks, CA: Sage.

Kuhn, T. (2012). Negotiating the micro-macro divide: Thought leadership from organizational communication for theorizing organization. *Management Communication Quarterly, 26*(4): 543–584. https://doi.org/10.1177/0893318912462004.

Lipsky, D. B., Seeber, R. L., & Fincher, R. D. (2003). *Emerging systems for managing workplace conflict: Lessons from American corporations for managers and dispute resolution professionals*. San Francisco, CA: Jossey-Bass.

McPhee, R. D., Poole, M. S., & Iverson, J. (2014). Structuration theory. In Putnam, L. L. & D. K. Mumby (Eds.), *The SAGE handbook of organizational communication* (3rd ed., pp. 75–100). Thousand Oaks, CA: Sage.

Mumby, D. K. (2013). *Organizational communication: A critical perspective*. Thousand Oaks, CA: Sage.

Nicotera, A. M. (2020). Organizing the study of organizational communication. In A. M. Nicotera (Ed.), *Origins and traditions of organizational communication* (pp. 3–17). New York: Routledge.

Oetzel, J. G., & Ting-Toomey, S. (2003). Face concerns in interpersonal conflict: A cross-cultural empirical test of the Face Negotiation Theory. *Communication Research, 30*(6): 599–624.

Patterson, T. E. (1993). *Out of order*. New York: Knopf.

Putnam, L. L., & Nicotera, A. M. (2009). *Building theories of organization: The constitutive role of communication*. New York: Taylor and Francis.

Rummel, R. J. (1976). *Understanding conflict and war, Volume 2: The conflict helix*. New York: John Wiley and Sons.

Searle, J. (1995). *The construction of social reality*. New York: Free Press.

Tajfel, H. (1982). *Social identity and intergroup relations*. Cambridge and New York: Cambridge University Press.

Ury, W. L., Brett, J. M., & Goldberg, S. B. (1988). *Getting disputes resolved*. San Francisco, CA: Jossey-Bass.

Wilmot, W., & Hocker, J. (2010). *Interpersonal conflict*, (8th ed.). New York: McGraw-Hill.

Unit One

Listen

2

Challenges to Effective Listening

We have two ears and one mouth so that we can listen twice as much as we speak.

Epictetus (50–135 AD, Greek philosopher)

Most likely you have heard this quote before. It may be used by angry parents who want their children to stop arguing, whining, or complaining and listen to them. In this context, it is no surprise if you saw that quote and rolled your eyes. This is a good example of one major challenge to listening – the belief that you already know what the person speaking is going to say. In this chapter, I rely heavily on previous research on listening[1] and related observations and results from my own research on conflict management, as well as experience as a mediator and supervisor, to define types of listening and describe the challenges to active, empathic listening. I will then identify and illustrate the advantages of listening and lay the groundwork for how we can practice listening that is engaged, acknowledges others, builds rapport, and nurtures relationships. This chapter will make it clear that listening is, in fact, the necessary starting point for creating an environment of constructive conflict management. Chapter 3 will go even further into illustrating what active, empathic listening looks like and demonstrating how to practice it.

Levels of Listening

Scholars have described different types or levels of listening. No doubt you have heard of the difference between hearing and listening. Hearing is one of our five senses, and if we are fortunate enough to have good hearing, we can hear many

---

[1] I am grateful to have found a 2009 dissertation by Clare Coburn on listening in mediation, which includes a comprehensive review of the literature on listening. I highly recommend this as additional reading to anyone who finds themselves interested in the material presented in Chapters 2 and 3.

Communication for Constructive Workplace Conflict, First Edition. Jessica Katz Jameson.

types of stimuli around us, in my case, the whirring of the dehumidifier in the hallway and the birds chirping outside my window as I write. We subconsciously (often) choose what we want or need to focus our attention on, and if something seems important, we may move from simply hearing it to more actively listening to what we hear. To be clear, in this book I am talking about listening as opposed to the physiological process of hearing. One typology describes four types of listening as *discriminative* (listening for new information, such as to learn a new skill), *evaluative or critical* (listening to respond/refute), *appreciative* (for pleasure, such as to music or entertainment), and *empathic* (listening for feelings or understanding) (Wolvin & Coakley, 1996).

As the above types of listening illustrate, our goals for the situation or interaction make all the difference in how we listen. Often, we enter into an interaction with the goal of persuading someone else to go along with our plan, such as a manager who needs employees to perform a task in a certain way or a salesperson making a pitch to a client. When our goal is to persuade others, we are listening to identify statements we can refute and correct or counter in order to be persuasive. This type of listening is necessary if the goal is to persuade others to behave in a certain manner or to sell a product. A major challenge in the workplace, however, is that employees become so accustomed to listening to persuade (or resist persuasion), that they do not practice listening in a non-evaluative way. This non-evaluative listening is necessary when we want to show others that we care about what they are saying and that they are truly being *heard*.

As will be discussed in more detail in Unit Two, *Engage*, a common reason organizational members often choose to avoid, rather than engage in, workplace conflict management is that they do not feel like anyone is listening. They believe either that by stating complaints or concerns they will face retaliation or that the process is futile because nothing will change anyway. This is the result of a workplace environment where organizational members see any challenge as adversarial and in which managers are always in the mode of evaluative or critical listening. Returning to the communication as constitutive of organization CCO framework described in Chapter 1, this style of listening constructs an environment that is adversarial and in which conflict, when it arises, is seen as competitive. Listening in a non-evaluative way, described in the above typology as *empathic* listening, is when the listener is truly listening to understand – not just to what the speaker is saying but also for cues to emotions that help understand why the speaker feels the way they do. When a listener shows this type of open and active listening, the speaker feels heard, and this creates a collaborative, rather than adversarial, interaction. If this becomes normative in the interaction of organizational members, it can indeed create an environment for constructive conflict management.

This idea is not new. In 2007, C. Otto Scharmer wrote a book about the need for a change in our institutions and the old patterns of interacting and collective behavior. He makes a point that is perhaps even more relevant today: "The crisis of our time reveals the dying of an old social structure and way of thinking, an old way of institutionalizing and enacting collective social forms" (Scharmer, 2007, p. 2). In order to break out of our old habits, Scharmer proposes that we need to be present in the moment and learn from the conversation and interaction at hand. As he describes it, we are typically listening from our own perspective and experience, with all its attendant biases, which creates a "blind spot." His listening typology therefore identifies types of listening that are from our own perspective and contrasts those with listening that is open to the speaker's perspective and experience. Scharmer's (2007) description of levels of listening is shown in Table 2.1. He describes *downloading* as listening from our own point of view and reconfirming our current beliefs or experience. The listener hears what is said and understands it only within the confines of his or her worldview and experience; there is no openness to engaging with what is heard. This may be because the listener is not that interested or motivated to listen more critically. The next level of listening is *object- or fact-focused* listening. As with the evaluative or critical listening described above, the listener is again listening from his or her perspective in order to focus on details to refute. This is what people often refer to as "listening to respond." This style has also been referred to as distributive listening (Mayer, 2000) because the goal is to distinguish your interpretation of events from mine – usually so that I can then attempt to persuade you of why you are wrong – a competitive and adversarial approach to conflict management. Coburn (2009) noted that fact-focused listening characterizes most legal and academic listening. The third and fourth levels of listening shift the focus from the listener's to the speaker's point of view. Scharmer's next level of listening is *empathic*. As described above, the goal of empathic listening is to understand what is being said from the perspective of the speaker, or to really understand their experience.

Table 2.1 C. Otto Scharmer's levels of listening.

Listening type	Definition
Downloading	Listening to what is said from one's own perspective only
Object- or fact-focused	Listening for information for the purpose of responding to or refuting specific points made by the speaker
Empathic	Listening to try to understand the perspective or experience of the speaker
Generative	Listening with the goal of imagining or creating a different future

Source: Scharmer, C. O. (2007) / Society for Organizational Learning.

This is the kind of listening we would expect from a counselor or therapist, or even a parent or friend when we are sharing a concern or a bad day. In empathic listening, the listener is not judging, evaluating, or trying to memorize the information being heard, but is there to be open to what the other is saying and wants them to feel they have been heard. Scharmer's fourth level is not described in other listening typologies, and he refers to this as *generative* listening. This level takes empathic listening one step further by using the information that is heard to help imagine a different future. It is worth taking a moment to reflect on this idea. If we are always listening to others from our own perspective or world-view, there is little room for growth. When we listen with the goal of understanding another's worldview, we open ourselves to seeing things in a new way and developing creative new approaches to problem solving. This is what Scharmer means when he says we need to change our current institutions and ways of collective action. In interpersonal conflict management, generative listening is what mediators strive to help the parties achieve, as they encourage disputing parties to listen empathically to each other and develop new ways to interact and work together in a more constructive environment (Coburn, 2009). An example of empathic and generative listening can be found in Box 2.1, which describes a mediation in which the parties listened to each other in ways they had not been able to without the help of the mediator, and how it changed the very nature of how they saw each other, their relationship, and possibilities for better communication moving forward.

The current social environment in the United States provides a perfect example of why Scharmer's (2007) notion of reinventing our institutions through how we listen and interact is so relevant and needed. As discussed in Chapter 1, an increase in protests about racial injustice in the United States and around the world in 2020 called for the dominant group, Whites in the United States, to engage in empathic listening to try to understand what it is like to be Black in America. Empathic listening needs to be followed with generative listening, openness to working collaboratively to build an anti-racist society that treats everyone equally and provides safety and social justice for all citizens.

Box 2.1   Familiarity Breeds Contempt

Roberta and Margaret work together in facilities management within a public university. They share an office that includes a computer and a telephone. There is a table between the two desks for the telephone, but the phone often ends up on one desk or the other depending on who used it last. Because the office space is small, Roberta and Margaret often bump into each other when they are in the office at the same time.

The office situation has created a stressful climate for Roberta and Margaret, who share supervisory duties over the housekeeping staff. While they work different shifts, their schedules overlap so that they can coordinate employee tasks. Roberta and Margaret are constantly bickering with each other and complaining about each other, and they undermine each other's authority with the staff. The rest of the department is experiencing the brunt of this conflict and have individually started to complain to the director of facilities. Academic departments have also begun to complain about poor service and maintenance standards and the director recognizes that action must be taken to manage this conflict. The director has tried to talk to Roberta and Margaret individually, but each one accuses the other of being uncooperative and neither one is willing to admit their role in this situation. For example, Roberta complains that Margaret's chair is always pushed all the way back and that she is disorganized. She also accuses Margaret of not communicating with her. Margaret complains that Roberta is always on the phone, and she keeps the phone on her desk rather than returning it to its appropriate place on the table. Margaret is also upset that even though Roberta has been working at this institution for 10 years (eight years longer than her), she refuses to answer any of Margaret's questions and often snaps at her when she asks.

The director recognizes that both of these employees are valuable – they both come to work on time and, despite their problems with each other, have a good work ethic and loyalty to the organization. She calls the human resources (HR) department for advice and learns about the possibility of mediation. She approaches Roberta and Margaret and strongly recommends that they try mediation because the department can no longer run this way. Roberta and Margaret both agree to give it a shot.

The mediators assigned to this case are a faculty member and a member of the HR department. Neither mediator has had any previous interaction with Roberta or Margaret. The mediators describe the mediation process, specifically pointing out that the goal of mediation is to help Roberta and Margaret create an agreement that will improve their working relationship. Roberta and Margaret both appear motivated to resolve their conflict so they can improve their comfort and satisfaction in the workplace.

Margaret was the one who originally went to HR with a complaint, so she is invited to speak first. She explains that she is very frustrated about their office situation and believes that the small space is the source of their problems. She confides that she has a bad back and must sit a certain distance from the computer keyboard, which means her chair is often pushed back, and she knows this is a problem when Roberta is in the office. She also complains that when the phone rings, it is hard for her to get to because it is always on

Roberta's desk, and out of her reach, rather than on the table between the desks, where it belongs. Margaret is also offended by the fact that Roberta is very short with her, and she is annoyed that Roberta will not answer her questions. The mediators ask Margaret a few follow-up questions to make sure she feels heard, and then they ask Roberta to share her view of the situation.

Roberta agrees that the office space is a problem. She is very frustrated about the chair, but did not realize there was a medical reason involved. She comments that she is on the phone a lot, and it is just easier to have it on her desk rather than constantly putting it back on the table when she hangs up the phone. She is upset about what she perceives as Margaret's lack of organization, which results in files not being put back where they belong, and sticky notes placed everywhere. She claims that every time she comes into the office there is a new sticky note on her computer with questions or assignments, and often the messages she receives are inaccurate. Roberta also cannot understand why Margaret has so many questions when she had the "same exact job" in her previous workplace, where she worked as many years as Roberta has. She perceives Margaret as lazy and a slow learner, and she does not feel it is her responsibility to get Margaret up to speed. Once again, the mediators ask a few clarification questions, and then they move on to set the agenda for the mediation by asking both Roberta and Margaret what the key issues are that need to be addressed in order for them to feel better about working together.

With the mediators' help, Roberta and Margaret identify three main issues that need to be worked out: the placement of the telephone and Margaret's chair, communication with each other about what has happened during their shift, and the organization of paperwork and files. They agree to start with the issue of improving their communication with each other. The mediators ask them to come up with specific examples of times they had difficulty communicating. Margaret tells the story of a time they had to coordinate the repair of a leaky roof, and she needed to ask Roberta to help her with the task. Roberta just said "you know where the forms are, get them signed and set up the work order." Margaret was hurt by Roberta's unwillingness to help, as she had never done this at a state institution before. Margaret pointed out that while she had held a similar job before this one, it was a private construction firm and their procedures were very different, which has made learning this job very stressful.

When Margaret had finished speaking, the mediators noticed a significant difference in Roberta's physical appearance and tone of voice. Roberta had clearly heard something new, which was confirmed when she said, "I really had no idea that things were so different where you worked before. When you got this job, I assumed you knew all the procedures. When you asked me questions, I thought you were just lazy and wanted me to do the work for you, now I understand why you had questions. It must have been really hard for you this past couple of years."

At this point, all eyes were on Margaret, who said, "you have no idea how much it means to me just to hear you say that you understand why it was hard for me." Margaret was a bit teary-eyed at this point, so a mediator jumped in and complimented the two for their good work listening to each other and pointed out that they had already made some real progress. At that point, the parties talked some more about specifics regarding how they might improve their day-to-day communication with each other and how to organize the office files. After 20 minutes or so of working out those details, a mediator said, "Okay, we have addressed the issues of improving your communication and organizing the office, now we need to talk about the telephone and the chair." Roberta and Margaret both looked at the mediators quizzically and laughed. Roberta said "The telephone? The chair? Who cares about that, that's not important, we've worked out our differences and those things don't even matter now." They agreed that nothing about the telephone or chair needed to be included in the agreement, that those were "little" things that were bothering them because of these larger misunderstandings they had. They both felt that their relationship was different now, and looked forward to returning to the office and a more cooperative, less stressful climate.

For Reflection and Discussion:

1) What do you think prevented Roberta and Margaret from directly discussing their issues with each other?
2) Why do you think the director chose to involve HR rather than talking to Roberta and Margaret more directly?
3) How do you think the communication styles of Roberta, Margaret, and the director hinted at in the first half of this case impact the workplace environment?
4) What do you think happened in the mediation session that enabled Roberta and Margaret to really listen to each other?

Source: B. C. McKinney & J. Bagnell (2012) / Kendall Hunt Publishing.

Challenges to Listening

If listening is so important, and if biologically we are predisposed to it with a body design that includes two ears, why is it so difficult? Several scholars have spoken to this either directly or indirectly. Starting with those who have directly addressed this question, Golen (1990) identified barriers to listening by describing what we might call dispositional attributions (explaining someone's behavior as a personality characteristic). His labels are lazy, closed minded, opinionated, insincere, bored, and inattentive. Egan (1998) has identified a slightly longer list of challenges to listening that seem to conflate types or levels of listening described above with some common barriers. His list, which is in the context of counseling, specifically includes inadequate listening, evaluative listening, filtered listening (cautioning awareness of labels as filters), fact- rather than person-centered listening, rehearsing (that is, preparing to respond), sympathetic (as opposed to empathic) listening, and interrupting.

While listening has not often been addressed directly in the conflict literature (for exceptions, see Coburn, 2009, 2012; Love, 2000), there is a lot of work on conflict that resonates with these ideas and explains what might be going on in conflict interaction that prevents effective and active listening. I will discuss these as bias, identity and defensiveness, and time.

Bias

We all make assumptions and have expectations about how the world works or how we feel it should work. When we see or hear something that violates our expectations, our first instinct is that it is wrong, or at least strange, and we decide whether to give it our attention. An example many can relate to is in politics. When you hear a politician or other person with views in opposition to your own discussing their opinions and ideas, you may feel yourself getting frustrated or even angry, and unless the issue at hand is very important to you, you might tune the person out – often literally by changing the station on the television or the radio or turning it off. When we are interacting with someone directly, we are probably engaged in fact-focused listening as described above: listening for what we can refute and rehearsing our response to prove the speaker wrong.

A less obvious type of bias is implicit bias, and this comes from even more subtle ways we have been socialized so that we operate within a set of assumptions and take certain things for granted. Implicit bias could be as innocuous as assuming that college classes will all take place in a classroom, so that when we suddenly have to take a course online (as most college students did in Spring of 2020), we are resistant and see it as a less valuable form of education because it feels uncomfortable and foreign. In terms of interaction with others, implicit bias can make us resistant to listening because our life experience and comfort have somehow taught us that certain people's ideas are not as valid, valued, or worth our attention. One example of implicit bias is based on where we were raised and how we hear different types of accents. As linguistics professor John Esling has written:

> Accent is the map which listeners perceive through their own ears rather than through their eyes to 'read' where the speaker was born and

raised, what gender they are, how old they are, where they might have moved during their life, where they went to school, what occupation they have taken up, and even how short or tall they are, how much they might weigh, or whether they are feeling ill or well at the moment. (Esling, 1998, p. 169)

You may recognize what Esling describes if you are from the United States and you have ever made assumptions about someone who had a New York, Boston, or Southern accent. Depending on where you grew up, and whether you identify with any of these groups, your assumptions will obviously be different. But the point is, we are making inferences about the speaker based on limited information and our place of origin, life experiences, and who we know, and this is a good example of implicit bias.

Many studies of diversity in group communication have revealed that certain members of groups are less likely to be heard than others, usually members of an underrepresented group in comparison to the dominant group structure. In the typical US workplace, this often includes women, African Americans, LatinX, and those born outside the United States. Stories abound of members of these groups who make a statement in a meeting that no one responds to, only to have a member of the majority group offer the same idea to resounding support or validation. This implicit bias has a real and lasting impact on the group and organizational environment, as some organizational members feel excluded, devalued, and ultimately may lose motivation and refrain from speaking up in meetings. Ironically, these members of underrepresented groups may then receive poor performance reviews or be passed over for promotion because they are viewed as less engaged members of the organization. This is another example of how communication constitutes the organization, as presented in Chapter 1. In this case, it is an example of how institutional racism (or sexism, etc.) persists in many organizations and institutions.

Identity and Defensiveness

As described above, our biases (both explicit and implicit) come from our worldview. This is a combination of multiple factors: where we were born or have lived, our parents' and family members' beliefs and values, our religious beliefs or the role of faith in our lives, how much we have traveled or been surrounded by diverse others, and much, much more. Our identity is critical to our self-definition; as Terrell Northrup (1989) has described it, identity is an individual's sense of "self-in-relation-to-the-world" (p. 55). Identity gives us a sense of predictability, providing us with expectations for how others will and should treat us. When we hear something that is counter to our beliefs, it can pose a serious threat to our identity, which will stimulate a defensive response and make it very difficult to listen, or at least engage in empathic or generative listening as described above.

Northrup describes a process of conflict escalation that begins with the perception of a threat and escalates to the point of intractable conflict, which refers to conflict that is highly resistant to resolution. Once someone feels that another person or group is threatening their identity, they assume a defensive posture to maintain their worldview and feelings of self-worth. When we are in defensive mode, we are not listening with an open and empathic mind, because we are listening in fact or object mode to refute. Northrup describes how we take this even further in distorting the information we hear to fit our pre-existing beliefs. The next stage of escalation is to physically separate ourselves from others to protect ourselves and avoid conflict. In this separation phase, we surround ourselves with people who think like us and will validate our worldview, helping us denigrate the other view (and importantly, people who hold that view). This process is currently being observed in polarized societies throughout the world. Whether people are divided by race, gender, politics, religion, or other identifications that threaten each other, the final stage is that parties, or members of each identity group, refuse to engage in empathic or generative listening, so they essentially collaborate in maintaining the conflict. Northrup describes this final stage of intractable conflict as collusion. In Chapter 6, a case study of certified registered nurse anesthetists and anesthesiologists illustrates how conflict between identity groups can come into the workplace, making people's jobs more difficult and threatening the organizational environment for constructive conflict management.

Time

Another category of challenges to listening has to do with the time that we are willing or able to devote to listening. Here I will discuss two sub-categories that help explain this challenge: (i) solution-orientation and (ii) need for processing time.

Solution-Orientation

It is not uncommon to listen to what someone is sharing with us, whether a friend, family member, or coworker, and immediately try to help them solve a problem they are experiencing. While this may be helpful, there are several disadvantages to offering potential solutions in this situation. One is that the speaker may not be looking for you to solve their problem. As Deborah Tannen (1986) has described, people often share their concerns or problems to build rapport – the interaction goal is to get validation and social support, and perhaps deepen a relationship. A second problem is that without a greater understanding of the whole situation, you might be giving bad advice. For example, when a coworker shares that she believes the boss is treating her unfairly by giving her more assignments than others, we may focus on the facts she is sharing and immediately suggest that she file a formal complaint against the boss with employee relations. But if we ask questions rather than jumping to a solution, we might learn that the boss is often praising her for the quality of her work, and this is why she is getting more assignments. Or we might hear that our coworker is caring for a family member that is ill, and it may be that she only perceives she is getting more work because she is tired and has not shared that information with her boss. This brief example illustrates differences between fact- or object-focused listening and empathic or generative listening, during which the listener pays attention to all of what the speaker is saying and feeling, with the goal of gaining greater understanding and finding new ways of thinking about a problem as opposed to the listener problem solving from within their current understanding or assumptions. Empathic and generative listening ultimately have the potential to develop solutions that result in improved outcomes as well as enhanced relationships (thus achieving both goals of problem solving and rapport-building).

Processing Needs

People differ in the length of time needed to process what they are hearing before they respond. There is evidence that, in general, people privilege speaking over listening, so those who speak more often are perceived as more engaged, or even more intelligent, than those who are quiet (Cain, 2012). You may have experienced this in a classroom where students who participate more often get more attention from the instructor, and likely receive higher grades for participation in class. Yet if you ask students why they don't speak up more, they may say that they need to take more time to think about what they heard and how they want to respond. These students will often say that by the time they knew what they wanted to say, the conversation had moved on to a new topic. Psychologists have associated this with the trait of extroversion and introversion (Cain, 2012). Extroverts are eager to engage in the conversation and are comfortable jumping in quickly,[2] while introverts take more time to process and reflect on what they hear before they respond. To connect this to the discussion of bias above, instructors have to be careful not to carry a bias toward more extroverted students. By speaking with the more quiet students (in a private meeting) and listening to why they are not speaking up in class, the instructor might develop ways to provide time for more students to process and feel comfortable participating, such as through small group activities or creating an online discussion board where students can share ideas later.

---

[2] Carl Jung introduced this psychological trait, and while many people think about extroversion and introversion in terms of how outgoing one is or how much people prefer being with others versus being alone, William McDougall interpreted this trait in terms of how much people reflect on what they hear before they respond (McDougall, 1923/1932, p. 184).

These differences in processing time may also challenge listening in interpersonal or dyadic conversations. For example, I have a tendency to respond quickly in interpersonal interactions, and if the other person gets quiet, I will often jump in with my own comments or observations. On more than one occasion I have realized that the other party was not finished with what they were saying; they were taking time to think about what more they wanted to say. In such cases, the other party felt interrupted and possibly disrespected. Good listening habits require paying attention to cues from the other party that may indicate they are still speaking or preparing to say more. This may require us to become a bit more comfortable with moments of silence, get better at listening to what is not being said, or pay close attention to affect and nonverbal behavior. Specific tips for active and engaged listening will be presented in Chapter 3.

A couple of additional comments are necessary regarding how much time one is willing or able to devote to listening. In the workplace, organizational members are typically juggling several roles, responsibilities, and tasks on any given day. There is an emphasis on time and efficiency that creates real barriers to the kind of active, empathic, and generative listening called for in this book. Managers are also expected to be problem-solvers (Karambayya & Brett, 1994), and therefore are likely biased toward trying to diagnose a problem swiftly, develop a solution, and move on to the next task. As described above, one downside of this is that the solution may not be the most optimal solution, or may not solve the underlying cause of the problem, and as a manager, it would be beneficial to develop deeper listening skills.

A second challenge to empathic listening is that the level of focus and attention it requires is mentally and physically exhausting. In mediation, for example, a third party is listening to disputants in order to understand their underlying needs and interests and help the parties brainstorm and develop an agreement that will allow them to move forward and meet all parties' interests. Having facilitated many mediations over the years, I have found that this level of listening is not sustainable for more than about two hours, and if I am honest, I know that I rarely devote this level of energy to listening unless I am in the mediator role. This will be discussed in more detail in Chapter 3, with implications for how we might be able to transfer this practice of listening to our daily activities.

Listening to Create a Constructive Conflict Environment: Fostering a Dialogue versus Debate Mindset

In the final section of this chapter I want to emphasize one overarching challenge to listening that connects back to Chapter 1: the fact that many of us (especially in the United States and other Western parts of the world) have been socialized to experience and understand conflict as adversarial. As described in Box 1.1

(the social construction of conflict in city government), when media report on conflict, they assume a rights- or power-based orientation, and this is also portrayed in fictional accounts of conflict (on television and in movies), as well as being evident in the metaphors we use to talk about conflict, such as "preparing to make our case" or "arming ourselves for battle." As long as we see conflict as the need to persuade or coerce others to see or do things our way, we are contributing to and reinforcing the social construction of an adversarial and competitive work environment. I refer to this in this section as a "debate mindset," because the goal of a debate is to argue for one side of an issue and research the opposing side in order to be fully prepared to counter their arguments. As seen in the judgment of legal cases or in debate (forensics) teams all over the world, whoever is better prepared and more skilled wins.

While I believe debate is a valuable skill and can be an appropriate way to critically examine and discuss important issues, there is a more cooperative alternative, known as dialogue. Morton Deutsch was an American social psychologist who is considered a pioneer in conflict studies. He was the first to talk about cooperative versus competitive environments, and specifically said that organizations can promote a cooperative climate, which will lead to greater cooperation and collaboration (while the reverse is also true if an uncooperative climate is promoted). While he did not talk about dialogue, per se, understanding the underlying features of dialogue and how they are different from debate can help organizational members think and act from a more dialogic, or collaborative, perspective.

The goal of dialogue is not to win, but to understand. While debate requires fact- or object-focused listening for the purpose of rebuttal, as described above, dialogue requires, at a minimum, empathic listening: listening to understand the issue from the other party's point of view. As an example of the difference, as I write this book there is a debate in the United States about the wearing of masks during the COVID-19 pandemic. People on both sides of this issue feel very strongly about their decision about whether to wear a mask. The interaction we typically see about this issue alternates between debate (often taking place on social media outlets, such as Twitter, and YouTube; see the case in Chapter 11) and direct confrontation. There have even been reports of violence, as mask wearers may get angry at those who do not wear a mask, while others angrily defend their right not to wear a mask and see it as an infringement on their individual rights. In debate mode, one type of argument revolves around whether the scientific evidence supports the belief that wearing a mask will prevent the spread of the virus. A second type of argument centers on individual rights, and whether any institution (private or public) has the right to force someone to wear a mask. Importantly, and as described above in the section on identity, as long as these are the dominant discussions, neither side will be able to engage in open, empathic, or generative listening to the other, as each side feels threatened by the other's argument. To take this a step further, there could be cultural differences at play. Geert Hofstede (1984) classifies different cultures (and by extension, different worldviews) as more collectivist or individualist. A collectivist culture emphasizes the common good and how people are connected, while an individualist culture emphasizes individual rights and independence. (Note that this also connects with Deutsch's ideas: if we see each other as more connected, we tend to emphasize cooperation, while if we focus on our independence, we emphasize competition). As long as the conflict about mask-wearing is managed as a debate or competition, the parties cannot communicate in ways that promote listening.

But what if we were to have a dialogue on the wearing of masks? A dialogue would include members of each viewpoint listening to each other with the goal of understanding the underlying interests, or why one either believes you should or should not wear a mask. This would require empathic listening – not seeing the other as the enemy, but seeing them as another human being that has certain views and feelings about an important issue. Because the goal of speaking in a dialogue is not to persuade or change someone's mind, we don't need to listen to refute (fact- or object- listening), and we do not need to feel a threat to our identity, because no one is challenging us. The question of how to approach a conversation (or conflict) as a dialogue, or more collaborative interaction, is an important one and, as shown in Box 2.1, it often requires the assistance of a third party, such as a mediator or group facilitator. Chapter 3 will focus on the specific skills we can develop and steps we can take to foster active, empathic listening and promote dialogue to create a constructive conflict environment.

Chapter Summary

This chapter described the different ways we listen in terms of four levels, *discriminative, evaluative or critical, appreciative*, and *empathic*, which is the one that helps us engage in dialogue and foster constructive conflict management. I then described a number of barriers that prevent us from empathic listening, including implicit and explicit bias, protecting our identity (which leads to defensiveness), and time. The final section of the chapter discussed the need to move from a mindset of debate, which is adversarial, to dialogue, where the goal is to better understand another person's views, values, experience, or interests. By using listening strategies that promote dialogue and understanding, we are more likely to foster a constructive workplace environment, and Chapter 3 provides specific strategies for effective, empathic listening.

Activities

1) **Political candidate dialogue?** One of the most common ways we see debate in action is during presidential and other political campaigns. In this situation, the purpose of the debate is both to provide insights into each candidate's positions on important issues and for each candidate to show that the other's approach is wrong. Develop an example of how you would design a public political candidate interaction based on principles of dialogue rather than debate. What could this look like? Who could facilitate this interaction? Where would you hold it? Who would be invited to watch and listen? Choose a social issue and try to develop some ideas about what the outcome of a political dialogue might be.

2) **Listening to those with divergent views.** For this activity you will need a partner. Choose a topic that you each feel comfortable discussing from opposing viewpoints (whether you are choosing a position that you actually agree with is not as important as imagining that you feel a certain way about an issue; whether you choose a "real" difference or role-play differences depends on your comfort and current relationship with the partner you choose for this activity). Take turns discussing how you each feel about the topic. Pay attention to how you are feeling as the discussion unfolds. Make note of when you feel defensive, whether you get angry or frustrated, when you feel you want to interrupt, etc. Reflect on what kinds of interactions – verbal or nonverbal for example – triggered various responses. Consider how you could manage or counter these "gut reactions" and work toward more open listening.

References

Cain, S. (2012). *Quiet: The power of introverts in a world that can't stop talking.* New York: Crown Publishing.

Coburn, C. (2009). When listening works: An exploration of mediators' experiences of their own listening and the listening of disputants. Dissertation submitted to School of Law, Faculty of Law and Management, La Trobe University, Bundoora, Victoria 3086, Australia. July 2009.

Coburn, C. (2012). Developing listening and suspension capacities for mediators. *Australian Dispute Resolution Journal, 23*: 99–105.

Egan, G. (1998). Attending, listening and understanding. In *The skilled helper: A problem management approach to helping* (pp. 61–79). Pacific Grove, CA: Brooks/Cole Publishing Company.

Esling, J. H. (1998). Everyone has an accent except me. In L. Bauer and P. Trudgill (Eds.), *Language myths* (pp. 154–158). London: Penguin Books.

Golen, S. (1990). A factor analysis of barriers to effective listening. *The Journal of Business Communication, 27*(1): 25–36.

Hofstede, G. (1984). *Culture's consequences: International differences in work-related values*. Thousand Oaks, CA: Sage.

Karambayya, R., & Brett, J. M. (1994). Managerial third parties: Intervention strategies, process, and consequences. In J. P. Folger & T. S. Jones (Eds.), *New directions in mediation* (pp. 175–192). Thousand Oaks, CA: Sage.

Love, L. P. (2000). Training mediators to listen: Deconstructing dialogue and constructing understanding, agendas, and agreements. *Family and Conciliation Courts Review, 38*(1): 27–40.

Mayer, B. S. (2000). *The dynamics of conflict resolution: A practitioner's guide*. San Francisco, CA: Jossey-Bass.

McDougall, W. (1923/1932). *The energies of men: A study of the fundamentals of dynamic psychology*. London: Methuen.

McKinney, B. C., & Bagnell, J. (2012) (Eds.). *Readings and case studies in mediation* (2nd ed.). Dubuque, IA: Kendall/Hunt.

Northrup, T. A. (1989). The dynamic of identity in personal and social conflict. In L. Kriesberg, T. A. Northrup, & S. J. Thorson (Eds.), *Intractable conflicts and their transformation* (pp. 55–82). Syracuse, NY: Syracuse University Press.

Scharmer, C. O. (2007). *Theory U: Leading from the future as it emerges*. Cambridge: The Society for Organizational Learning.

Tannen, D. (1986). *That's not what I meant!: How conversational style makes or breaks relationships*. New York: Morrow.

Wolvin, A., & Coakley, C. G. (1996). *Listening* (5th ed.). Boston, MA: McGraw-Hill.

3

Listening as Reflective Practice

We have to learn to listen to ourselves before we can really understand others.

Edgar Schein (professor of management)

Wisdom is the reward you get for a lifetime of listening when you would rather have talked.

Mark Twain (1835–1910, author)

In Chapter 2 I discussed the many obstacles to effective, empathic listening and introduced the idea of using a dialogic mindset to move away from adversarial and evaluative approaches to listening and move toward listening to understand and engage in collaborative problem solving. The notion of listening as a "reflective practice" is not new. Organizational development scholars Edgar Schein (1969, 1993) and Donald Schön (1983) made the ideas related to reflective practice popular in the 1980s or even the 1960s. It is also important to recognize the contributions of David Bohm (1996; Bohm, Factor, & Garrett, 1991), whose thinking on dialogue has highly influenced the way many scholars think and write about the process. This chapter describes and expands on the role of listening in a reflective process that includes two subsections to illustrate: (i) how we can *listen to ourselves* to better understand our emotional responses, assumptions, and biases that get in the way of effective listening, and (ii) how we can *listen to understand others*, which creates the conditions for dialogue. Previous theory and research suggests that when organizational members practice this type of listening, it will promote authentic leadership, foster interpersonal connection, and create a culture of constructive conflict management.

Communication for Constructive Workplace Conflict, First Edition. Jessica Katz Jameson.
© 2023 John Wiley & Sons, Inc. Published 2023 by John Wiley & Sons, Inc.

Listening to Ourselves

Edgar Schein's quote at the opening of this chapter comes from his essay on dialogue, culture, and organizational learning (1993). Here he describes that dialogue requires listening to understand where another person is coming from. In order to do this, we have to listen without concern for protecting our own assumptions, values, and worldview. This kind of listening may also be defined as a self-awareness that leads to self-monitoring. Self-awareness involves reflecting on how your own worldview, which comes from family, culture, religious views, political leanings, profession, and life experience, impacts what you hear and how you interpret what you hear (Astor, 2007). For example, imagine you are talking to a friend who is looking at their cell phone during your conversation. While your experience tells you that many people look at their phones while engaged in conversation, you still find yourself getting angry, thinking "I really need a friend right now, what is so important that she is looking at her phone rather than paying attention to me?" If you are practicing self-awareness in that moment, you will pause and reflect on your emerging anger and, rather than assuming the worst and acting on it, you might acknowledge what is happening and demonstrate curiosity by asking, "Is everything okay?" While this is a simple example, that moment of inner listening may make the difference between saying something you regret and showing compassion or concern.

Bohm (1996; Bohm, Factor, & Garrett, 1991), originally referred to this act of noticing your emotions and reflecting rather than acting on them as "suspension," coming from the idea of suspending judgment or avoiding the urge to attack another person's idea or statement. In her study of how mediators engage in listening, Coburn (2012) describes suspension as "the ability to listen to ourselves, to listen within, and to discern our own emotions, reactivity, prejudices, habits and patterns" (p. 100). She explicitly connects the process of suspension to reflection when she writes, "if we can suspend certainty, then we may bring an attitude of inquiry, a capacity for reflection-in-action" (p. 102). This idea of listening to ourselves is an important first step in non-evaluative listening, which enables us to listen with openness and empathy that leads to greater understanding and, ultimately, collaborative problem solving.

A workplace example may help illustrate the value of inner listening. In a team meeting, someone may present an idea that displays a lack of knowledge about a client that you work with closely. As they continue to talk and others expand on the original idea, you may find yourself getting frustrated and defensive. You may be thinking that, based on your history with the client, you have a good sense that this client would respond negatively to the ideas currently being developed by the group. Importantly, as you are having this inner dialogue about your frustration and what you "know" about the client, you are no longer listening to the group conversation. You have made an evaluation that this will not be valuable, and in doing so you may miss out on new information team members are sharing. Rather than continuing to rehearse what you want to say next, you might consider asking a question to help you better understand where they are coming from and why they may think this is an idea worth pursuing. By genuinely asking about evidence or data on which their idea is based, you then open the door to share additional information with the team in a non-defensive way, leading to more openness. The two brief sample conversations that follow illustrate the difference between a defensive reaction versus a thoughtful response that can result from listening to oneself:

Defensive reaction:

BOB: I think we need to come up with a rebate plan to encourage customers to increase their inventory and prevent the need for urgent requests that our production schedule cannot meet.

JOCELYN: That is a great idea; it creates a huge problem for customer service when they have to tell one of our biggest customers that we cannot fulfill their orders.

YOU: We have had a rebate plan for the last 10 years; where have you all been?

BOB: Well that plan clearly isn't working so you must have dropped the ball or it isn't being implemented properly. If we use my plan. . .

Note that in this scenario, conflict escalation ensues, and you and Bob are increasingly defensive, accusatory, and angry.

Response using the inner process of suspension:

BOB: I think we need to come up with a rebate plan to encourage customers to increase their inventory and prevent the need for urgent requests that our production schedule cannot meet.

JOCELYN: That is a great idea; it creates a huge problem for customer service when they have to tell one of our biggest customers that we cannot fulfill their orders.

YOU: Can you say more about the urgent requests we have been getting and how these are creating a problem for our company?

BOB: Based on our data since the last annual report, this customer has requested expedited shipping six more times than usual over the previous year.

YOU: Okay, so I'm hearing that the issue may be more related to order fulfillment as opposed to inventory. Since we already have a rebate program in place, we may need to search for a solution related to shipping rather than purchasing, do you agree?

Note how this response may lead to further collaborative discussion of the causes of the problem and potential solutions.

An important component of listening to oneself and self-monitoring before we respond is emotion regulation. Emotion regulation is the psychological process of being aware of our emotions and regulating them, usually through either cognitive reappraisal or emotional suppression (Ochsner & Gross, 2005). Cognitive reappraisal involves asking yourself questions such as "why do I feel this way," "is there someone to blame," or "does this emotion serve me?" (Lazarus, 1991). The goal is to see if we can reframe the situation to better cope and respond. The second route to emotional regulation is to suppress it, which may be valuable in the moment (for example, if you are feeling angry, it may be prudent not to express anger in a conversation with your boss). While emotional suppression should probably not be used as a long-term strategy, it can serve as a valuable skill for listening.

As noted in the work of Coburn (2012), there are good insights on how to practice inner listening from studying mediators. We learned in Chapter 2 that mediators are third parties who help parties in conflict come to mutual agreement. In order to be successful, they need to appear neutral so that one party does not feel the mediator is siding with the other. Of course, mediators are human and they have their own views, values, and biases, which means they have to be able to listen to themselves and monitor their responses to disputing parties, especially when both parties are in the room at the same time. Coburn provides several examples of strategies mediators use to self-monitor. Most important is that they are able to "catch themselves" in the process of evaluating what a party is saying, getting angry, or making assumptions about a party based on stereotypes. One mediator Coburn interviewed described her inner dialogue, moving from evaluating the person as "strange" to realizing that she needed to ask questions to better understand where the party was coming from:

> Even if on the first reaction you think "That's really strange and how can somebody think that way!" [you have] to put that aside and think, "Well, I want to know why the person thinks that way". Even if on that first reaction you went, "Huh, that's strange". Well, [instead you] say to yourself, "Hey, hang on, put that aside", and think, "I really want to see how they tick." (Coburn, 2012, p. 102)

Based on the several examples shared in this opening section, listening to oneself consists of the following practices, all of which can also be categorized as "reflection-in-action" (Schön, 1983):

- Self-awareness: Be aware of your initial reaction to what someone is saying, whether it is a judgment or defensiveness you may feel when someone says or does something that you feel is disrespectful or wrong.

- Self-monitoring: Once you practice awareness, you have the ability to control your response based on what is most appropriate for the given situation (bearing in mind the desire to have a productive conversation and maintain a good relationship with the other person).
- Suspension: Use that awareness to suspend your assumptions and be open to different possibilities, such as:
  - Intent: I am assuming s/he intends to insult or question me, but they may not realize what they are saying hurts my feelings.
  - Values: I am assuming that person's actions are due to a certain value system, but that may not be accurate.
  - Hypotheses: I am assuming that this is the reason why this happened, but I may be wrong.
- Emotion regulation: Once you suspend judgment, you can recognize the emotion that you are feeling, name it, and set it aside until you have more information rather than responding instinctively.
- Curiosity and openness: Respond with curiosity rather than judgment by asking questions such as "Why do you feel that way" or "Can you say more about why you think that is?"

This first step of inner listening thus paves the way for listening to others with a goal of understanding, rather than persuading, arguing, or imposing your views and values on the other.

Listening to Understand Others

As described in Chapter 2, there are big differences in how we listen when our goal is to win an argument as opposed to when our goal is to understand another person's (or group's) opinion, perspective, or experience. A goal of truly understanding another person means letting go of assumptions, implicit bias, or expectations, and being truly open and curious, as described above. Scholars have found that conflicts that are intractable – which means they are resistant to resolution – are overly simplified by parties who are closed to any new information (Kugler & Coleman, 2020). One of the most famous models of conflict escalation is described by John Gottman as the "four horsemen of the apocalypse." The model includes criticism, defensiveness, contempt, and stonewalling (Gottman & Silver, 1999). While these ideas were developed in studies of behaviors that predict divorce, they can be applied to nearly all types of interpersonal conflict. This is relevant to effective listening because when conflicts begin with criticism, which is heard as an attack, the listener immediately stops listening and moves to defensiveness, as we saw with Carl in Box 3.1 above. In contrast, conflicts tend to de-escalate and move toward discussion and resolution when parties remain open. This requires use of

---

Box 3.1   How Defensiveness Prevents Listening to Understand

Carl is the director of marketing at an agency where he has worked for about 10 years. He is generally liked by his staff and does a great job of attracting and maintaining clients. Carl is constantly juggling multiple projects and delegates heavily to the administrative assistants in the office. Carl has become particularly dependent on Joanna because of her organizational and writing skills. When Carl is feeling stressed, he is often seen dashing through the office, talking out loud to himself, and, occasionally, barking orders at others. At times, Carl can be loud and aggressive. Most of the employees laugh off Carl's behavior and attribute it to his "Type A" personality, telling themselves and others that this is what makes their firm successful. Carl generally calms down and returns to his normal, jovial self by the end of the day.

Joanna likes her job and many of the people at the firm, so she tries her best to accept this behavior from Carl as "just the way he is." However, the more he has delegated tasks to her, the more uncomfortable she has become with Carl's communication style. She is particularly offended by his loud manner, as she feels she is on the receiving end of his aggression when she is doing her best to help him. She knows that Carl is popular with her coworkers and customers, so feels she has no one to turn to. One day he barges into her workspace and demands, "Where is the damn ad copy I asked you for?" Joanna decides this is the last straw and she gathers the nerve to go to the human resources (HR) office to report the increased stress she is feeling on the job and her perception that Carl is creating an uncomfortable work environment. HR offers to investigate, but Joanna is concerned about upsetting Carl and jeopardizing her job. She asks if there are any other options. The HR counselor suggests that he could facilitate a conversation to help her talk to Carl directly about how his communication style is affecting her. She agrees she would be willing to try this.

Carl is a bit taken aback by the request from HR to attend a facilitated session with Joanna, but he does not want to lose a capable employee so he agrees. The HR counselor brings Carl and Joanna to her office and starts by asking Joanna to explain the difficulty she is having. Joanna calmly describes that she gets very anxious when Carl yells at her and does not feel this leads to the most effective work on her part. Carl immediately interrupts to say he does not yell *at* Joanna; yelling, and occasional profanity, is just a habit that comes out when he gets stressed. He reminds Joanna that this is a demanding job, and he is responsible for making sure they get and keep their clients. He goes on to say that if he does not get the job done the firm will close, and they will all be out of a job. At this point Joanna does not feel safe, and she remains quiet. Recognizing the situation is uncomfortable, Carl says, "I know I take some getting used to, but my bark is worse than my bite." Joanna sees that Carl is trying to take some responsibility, and she thanks him just to end the interaction and get out of the HR office. She does not feel heard, and she leaves the HR session with little confidence that anything is going to improve.

For Reflection and Discussion:

1) What do you think prevented Carl from effectively listening to Joanna? How could Carl have used the five principles of reflection-in-action discussed above (self-awareness, self-monitoring, suspension, emotion regulation, and curiosity/openness) at any point during his interactions with Joanna? (What kind of inner dialogue might he have with himself?)
2) Write a script between Carl and Joanna to demonstrate how this conversation might have gone if each of them were using these principles of reflection-in-action.
3) Contrast the outcome of this conversation to the case in Box 2.1, the conflict between Roberta and Margaret. What are some differences that may have led to more effective listening and understanding in Box 2.1 in contrast to the interaction between Carl and Joanna?
4) How does the response of employees to Carl's behavior impact the organizational environment and what is considered acceptable? How would you analyze the phases of this conflict using Rummel's conflict helix (see Chapter 1).

the five principles of reflection-in-action described above. It is also worth noting that this is not easy, and, in a special journal issue devoted to listening, Kugler and Coleman (2020) describe that effective listening requires parties to "engage in higher levels of cognitive, emotional, and behavioral complexity" (p. 213). The kind of empathic listening being described here is complex, as it requires self-awareness, emotion regulation, nonjudgment, and openness to refrain from reacting with instinctive defensiveness. As illustrated in Box 2.1 in the previous chapter, it is often more likely for parties to listen effectively in a facilitated session, such as mediation, in which a third party sets ground rules and creates an environment to support these more complex and reflective behaviors. In fact, other scholars in the same special issue on listening point out that difficult inter-group conversations, such as those that might occur between Jews and Muslims who work together in Israel, for example, are most successful when they are "long-term, gradually evolving, and facilitated dialogue processes" (Maoz & Frosh, 2020, p. 205). The subsequent paragraphs summarize research on the conditions for effective dialogue and, by extension, the way parties must prepare themselves for the type of listening that is a prerequisite for success. As you will see, there is substantial overlap with ideas described in the first section on listening to oneself, self-awareness, and self-monitoring. The three conditions for effective listening and dialogue described below include (i) letting go of defensiveness and assumptions; (ii) being inclusive of all voices; and (iii) asking questions rather than persuading. Because these conditions and behaviors require a lot of reflection and are new to many people, the chapter includes tips from research on mindfulness on how we can practice self-awareness and non-evaluative listening (see Box 3.2).

Box 3.2   Listening through Mindfulness Practice

The ideas about effective, empathic listening described in this chapter are counter to patterns of judgment about whether the speaker is a threat that are deeply ingrained and, in some ways, physiologically designed to protect us from harm. Changing habits of judgment and defensiveness takes practice, and one way to do this is through mindfulness practice. Mindfulness has received a lot of attention and is often misunderstood. While its origin is in Buddhism, it is not a religious practice, but a way of staying present in the moment and not allowing our thoughts to take over, which can escalate emotions such as stress and anxiety (for example, when all you can think about is a paper deadline or a difficult conversation you need to have with a friend). Mindfulness practice can be done in about 5–10 minutes per day and involves trying to stay in the moment as much as possible. This is often done by focusing on the breath, as that is something we all have and constantly do, so it is always there. While sitting with a straight back (in a chair or on a cushion), close your eyes and pay attention to your breathing as it goes in and out. As you sit, thoughts will come to your mind. The goal is to acknowledge the thought, but not to judge it as good or bad, and then let it go (it can help to visualize the thought as a cloud moving past you). Then return to the breath (counting the in and out breaths can also help you focus). The idea is to remind us that thoughts do not have to be dwelled upon; we can set them aside and give them attention later. By practicing this for 10 minutes each day, you can start to become more self-aware, which can lead to greater self-monitoring, suspension of judgment, and openness to what is happening in the moment. There are many apps out there that can guide mindfulness meditation practice, and many of them are free.[1]

Let Go of Defensiveness and Assumptions

When we believe we are under attack, we simultaneously put up our defenses and go into fight or flight mode. Once that happens, we either try to exit the situation as quickly as possible (sometimes an appropriate action, to be discussed further in Chapter 4), or we go on the offensive. This is a healthy and natural response designed to protect ourselves, but it is counterproductive when the goal is to have

---

[1] *Calm* is a great app, but there is a cost for full access. Another one is *Aura*. There are countless others worth investigating, and ancillary benefits may include emotion regulation, decreased stress and anxiety, and improved interpersonal relationships. Adapted from Davis & Hayes, 2011.

a difficult conversation. A good example of how this often happens in the workplace is an employee feedback session. It is part of a supervisor's job to let employees know when they are performing well, along with taking corrective action when someone makes an error or is not performing to expectations. The challenge here is how to listen to negative feedback without getting defensive. While the delivery of the feedback is important to creating a supportive climate that does not attack or criticize (to be discussed more in Chapter 4), the listener can also control how they attend and respond to corrective feedback. Based on the "four horsemen" model of conflict escalation, we know that criticism leads to defensiveness, so the goal for the recipient of the feedback is not to hear the feedback as a personal critique. This is much easier said than done, yet the principles of reflection-in-action described earlier provide guidance here. As an example, imagine a supervisor (or an instructor) who indicates reports have been turned in that include errors, and you need to take the time to proofread your work before you turn it in. You might interpret this as a personal attack, thinking that the supervisor is accusing you of sloppy work and perceiving that you do not do your job well. If you are *self-aware*, you will recognize you are jumping to this conclusion, and you can practice *suspension* to set aside this assumption so you can listen attentively and learn more from the speaker. This *self-monitoring* allows you to *regulate your emotions*, so instead of getting angry, you might say to yourself "it is my supervisor's job to make sure I am working correctly, this is not personal, and I need to hear it and adjust my behavior appropriately." You might then use *curiosity* to ask questions to help clarify what you are hearing and develop a collaborative solution. When the supervisor has finished speaking, you might ask, "Can you show me a specific example of where my report did not meet the standards?" This will make sure you know specifically what you did wrong, and you don't have to guess. You might also ask something like, "Do you have any specific strategies you use to proofread your work that I can learn from?" This sort of response helps "close the loop" on the feedback, so that not only are you learning more precisely what went wrong, but you also have a specific plan for moving forward in a more positive and productive way. A benefit of this model of listening and responding is that you leave the interaction feeling more confident in moving forward, rather than leaving with a lack of clarity, hurt feelings, and possibly frustration or anger with your supervisor, which can have long-term effects on the relationship and your work climate.

In the example of a feedback session, the criticism may be felt as an individual or personal attack, but even more complex emotions may develop when we perceive an attack on a group we identify with. As an example, imagine you are an accountant who has been assigned to a work team that consists of coworkers from sales, customer service, and marketing. During a team meeting, you offer a comment on the effect of the team's proposal on the company bottom line, and one of the team members responds by saying, "all you accountants think about is balance sheets." In this case, suspending judgment of this comment as an attack may be harder because it is a criticism of an important identity group. If you let this comment go, you may feel disloyal to your professional group, in addition to feeling a personal attack. Ellis (2020) describes how this feeling of disloyalty is likely to make difficult conversations especially difficult when the identity group is more central to our identity, such as race, ethnicity, or religion. Yet even in this example, by being self-aware and using our self-monitoring skills, we can listen to what the person is saying and suspend judgment, responding with objective facts and curiosity, such as by saying, "Well yes, it is the job of accountants to pay attention to the projected costs and revenue of various proposals. I want our team to succeed, so can we discuss possible revisions that will increase the likelihood that management will accept this idea?" Contrast this with the kind of response that might first enter someone's mind, such as, "No kidding you jerk, why do you think I'm on this team?" You might take a moment here to reflect on how the conversation is likely to move forward – and the longer term effect on the team – based on which of the two responses are offered. Suspending defensiveness is hard, but the benefits to relationships and creating a workplace environment that supports collaboration and dialogue are well worth the effort.

In addition to using suspension to avoid hearing a criticism as an attack, we can also practice self-awareness and self-monitoring to suspend the assumptions and stereotypes we may have about the speaker (Ellis 2020). We should not assume that we know a person's intent, views, or values. In the first example of a feedback session with a supervisor, an employee might assume that the supervisor does not like them. This assumption will influence the interpretations of the message in a way that presumes an attack and discourages listening. Even more troubling in the workplace (as well as in society in general) is when we assume we know about the other's views and values based on their identity group (political party, skin color, religion, place of birth, sex, etc.). Because the workplace is filled with employees from diverse backgrounds, there is a danger of "moral exclusion," which occurs when we believe members of another identity group are so morally inferior that they do not deserve to be listened to (Dorjee & Ting-Toomey, 2020; Maoz & Frosh, 2020). In difficult cross-cultural conversations, Broome (2013) has described that it is one role of a facilitator to "nurture respect for the other by encouraging deep listening," which is the kind of listening described in this chapter. Ellis (2020) describes a three-step process originally proposed by Gaertner and Dovidio (2000) that helps move beyond assumptions and stereotypes by attending to the language we use to describe the self and the other. This three-step process includes: (i) Decategorization: instead of putting people in a category (e.g., all accountants only care about numbers), think of the person speaking as an individual (e.g., Jeff is a unique individual who happens to be an accountant); (ii) Mutual differentiation: consider how the speaker and the listener are both unique individuals (e.g., Jeff is an accountant and I am in sales, it is natural that we are going to see things differently based on our training and experience); and (iii) Recategorization: in this step we come up with a new way of thinking about the other in place of our initial assumption or stereotype (e.g., Jeff is a teammate and he cares about the success of the team). When we recategorize an "other" in a new way, this may also allow us to rehumanize them (Maoz & Frosh, 2020) and, therefore, see them as having an important point of view and worth listening to. This leads to a second condition for effective listening and dialogue: inclusivity.

Be Inclusive

Inclusivity is a word that is often used, and often in conjunction with diversity, but the difference between the two is not always well understood. A diverse organization includes members who come from many different backgrounds. This diversity may refer to age, sex, race, ethnicity, sexual orientation, ability, and religion, for example. At one time, there was a big focus on increasing diversity in our organizations and institutions, and this is still an important value. However, we have learned that just having diversity is not enough to improve equality and fairness. It is not enough for organizations to have diverse members; organizational members need to value their contributions and include them in the decision-making process. The realization that members from underrepresented groups, such as African Americans and other Black persons, LatinX, Muslims, and those who identify as LGBTQ, are often treated differently than members of the majority group (usually White, Judeo-Christians in the United States) has led to more focus on inclusiveness.

We are inclusive when we listen to everyone and value their input equally. This is a corollary to the above discussion of suspending assumptions and stereotypes. We should not assume that because someone is Black or White they feel the same way about law enforcement, or assume that because someone is a Democrat or a Republican they all feel the same way about health care. One reason we want diversity in our organizations (aside from the obvious moral imperative) is that we want and need multiple perspectives to engage in critical thinking and effective collaboration and problem solving (Ellis, 2020; Dorjee & Ting-Toomey, 2020). If we are not inclusive by listening to, hearing, and acknowledging multiple perspectives, we are being disingenuous about and defeating the purpose of having a diverse organization.

A major challenge to inclusivity and effective listening that will be discussed throughout this book is power. Rummel's model of conflict described in Chapter 1 pointed out that a major stage of conflict revolves around how power is balanced during conflict. You may recall that conflict parties may use coercive or non-coercive power in this power-balancing phase. Coercive power is often used by those who have more power because they can effectively shut down the others.

One way to shoot others down is by refusing to listen because a conversation is uncomfortable. Note how Carl ends the conversation with Joanna in Box 3.1 by trying to explain that this is just the way he is and that his "bark is worse than his bite." At that point, Joanna is not in a position to push back as Carl has power over whether she keeps her job. Yet Carl's intentions are less important than the *impact* of his words, which may be creating a hostile environment for Joanna. These power dynamics also come into play in conversations between members of majority and underrepresented identity groups. In Robin DiAngelo's (2018) book *White Fragility*, she illustrates how White people often shut down conversations about racism because they feel they are being accused of being "bad people." Yet because the United States has a history of racism that has been institutionalized and reinforced over the years, charges of racism don't need to be heard as personal attacks as much as a reminder that we have important work to do to overcome ideas, assumptions, and behaviors that have the effect of marginalizing and oppressing people from underrepresented groups such as those who are Black, Brown, or LatinX. When a member of the dominant White identity group says, "I'm not racist" and is unwilling to continue the conversation, it is an important example of not listening, not being curious and open, and as a result, racism continues to be perpetuated. This also results in a lack of inclusiveness, which is often invisible (to members of the majority group) in meetings and even social gatherings where voices and experiences of members from underrepresented groups are unheard and unrecognized.

One way of facilitating inclusivity is to create agreement on ground rules for difficult conversations or even team meetings. Ground rules might include principles such as making sure everyone participates and requiring speakers to provide clear evidence and data to support arguments. Importantly, Ellis (2020) points out that participants must be open to different views of what counts as evidence. While in the West (North America, Europe) we tend to privilege rationality and facts, other cultures see narratives and lived experience as important types of evidence. When a more powerful group says another person's evidence does not count, they are using power to shut down dialogue and reduce inclusivity (Ellis, 2020). The antidote to this is to focus on curiosity and openness by asking questions and listening to the conversation that unfolds.

Ask Questions

As illustrated above, an important way to engage in active, empathic listening and practice openness and curiosity is to ask questions. This allows us to avoid assumptions and move toward understanding and is a condition for dialogue. This emphasis on inquiry over advocacy (trying to persuade others to our view or "win" the argument) has also been shown to be a characteristic of high-functioning teams. In observations of hundreds of teams, Losada (1999) found that those whose communication included more instances of inquiry than advocacy had team members that were more engaged and satisfied and the teams were more innovative and productive. When we are in a diverse group or talking with someone from a different cultural background or identity group, conflict may be triggered because we are confronted by a different set of expectations about appropriate behavior. Asking questions enables us to learn more about other worldviews and expectations rather than falling back on assumptions. One challenge of asking questions is figuring out what to ask and asking in a way that is nonjudgmental. Several scholars and practitioners offer suggestions for how to ask useful questions that can lead to understanding.

A YouTube video provides an excerpt from a workshop facilitated by Dan O'Connor, a consultant and trainer with an organization called Power Diversity. In the clip from a business communication workshop, O'Connor (2009) suggests that any awkward moment where one feels offended or disrespected can be addressed by asking one of four "magic phrases." They all begin with the comment: "That's interesting" followed by one of four prompts: "Tell me more"; "Why would you say that?"; "Why would you do that?"; "Why would you ask that?"

As described by O'Connor, asking such questions helps to get more information and allows one to collect oneself before making a hasty response that is likely to escalate an awkward situation. Note how this language sounds a lot like what was described when I covered the concepts of self-monitoring and suspension. While these phrases are consistent with the discussion of the value of inquiry, I would add that one must be very careful in how one asks these questions to reduce the potential for defensiveness. If the question is asked in a polite, supportive style, the continued conversation might allow the listener to learn something new and change their initial opinion of the communication as offensive. The way these questions are posed will make all the difference in whether conflict escalates or an engaging dialogue ensues.

Another example of the kinds of questions that can lead to dialogue and greater understanding in difficult conversations comes from Kenneth Cloke (2020), a nationally recognized mediator who has authored many articles and books on conflict resolution and is Director of the Center for Dispute Resolution in Santa Monica, California. Given the adversarial political climate of 2020, he wrote an article for a newsletter on Mediate.com that includes "50 questions you can ask friends and relatives in political arguments." While the dialogue that we want to foster in the workplace may not be about politics, per se, the questions Cloke suggests offer models of the types of questions that encourage others to expand on their statements so we can better understand where they are coming from and, to the central point of this chapter, show that we are actively listening. Many of the questions suggested by Cloke are relevant to any topic, such as, "What life experiences have you had that led you to feel so passionately about this issue?" or

"Do you have any doubts or grey areas about this that you would be willing to discuss?" Note how these open-ended questions invite others to reflect on and consider where their views come from or look for possible points of common ground between the speaker and listener.

An article by Miles (2013) provides strategies for asking questions in negotiation. He underscores the important point that by asking good questions in a conflict situation, we learn more about the other party's underlying interests and concerns and this can help us find creative solutions that meet both (or all) parties' needs. Miles points to research on negotiation that has concluded, "less than 10 percent of a typical negotiation conversation involves sharing information" (p. 384). It may be intuitive that parties to a negotiation will resist sharing information, as we typically think of negotiations as adversarial, competitive interactions where the goal of one party is to get the better deal or outcome. Yet we can also approach negotiations as more collaborative or integrative, meaning that the goal is for both parties to maximize their outcomes while maintaining a positive relationship. This will be discussed further in Unit Two on engaging conflict. For now, the main point is to consider that asking questions facilitates active, empathic listening and promotes dialogue, or collaborative conflict management and problem solving. The discussion of asking questions during negotiation reminds us that such questions should be asked in a way that is authentic, showing the other party the question comes from a desire to learn rather than manipulate the other into providing information to be used against them. When we use communication and questions to better understand others and their experiences rather than to debate and persuade, there is tremendous potential for creating a relationship and environment of collaboration.

Chapter Summary

The goal of Chapter 3 was to provide specific ideas and practices to help us become more effective, empathic listeners, as this is the first step of the LEARN framework toward developing constructive workplace environments. The chapter described five practices that support reflection-in-action (Schön, 1983): self-awareness, self-monitoring, suspension, emotion regulation, and curiosity or openness. Working on reflection-in-action helps us stay focused on the present moment, or conversation, rather than getting lost in thoughts or unhelpful judgments and assumptions about the other(s) we are communicating with. The chapter then turned to how we can listen with the goal of understanding the other speaker and where they are coming from. This builds empathy and reduces our reliance on assumptions that can get in the way of effective listening. Conditions for listening to understand (which is also what supports dialogue, as opposed to a debate mindset) include

(i) Letting go of defensiveness and assumptions (which are supported by listening to ourselves!); (ii) Being inclusive, which involves treating everyone as valuable and seeing everyone's contribution as important; and (iii) Asking good questions, which refers to asking open-ended questions geared toward understanding why someone believes what they do or supports a certain outcome, and asking authentically with a goal of understanding and collaborating, as opposed to persuading to try to win an argument. When we listen in this way, we are actively and authentically engaging with another, and this is the next step in the LEARN framework that is discussed in Unit Two, Chapters 4 and 5.

Activity: Non-evaluative Listening

Step 1. This activity requires you to work with a partner. Each student should plan to describe a current problem or conflict you are experiencing. Decide who will be the speaker and listener for the first round. The most important rules are that the student in the listener role CANNOT:

1) judge or evaluate the validity of the speaker's problem, concerns, or needs, or the actions they have taken so far
2) offer a solution to the speaker's problem or conflict.

The listener SHOULD ask questions to help the speaker become more self-aware, identify assumptions they are making, and better understand the problem or conflict and come up with ways they can manage it.

Step 2. After about 5–10 minutes, switch roles.

For Reflection and Discussion:

1) Was this activity difficult to do? Why or why not?
2) What kinds of questions were most valuable for helping the speaker gain self-awareness or other insights?
3) What kinds of questions helped the listener better understand the problem from the speaker's point of view?

References

Astor H. (2007). Mediator neutrality: Making sense of theory and practice. *Social and Legal Studies, 16*(2): 221–239. https://doi.org/10.1177/0964663907076531.

Bohm, D. (1996). *On dialogue*. New York: Routledge.

Bohm, D., Factor, D., & Garrett, P. (1991). Dialogue – A proposal. Retrieved October 18, 2020, from http://www.david-bohm.net/dialogue/dialogue_proposal.html#5

Broome, B. (2013). *Building cultures of peace: The role of intergroup dialogue*. In J. G. Oetzel and S. Ting-Toomey (Eds.), *The SAGE handbook of conflict communication* (2nd ed., pp. 737–762). Thousand Oaks, CA: Sage.

Cloke, K. (2020). 50 questions you can ask friends and relatives in political arguments. Mediate.com, December 2020. Retrieved December 24, 2020, from https://www.mediate.com/articles/cloke-50-questions.cfm

Coburn, C. (2012). Developing listening and suspension capacities for mediators. *Australian Dispute Resolution Journal, 23*: 99–105.

Davis, D. M., & Hayes, J. A. (2011). What are the benefits of mindfulness? A practice review of psychotherapy-related research. *Psychotherapy, 48*(2): 198–208. https://doi.org/10.1037/a0022062.

DiAngelo, R. (2018). *White fragility: Why it's so hard for white people to talk about racism*. Boston, MA: Beacon Press.

Dorjee, T., & Ting-Toomey, S. (2020). Understanding intergroup conflict complexity: An application of the socioecological framework and the integrative identity negotiation theory. *Negotiation and Conflict Management Research, 13*(3): 244–262. https://doi.org/10.1111/ncmr.12190.

Ellis, D. G. (2020). Talking to the enemy: Difficult conversations and ethnopolitical conflict. *Negotiation and Conflict Management Research, 13*(3): 183–196. https://doi.org/10.1111/ncmr.12187.

Gaertner, S. L., & Dovidio, J. F. (2000). *Reducing intergroup bias: The common ingroup identity model*. New York: Psychology Press.

Gottman, J. M., & Silver, N. (1999). *The seven principles for making marriage work*. New York: Three Rivers Press.

Kugler, K. G., & Coleman, P. T. (2020). Get complicated: The effects of complexity on conversations over potentially intractable moral conflicts. *Negotiation and Conflict Management Research, 13*(3): 211–230. https://doi.org/10.1111/ncmr.12192.

Lazarus, R. S. (1991). *Emotion and adaptation*. New York: Oxford University Press.

Losada, M. (1999). The complex dynamics of high performance teams. *Mathematical and Computer Modeling, 30*: 179–192.

Maoz, I., & Frosh, P. (2020). Imagine all the people: Negotiating and mediating moral concern through intergroup encounters. *Negotiation and Conflict Management Research, 13*(3): 197–210. https://doi.org/10.1111/ncmr.12189.

Miles, E. W. (2013). Developing strategies for asking questions in negotiation. *Negotiation Journal, 29*(4): 383–412. https://doi.org/10.1111/nejo.12034.

Ochsner, K., & Gross, J. J. (2005). The cognitive control of emotion. *Trends in Cognitive Sciences, 9*: 242–249.

O'Connor, D. (2009). Four magic phrases you can use to respond to ANYTHING (Video). Retrieved January 1, 2023, from https://www.youtube.com/watch?v=g5RknemM8Hw&feature=related

Schein, E. H. (1969). *Process consultation: Its role in organization development.* Reading, PA: Addison-Wesley.

Schein, E. H. (1993). On dialogue, culture, and organizational learning. *Organizational Dynamics, 22*(2): 40–51. https://doi.org/10.1016/0090-2616(93)90052-3.

Schön, D. A. (1983). *The reflective practitioner: How professionals think in action.* New York: Routledge.

Unit Two

Engage

4

Obstacles to Engaging Conflict

Not everything that is faced can be changed, but nothing can be changed that is not faced.

James Baldwin (1924–1987, author and civil rights activist)

The E in the LEARN framework stands for *Engage*. When you feel that someone has treated you in a way that is unfair or disrespectful, or they have an idea that you disagree with or you believe interferes with achieving your goals, one of the first questions you may ask yourself is: "Should I say something, or should I let it go?" This chapter describes the variety of reasons, some of which are quite reasonable, why we often choose the latter. Yet, as Baldwin famously reminds us in the opening quote, if we do not engage in the conversation, and are not willing to risk the conflict that ensues, nothing will change. We become complicit in the problematic behavior, whether it is injustice, disrespect, or creating a work situation that we do not agree with, when we choose to avoid conflict. Further, research has shown we actually create a more stressful work climate for ourselves when we avoid conflict (Friedman et al., 2000). Importantly, there are many ways to engage conflict that can help the interaction go more smoothly. The word *engage* is intentional because it is in contrast to the idea of *confronting* another. Confrontation has a connotation that suggests an adversarial, combative stance. Engaging, on the other hand, invites others to connect with us and suggests an open conversation that others want to participate in. The goal of this chapter is to discuss the many obstacles to engaging workplace conflict, such as protecting individual safety, preserving interpersonal relationships, and managing one's position and reputation. It is important to remember that the decision about how to respond to a potential conflict situation is not binary: it is not just *whether* to engage, but also *how* to engage. The next section reminds us that there is a range of conflict styles we can choose to engage conflict.

Many studies of workplace conflict management behavior have been based on the concept of *conflict styles* (Thomas & Kilmann, 1974; Rahim, 1983, 2011). This literature is useful in articulating people's tendencies toward one or more of five styles or approaches to conflict. While the labels vary depending on the instrument used, the framework is based on the dual-concerns model of concern for self and concern for other (Blake & Mouton, 1964; see Figure 4.1). According to the dual-concern model, when there is low concern for self and other in a given conflict situation, people will choose to *avoid*, which typically means their needs will not be met. When there is low concern for self and high concern for other, people will *accommodate* the other party by meeting their needs. When there is high concern for self and low concern for other, people will *compete* to get their own needs met. When there is high concern for self and other, people will *collaborate*, attempting to meet all parties' needs. The model suggests a middle ground, *compromise*, used when people have some desire to get both their own and the other's needs met, but parties are willing to give up some needs in order to resolve the conflict.

A major limitation of the dual-concerns model is an over-simplification of the explanation for why people choose to avoid or accommodate in conflict. My research on organizational conflict management began with an attempt to develop a

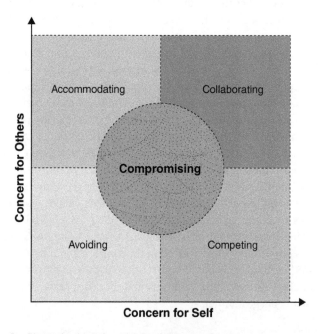

Figure 4.1   Conflict styles based on the Dual Concerns Model.

framework organizational members could use to select the most appropriate conflict management strategy based on the characteristics of a given conflict. The most consistent results from my early research suggested that: (i) participants believed it was better not to deal with conflict at all if you could not resolve it yourself, and (ii) participants did not perceive there was anyone they could turn to for assistance with conflict management. In other words, there was a strong consensus among over 600 participants in this study that workplace conflict should be avoided if it cannot be easily resolved among the parties directly involved in the conflict (Jameson, 1999, 2001). This research suggests that employees avoid conflict not out of low concern for self, but actually out of a very *high* concern for self (and sometimes, other).

My findings were consistent with other research concluding that people often avoid rather than engage conflict in the workplace (Lovelace, Shapiro, & Weingart, 2001). This reality can be juxtaposed with laboratory and field studies that have nearly unanimously concluded that collaboration is *perceived as* the ideal conflict style as it has the best long-term implications for relationships and effective problem solving (Gross & Guerrero, 2000). On the other hand, some have suggested that a combination of competing and collaborating can achieve the most optimal outcomes (Pruitt, 1995). It probably goes without saying that the selection of the most productive or practical conflict style will depend on the characteristics of the specific conflict (the parties involved, the issue, the urgency, and the organizational culture all being important factors).

It is also important to note that there are cultural differences in how people orient to conflict and how they believe it should be engaged. The preponderance of research has concluded that nations with high collectivist values and high power distance (such as China, India, and Japan) are less confrontational and assertive and more cooperative than those with high individualist values such as the United States, Canada, the United Kingdom, and parts of the European Union (Ting-Toomey, 1988). One study comparing South Korean and US employees, for example, found that South Koreans preferred collaborating, compromising, and accommodating, while US participants preferred the avoiding style (Kim & Meyers, 2012). This underscores the challenges to engaging conflict and an underlying goal of the LEARN framework presented here, which is to identify and describe communication tools that emphasize solidarity, respect, face saving, inclusivity, and collaboration. It is therefore my hope that the idea of engaging conflict shared here transcends cultural boundaries.

Two of the main reasons employees in the United States provide for not engaging conflict are (i) concern for retaliation or other negative consequences, and, relatedly, (ii) belief that engaging in the conflict won't change anything. The case below describes how one organization reinforced these concerns even in the midst of trying to create a more open and collaborative conflict management environment.

Having made the point that organizational leaders should desire an environment conducive to engaging conflict, the remainder of this chapter goes into more detail about the major obstacles to creating such an environment. These include common employee narratives about conflict, perceptions of power difference, threats to individual and group identity, and managing the emotions that accompany conflict. Readers may note some overlap among the obstacles to engaging conflict and obstacles to effective listening described in Chapter 2.

Employee Conflict Narratives

My early research on organizational conflict consisted of a series of 12 focus group interviews including 92 participants and resulting in three sets of conflict narratives. Referring back to the communication as constitutive of organization (CCO) perspective, these narratives describe how organizational members develop a shared understanding of conflict and their options for managing it. Two of these narratives, *conflict as political maneuvering* and *conflict as mission impossible*, illustrate why organizational members often choose to avoid, or disengage from, conflict. Importantly, a third narrative was also discovered, which presented *conflict as collaborative problem solving*. This more optimistic and hopeful portrayal of conflict will be discussed in Chapter 5 on *Changing the Rules of Engagement*. In the succeeding sections I have selected from the focus groups portions of text that illustrate each of the first two themes that help explain why employees often choose to avoid conflict or engage in less constructive ways.

Conflict as Political Maneuvering

Organizational conflict is often described as a political game in which members attempt to achieve personal or organizational goals, sometimes at the expense of other members. Whether it is through the exercise of the organizational member's own power, status, or authority; coalition building; or alignment with a more powerful employee, this narrative suggests most participants either witnessed or engaged in acts of political maneuvering within their organizations.

The first example illustrates use of positional power to settle a conflict without taking the time to understand the problem:

> *The head boss said they had to work it out or he was going to take someone's job away. And I thought that was a rather ridiculous way of dealing with it because these people had to continue to work together forever, so threatening them that they have to work it out is not going to maintain that relationship.*

Several participants told similar stories, and in each case focus group members agreed they had seen managers use this tactic. They further reported that this strategy kept the conflict under the surface because it directly encouraged employees to hide the conflict. This leads to a lack of confidence in management and decreased employee morale.

Additional stories described the negative impact of managers who used their power to avoid conflict, rather than taking time to fully understand the underlying issues. One participant described a situation where a decision had to be made about how to delegate a task among three groups, and the manager made a quick decision without fully assessing the situation. The boss said to this employee:

> *"Your group is going to handle it," and within a couple of weeks she sees our team slowly but surely drowning and she said, "what's going on?" And I was thinking, if you had really taken the time to see who could handle the accounts and who couldn't, you would have seen it definitely wasn't us.*

A final example of a manager's use of power to avoid directly addressing a relational conflict illustrates how it resulted in escalating the conflict:

> *So finally I went to resign, and my boss was like "no, it's not you, it's her."... His way of dealing with it was to promote me to office manager. Well here's someone who is already bitter towards me and I'm thinking well that just exacerbated it, she hated me.*

Another set of participants described seeking out a powerful third party to address or resolve conflict:

> *I was having trouble with this one woman who was never going to meetings; she was a very critical person, and she was the one who needed to say yea or nay. And she wasn't going to meetings, and finally I went to my director because I didn't know what to do ... So she actually called this other woman and said, is this supposed to be your department or is this supposed to my department? And the woman said it was her department, so my boss said, well, then you need to be there [at the meetings], and she's been going to the meetings now ...*

While going to a powerful third party can be effective, it can also create additional organizational conflicts, as in the following example, in which the participant felt he was put in the middle of someone else's conflict:

> *... So my director asked me about it, he said, "apparently you don't have the time of the day for [the clients]" and I said "no, my supervisor told me not to*

call them," and at the same time, [the supervisor] walked in, so right there in front of him I said, "that's what you said to me, isn't it?" So I kind of let the cat out of the bag.

The interview participant went on to describe that the supervisor became angry with the participant and asked, "why'd you say that in front of [the director]?" The participant responded with, "I'm not getting involved in your political crap between you and him upstairs, if you're not gonna back me, then too bad."

Focus group participants also shared many situations in which coworkers were relocated, and in some cases even promoted, to separate them from colleagues with whom they could not collaborate. These responses to conflict send a message from leaders that "bad" behavior is rewarded rather than corrected and fuel the belief that engaging in conflict is futile, fostering a climate of silence (Morrison & Milliken, 2000).

We have a gentleman who was assistant manager of a program, and he just happens to be the best friend of the CEO. He was doing his job very poorly, the customers complained, the co-workers complained, his boss complained, so it was handled by promoting him to create a new department . . . There's just a refusal to admit that a problem exists, due to the friendship I guess.

Several participants described a culture of retaliation and revenge that also influenced conflict behavior:

We are a smaller organization, so things that happened months ago people still remember, and if they have not gotten revenge, they are going to somehow seek that out.

We're very level conscious, and if that dispute is with your manager or your manager's manager or even a manager that you don't report to but is in authority higher above you . . . that can be very difficult because that is a sign of power and you have to be very careful about how you tread on those relationships because that can make or break your career with this company.

In summary, this first narrative demonstrated that participants often experienced conflict as a form of political maneuvering, driven by competing interests and multiple agendas, and managed through personal power or networks. Managers frequently asserted their power or authority in an attempt to make conflict go away without solving the real problem. The use of a powerful person in one's organizational network may be effective but may also be perceived as using friendships for personal gain. This concern for one's reputation and how one might be perceived by others helps explain why employees often choose to avoid conflict altogether, which is further developed in the narrative of *conflict as mission impossible.*

Conflict as Mission Impossible

Participants often described conflicts as interpersonal problems that were impossible to solve; thus this theme of *mission impossible.* Relational histories, personality clashes, perceived irrational behavior, and lack of conflict management skills were presented as factors that prevent conflict resolution. Participants often indicated that conflict becomes a mess when personalities get in the way, or, as one participant put it, "human chemistry is the one thing you can't fix." Participants often described irrational or incompetent coworkers who had been with the organization a long time:

> My first job out of college, the woman I worked with directly had been there for 13 years in the same position I was, and she hated me from day one. It didn't matter what I did. It was an administrative assistant position, and my first day on the job she said to me, "it's a shame you went to college for four years to be a secretary." That's how the atmosphere started. So this went on for two years, every day she would take things off my desk, and there was just constant tension, and I would just ignore it.

The mission impossible narrative suggests that employees often perceive conflicts as impossible to resolve because they do not have the skills to manage them constructively. Although some participants described attempts to address conflicts that involved personality clashes, personal histories, or stubborn individuals, the stories emphasized that relational conflicts were not considered worthy of attention in the workplace. In the examples that follow, managers were described as not handling these situations well.

> It was obvious to the people involved in the conflict what was going on and even to observers, that the people who were in a position to do something about it or intervene basically ignore the situation . . . no one else was taking action to do anything about it. And other observers were affected by it because they wonder, "why isn't someone doing anything about it?"
>
> In my company they hire a lot of young people and turnover is very high, so they figure they don't need to worry about a problem because it will just go away. Although maybe if they did pay attention to the problem, turnover wouldn't be so high . . .

As the above examples illustrate, conflict management was often left to employees to handle on their own, yet this created a paradox. On one hand, participants suggested that many employees lacked conflict management skills. On the other hand, they noted that even when conflict management resources were available, organizational members appeared incompetent if they used them. One participant described an email from the HR department offering to help with conflict, but perceived it as disingenuous:

> *Yesterday they sent out an email concerning conflict resolution. Basically it said, "it is the manager's role and responsibility," but it said you are not alone, you have all these other groups that can help you if you need help; but it was like personnel, personal advising services . . . but basically it said it's the manager's role.*

Participants also reported that supervisors viewed them as incompetent when they were unable to resolve the conflict on their own:

> *When we were all together in the same room they [the supervisors] pretty much were like, "you guys need to work this out," they realized that they did not need to be there and couldn't figure out why they were called into this room to discuss this, that it was really something we could have worked out ourselves.*

Similarly, the following stories describe the common perception of what happens when the HR department gets involved in handling the conflict:

> *A lot of HR people don't have any skills to negotiate, not any more than any of us do, probably haven't even taken a course. . . I would never think of going to HR to mediate because I wouldn't think they'd have the skills to do it. I've worked in three large companies, and I've had yet to see an effective HR department.*
>
> *And they've done particular training, and they have people with good social skills, but they seem to spit out whatever they've read in organizational behavior class, but they're not really helping you . . . So you may go in with a dispute, and they just give you all these fluffy words, and an hour later you come out saying, "what was that all about?"*

A variation on the narrative of not using available resources was a story of an organization in which employees were ridiculed when they used their conflict training. In this case, three focus group participants were from the same organization, and they described the use of LET (Leadership Effective Training; names are pseudonyms):

> PETE: *We go through the LET seminars, which teach self-mediation skills. It says, "here's the tools you need to properly listen to the person and get your point across" . . . and they actually do work, especially for people who don't have that skill . . .*

The moderator asked if people use LET, and one participant said they did, but another was not convinced, suggested by the following exchange:

> JEREMY: *Unnnng [Groan and eye-roll]. I don't necessarily buy into it because everyone in the company is required to take it, and if you hear someone using it you get really pissed that they're trying to "LET you."*
>
> PETE: *I can agree if it's done poorly . . . it does look a little corny sometimes, but I think it does work well for the unskilled.*
>
> JEREMY: *I think it works best when the person you're using it on doesn't know you're using it. Like I use it on my wife, and it works real well. But if I were to use it on [Louis], he'd probably pick on me and say, "why are you trying to LET me?"*

Personality clashes, supervisor interference, and the expectation that individuals should be able to handle conflicts on their own despite a lack of any training all constitute the narrative of conflict as mission impossible. The stories told by focus group participants paint a powerful picture of how conflict is often experienced in the workplace. In these stories are echoes of the same narratives heard from focus group and individual interviews with Unity Hospital staff (described in Box 4.1): stories of retribution, use of power, limited employee voice, and the perception that there is no point in rocking the boat.

Individual follow-up interviews with managers in our focus groups provided further explanation for these experiences of workplace conflict. When asked how they resolved conflicts among employees, managers conveyed the importance of taking care of conflict "close to home." In other words, they would be seen as incompetent if they went to another party for assistance with conflicts among their staff. This is an example of why mediation and other alternative dispute resolution (ADR) programs are underutilized; the very people they are intended to help are those who believe they will be penalized for using them. Fear of being seen as incompetent or unprofessional is a central theme explaining why conflict is either avoided or handled poorly.

The conflict narratives described above are significant because focus group participants were diverse members of a variety of organizations and industries.

Box 4.1   Conflict Norms at Unity Hospital

The history of management–employee relations at Unity Hospital (a pseudonym) created a belief among employees that the human resources (HR) department worked on behalf of management and not employees. This perception created a pattern of conflict avoidance as employees believed that engaging conflict would result in retaliation. When new leadership came to the HR department, they were determined to change this reputation and instill trust and confidence in both employees and management. The new HR director believed that one way to achieve this goal would be to involve everyone in the design of a new employee grievance process. They hoped to use principles of dispute system design to implement an approach to conflict management based on resolving the underlying interests of parties rather than using an adversarial, rights-based approach (Ury, Brett, & Goldberg, 1988). This case study describes results of a three-year study of Unity Hospital's new dispute system that included document analysis, surveys, interviews with supervisory and non-supervisory staff, a focus group interview with managers, and a focus group interview with employees. Note that all interviewees were non-medical staff, either administrators or employees in support positions, such as housekeeping and technical support. The case illustrates how employee beliefs and how employees talked about conflict with each other were major obstacles to constructing an environment for engaging conflict.

Interviewees shared stories of supervisor retaliation after learning an employee had consulted the HR office about a conflict. According to one focus group participant, it was hard to stop retaliation because it was impossible to prove – supervisors could easily justify giving an employee a bad shift or denying a vacation request by claiming they had no one else available to work at that time. One of the supervisors said, "When I recommend that employees go to HR, it motivates them to settle it here [in the department]; they are afraid of supervisor retaliation and unfortunately they are right because some supervisors do retaliate." When supervisors engaged in retaliatory actions, it reinforced and deepened the pattern of conflict avoidance. Employees learned not to complain or talk to the HR department and warned coworkers to do the same.

According to focus group participants, the actions of the HR department further intensified the pattern of avoidance. One employee who sincerely believed the HR department wanted to be fair described them this way: "Many times when an employee contacts employee relations, they contact the supervisor to get their side of the story, but no one contacts the employee, so there is still a perception of management bias." Despite the new HR director's verbal commitment to fairness and neutrality, the staff's actions reinforced the perception that employees would not be treated fairly.

The pattern of avoidance was also deepened by the actions of Unity Hospital's senior leadership. Employee climate surveys indicated that even though training programs were valued at Unity, they were not made available to line staff. This was true of a variety of trainings offered at Unity, including mediation and arbitration training, which was only offered to supervisors. When I asked staff members why they could not participate in training, they said the training was not offered at times they could attend and they could not get time off during their shift. By communicating the value of training but not allowing equal access, Unity illustrated a paradox of participation (Stohl & Cheney, 2001) that excluded certain voices and maintained the perception that engaging conflict was futile.

Unity Hospital invested considerable resources into the development of their dispute system process to change this perception, yet communication about the program was confusing and did little to change employees' perceptions about the safety of engaging in conflict. While the brochures mentioned mediation, for example, it was not always clear who would mediate the conflict and what conflicts were suitable for mediation. The ambiguity of options available to get help with conflict undermined the HR director's desire to counter the pattern of employee conflict avoidance described above.

Importantly, evidence suggested that when employees did use the new mediation process, they were very satisfied. Surveys of employees who had used mediation indicated high levels of satisfaction with the HR department. If stories of these satisfied employees had circulated through employee networks, there could have been more adoption of mediation and the new dispute system. Unfortunately, rather than building this more positive narrative, employee experiences with and stories about the previous system reinforced the perception of retribution, and the pattern of conflict avoidance was too culturally embedded to create widespread institutionalization of the new mediation process.

For Reflection and Discussion:

1) Thinking back to the obstacles to effective listening and the model of conflict escalation described in Chapters 2 and 3, why do you think a supervisor would retaliate against an employee who filed a complaint with HR?
2) Think about your own experience as an employee or a student. In what situation might you use a dispute resolution process like the one at Unity Hospital? Why would or wouldn't you seek help to resolve a conflict?
3) Can you come up with any ideas for how Unity Hospital could promote a new set of narratives about how to manage conflict? What would have to change?

The themes provide a snapshot of the type of communication that occurs when people talk about conflict and how this socially constructs the options organizational members see as available for engaging it. Research shows three central obstacles to engaging in productive conflict management, all of which are illustrated in the above narratives: power, identity, and emotion.

Power

Most workplaces have a formal or informal hierarchy. In business organizations, the CEO may not be questioned. In healthcare and academic settings, status may be afforded to people with certain credentials, like an MD or PhD, which may be intimidating to those without such credentials who do not feel their beliefs or ideas will be heard. Organizations with a culture that privileges hierarchy and status have to work harder to create environments that encourage employees to engage conflict to overcome this perception and power dynamic. One major challenge is overcoming some very basic patterns of human interaction that often reinforce power differences.

Dyadic Conflict Communication Patterns

In the *Pragmatics of Human Communication*, Watzlawick, Bavelas, and Jackson (1967) presented two common patterns of human interaction. Symmetrical escalation occurs when parties compete for power by matching each other's moves. When one party yells, the other reciprocates by also yelling. In contrast, complementary patterns of dominance and submission occur when one party makes a move to gain power and the other submits. Neither of these patterns are particularly helpful in a conflict situation. During symmetrical escalation, parties are engaging in conflict but not actively listening to each other as they are embroiled in a power contest. Escalation can go as far as a physical altercation, and it is easy to see where people who get into this pattern would find it better to disengage.

In complementary patterns, one person will typically get their needs met while the other continues to accommodate. This finding is supported by Morrison and Rothman (2009), who demonstrate that people who perceive themselves as having lower power will most typically submit to someone with higher power. This pattern is not sustainable, however. Eventually the submissive member will become frustrated and will take action to resist the person with more power, which may escalate conflict (a specific example of this is decribed in Chapter 6, Box 6.1). Other impacts of accommodating might include excessive absences, theft, absenteeism, and other antisocial workplace behavior (Trudel & Reio, 2011). Because many people in the United States learn to either directly engage conflict to win or run to avoid conflict, it is no surprise that the dominant conflict pattern is adversarial.

Patterns of Power in Work Teams

Status and hierarchical distinctions also have a chilling effect in work groups and teams. Consider a healthcare team working on a patient with a complex illness. This team may include a resident, a nurse, a medical specialist, a psychological counselor, a rehab specialist, and a pharmacist (to name a few). Each of these team members has important expertise to contribute to the patient's care, but each also has his or her own interests, priorities, and schedules to maintain. The best interests of the patient require that the team share information and collaboratively develop a treatment plan, but the institutional structure and culture (i.e., the pressure to treat many patients in a single day) is such that team members may communicate solely by notes on the patient's chart or brief "corridor conversations" as they pass each other in the hallways in between patients (Ellingson, 2005; Long, Iedema, & Lee, 2007).

Nonprofit boards of directors share dynamics found in workplace teams. Composed of volunteers from diverse backgrounds, these groups are further challenged by the fact that they only meet monthly or quarterly, so the members may not have much relational history. Status is often conferred on board members based on their length of service to the organization, association with a high-status profession such as a law office, or a specific expertise such as accounting. In a two-year study in which we observed a full year of board meetings for four unique organizations, we found it was common for members with more tenure on the board to dominate meetings. Interviews with board members confirmed that newer members often perceived themselves as accommodating others. We also found that members often accepted the reports of officers, such as the treasurer, without asking any questions, allowing their conclusions to go unchallenged even when obvious errors were included in the report (Metelsky & Jameson, 2013). Since all board members have an ethical obligation to understand financial reports and other important organizational documents, difficult questions often need to be asked, regardless of status or hierarchical norms. Yet volunteers, who are typically motivated by intrinsic rewards, are especially unlikely to wish to endure uncomfortable interpersonal interactions. My research and that of others has found that board members are particularly prone to politeness and conflict avoidance (Jameson, 2007; Kerwin, Doherty, & Harman, 2011; Leslie, 2010). This explains how nonprofit organizations have sometimes made inappropriate financial decisions that ended up as front-page news, limiting the organizations' ability to achieve their missions and damaging trust and credibility across the nonprofit sector.

Detrimental Impacts of Using Power to Suppress Conflict

The media is filled with stories of employee silence in corporate settings with far-reaching implications. High-profile examples exist in the auto industry, where in 2014 Toyota issued recalls affecting over 6 million vehicles due to problems with braking and acceleration while GM recalled nearly 7 million vehicles. In both cases mechanical failures led to fatalities, and the problems were known at least 10 years before recalls were put in place (Yan, 2014). News reports indicate that some employees knew there were issues, but were silenced or otherwise convinced that they should not be concerned.

The fact that the auto industry has experienced this problem before (Ford Pinto, Ford Explorer, Firestone Tires) further illustrates the pervasiveness of the problem. On Wall Street, former companies such as Enron and Lehman Brothers are household names because of financial decisions that protected highest-ranking executives while depleting employee retirement programs and corporate stock, and ultimately destroying the organizations (Eichenwald & Henriques, 2002; Harress & Caulderwood, 2013). Importantly, there were employees who attempted to engage in conversations about what they were seeing as unethical or poor business practices. Sherron Watkins has become famous for her memo to then Enron president Ken Lay about what she saw as problematic accounting. An interview with *Time* magazine reports that Watkins was made irrelevant at the company and left within the year (Lacayo & Ripley, 2002). Lawrence McDonald, a vice president of Lehman Brothers, also reported being "pushed out" when he tried to raise issues of poor financial management (Harress & Caulderwood, 2013).

The unwillingness of employees to speak up about concerns in their organizations is described in great detail by management scholar Elizabeth Wolfe Morrison and her colleagues (Morrison, 2011). Morrison and Rothman (2009) argue that those with higher power overestimate their own competence and simultaneously undervalue input from subordinates. As a result, managers may unconsciously communicate to employees that their input is not welcome. On the other side of the relationship, those with lower power tend to overestimate the potential costs of speaking up, focusing on the risks rather than rewards. These cognitive biases combine to create a cycle of silence (Morrison & Milliken, 2000). Morrison's research underscores the interplay between perceptions of power and employee concerns about how they are viewed by others in the organization. Issues of individual identity and the negotiation of relationships are a second obstacle to engaging in productive conflict.

Identity

The focus group narratives described above revealed that employees are very concerned about how they are perceived by others in the organization. Employees do not want to be seen as troublemakers and do not want supervisors to believe that they cannot handle conflict on their own. As described in Chapter 3, when an employee's main goal in communication is focused on protecting identity, it leads to defensiveness and an adversarial pattern that prevents effective listening and impedes engaging conflict.

Why Adversarial Patterns Persist

There are many theories of human behavior that provide insight into adversarial patterns. I focus on two that I have found especially helpful: attribution theory (Heider, 1958) and verbal aggressiveness theory (Infante & Wigley, 1986). Attribution theory posits two types of attributions used to explain behavior: dispositional and situational. Dispositional attributions explain another's actions as the result of an internal trait or characteristic, such as, "she does not engage in conflict because she is a very quiet person." Situational attributions suggest others' actions are influenced by external factors or events, such as, "she does not engage in conflict because her company is downsizing and she wants to keep her job." A component of attribution theory known as the fundamental attribution error (Jones & Harris, 1967; Ross, 1977) is especially helpful in making sense of the common adversarial narrative described above. The fundamental attribution error explains that people are more likely to use dispositional attributions when observing others' unacceptable or problematic behavior (e.g., "he was late to work because he is lazy"), whereas they are more likely to use a situational attribution to explain their own bad behavior ("I was late to work due to traffic"). It is easy to place blame on the other party in a conflict situation if their behavior is perceived to be internally motivated (and assumed to be intentional) while seeing one's own behavior as externally influenced (and thus out of our control). While attribution theory describes a psychological process, it explains the predominance of adversarial communication.

Another aspect of attribution bias is that when a person achieves success (a big deal is closed, a great idea presented), they typically use a dispositional attribution, suggesting that their success was internally motivated, while failures are attributed to extenuating circumstances. The implications of attribution bias suggest the benefits of being more reflective about possible sources of another's behavior before assuming a dispositional character flaw or negative intent. Engaging in conflict by being inquisitive, rather than blaming, is one way to alter the rules of engagement and create more engaging communication. Alternative explanations for another's behavior may also come from awareness of their level of comfort with conflict, as demonstrated by the theory of verbal aggressiveness.

Verbal aggressiveness theory, originally developed by Infante and Wigley (1986), describes a trait that falls on a continuum from verbal aggressiveness to argumentativeness. Although being *argumentative* is typically considered a negative characteristic (given the negative social construction of conflict), the theory suggests that argumentativeness is the more constructive communication style. The trait of argumentativeness describes people who are comfortable with conflict. These are effective communicators who can separate a conflict over interests or ideas from personal attacks. They are adept at using facts, logic, and examples to support their views or ideas. The theory postulates that verbal aggressiveness is the opposite trait. People high in verbal aggressiveness are uncomfortable with conflict and cannot easily provide the evidence to support their beliefs. As a result of this discomfort, they become more defensive when faced with conflicting views or criticisms of their ideas. Failing to easily cite the relevant facts and evidence for support, they are likely to become frustrated and thus move to personal attacks and escalated conflict behavior.

How another party responds to the person who is high in verbal aggressiveness is likely to make the difference in the patterns that develop. For example, if one party reciprocates another's verbal aggressiveness, symmetrical escalation and the bilateral adversarial narrative are likely to ensue. Alternatively, one might be intimidated by verbal aggressiveness and easily back down, leading to the potential for complementary interaction (accommodation), as described above. A party who is high in argumentativeness may try to change the nature of the interaction by focusing on the task at hand or the problem to be solved. While this may be successful in de-escalating the conflict, it is critical to remember that people who are high in verbal aggressiveness will find any disagreement uncomfortable and likely perceive it as a personal attack. They may therefore continue to escalate the conflict despite the other party's best intentions. The party who is high in argumentativeness may get frustrated by this response and ultimately reciprocate the verbal aggression.

As with attribution theory, the implications of verbal aggressiveness theory suggest the need for reflection and heightened awareness of possible causes of another's behavior. In an interaction with someone who is high in verbal aggressiveness, there will need to be more meta-communication – talking about the interaction event – (Tannen, 1986) in order to engage in a productive conversation. For example, when interacting with someone perceived as high in verbal aggressiveness, one might directly state that one's intent is to better understand the person's views, not to criticize or judge. On the flip side, for people who perceive themselves to be high in verbal aggressiveness, self-awareness will be key to reflecting on their own responses to others and working on the ability to hear ideas or arguments as attempts to resolve a problem or disagreement rather than as a personal attack. The more successfully interaction can be reframed as a conversation as opposed to a conflict, the more likely people will experience engaging and productive dialogue. Reframing will be covered in Chapter 5.

These theories provide two potential explanations for interpersonal behavior during conflict. While people cannot control how others communicate during conflict, they can control how they make sense of the other's behavior, which influences how they respond. By considering different causes for behavior, such as aspects of the situation or their level of comfort with conflict, the rules of engagement can be altered.

Further, the relevance of someone's personal identity as a competent employee or a caring coworker is also related to their level of identification with their work group or organization. While an emphasis on power may lead to employees not wanting to rock the boat, greater organizational identity (when being a part of an organization or team is central to one's sense of self) may lead to higher likelihood of speaking up in one's group or organization. Morrison, Wheeler-Smith, and Kamdar (2011) conducted a field study confirming that engineers with strong work group identification were more likely to speak up and contribute to their work group efforts. By extension, this finding suggests that high identification with a group or organization provides a level of confidence and commitment that would compel one to engage in conflict. Morrison et al. (2011) found this relationship was mediated by what they call "group voice climate," or the shared belief that it is safe to share ideas and disagreement. High group voice climate might share similarities with Losada's (1999) description of teams that had greater inquiry over advocacy (see Chapter 3): when the atmosphere is one that welcomes questions and greater understanding, everyone's voice is included and valued. Unfortunately, in too many workplaces the fear of speaking up is greater than the perception of benefits to sharing one's ideas. This experience of fear leads us to a discussion of emotion as an obstacle to engaging conflict.

Emotion

Emotions are a strong force in conflict communication, and one of the most common emotions related to conflict is fear, sometimes for personal safety, but also fear of damage to one's reputation, livelihood, or relationships. When scholars talk about emotion in conflict they often emphasize anger, guilt, shame, and contempt – emotions that often arise when conflict comes to the surface. Yet fear is what keeps conflict underground. As has been discussed, fear of negative repercussions is the most commonly cited factor in explaining an employee's organizational silence (Morrison & Milliken, 2000; Morrison, 2011). Notably, and as described in Box 4.1, those repercussions often come from supervisors. Yet just as supervisors can punish employees with poor schedules or increased workloads, coworkers can "punish" supervisors by withholding information or through lack of engagement in meetings or social events. As illustrated by the focus group data described above, people often fear retaliation and damage to their reputation when faced with workplace conflict.

Another source of fear is that of disrupting group or organizational harmony. A nonprofit board member described his perception of what happened when a difference of opinion occurred during a meeting: "It was just about to get good and someone jumped in and said, 'you're both saying the same thing,' but the thing is, they were not!" This statement reflects that group members may use communication strategies to gloss over or defuse a conflict rather than engage it. There is a fear that conflict will disrupt the meeting and destroy group harmony. Obviously, whether groups are more likely to engage or avoid conflict depends on a number of variables: whether there is a skilled facilitator within the group, how group norms have developed, status differences among group members, and the nature of the conflict itself. Nevertheless, the fact remains that conflict brings with it a range of emotions that can hinder effective communication. A study of the metaphors participants in a training session used to describe the experience of emotion in conflict helps further illustrate this point (see Box 4.2).

Box 4.2   Like Talking to a Brick Wall

In an advanced training workshop on how to deal with parties' emotions, a partner and I facilitated an exercise in which we asked mediation workshop participants to identify metaphors that described their experiences of emotion in conflict (Jameson, Bodtker, & Jones, 2006). Their responses provide evidence of the challenges presented by the strong emotions that accompany conflict. Since parties often blame each other for the conflict (at least initially), *anger* is one of the most commonly experienced emotions during a conflict. Workshop participants described anger as a "flash," "wind," "simmering teapot," "bullet," "bear," "tornado," "drowning," and "having amnesia." Many of these are obvious: a *simmering teapot* is ready to "blow off steam"; a *bullet* is unstoppable and can inflict great pain and damage – you can't take it back, and it has tremendous force. Like a *flash*, anger can come on quickly and without warning; and, like a *bear*, it can be frightening and dangerous. One metaphor we had not heard before was anger as "*having amnesia.*"

The amnesia image suggests that the brain isn't working as it should. An amnesiac feels panic and a loss of control. When someone is angry, this metaphor suggests, they lose control and fail to recognize the damage they might inflict on others. They might momentarily forget the history and significance of their relationship and previous investment in it. In the heat of the moment, a person experiencing anger cannot see the big picture, which reduces their ability to manage cognitive complexity, to see nuance, or accept another person's point of view. It is interesting that anger was perceived as accompanied by the fear of not being able to control oneself. Many participants suggested that when they feel anger personally they are most likely to avoid or disengage, at least until they can calm down. While this is not necessarily a bad strategy, it is important that parties are able to confront the conflict at a later time, and all too often the issue is left ignored until it is triggered the next time and the cycle starts all over again. Further, the memory of a negative interaction lingers and makes it more difficult to engage in future contact, harming relationships with coworkers (Gayle & Preiss, 1998).

Once anger subsides, it is not uncommon for one or more parties in a conflict to feel *guilt*. This can occur when someone acknowledges their own contribution to the conflict. Participants reported that guilt was like "an internal nagging," "a hamster on a treadmill," or a "hot potato" (wanting to pass it along to someone else). Because guilt is a self-conscious emotion, the person who experiences guilt is inwardly focused. Paradoxically, to alleviate guilt people often focus on meeting the other party's needs, which causes them to make concessions or accept agreements that are not in their best interests. This is an example of choosing avoidance to reduce uncomfortable emotions. When one chooses to avoid or accommodate, however, the other party has no need to acknowledge the role they played in the conflict. This is another example of the negative consequence of avoiding conflict. The decision not to engage in conflict results in an inability to get needs met, relational damage, and disruption to workplace productivity.

A final example is the emotion of *contempt*. To feel contempt is to feel morally superior to another, and one usually expresses contempt by denigrating the other. Contemptuous communication that belittles the other party leads to defensiveness and is a key contributor to conflict escalation. One participant suggested that dealing with someone who feels contempt is "like talking to a brick wall." It is hard to get through to someone who feels contempt, and, as one participant said, "it hurts if you run into it." One who feels contempt has a barrier around them and is inaccessible. Another metaphor used for contempt was one of "erosion." Like a major storm, contempt can erode the foundation of a relationship. When people feel contempt, they distance themselves to the point where they cannot relate to others. Similarly, the targets of contempt also feel as though they are being "eroded." Another participant suggested that receiving another's contempt is like acid eating away at you. When people perceive they are the target of contempt, they are likely to run and hide to avoid the feeling of being belittled.

For Reflection and Discussion:

1) Consider a time you were in a conflict that was difficult to resolve. What emotion(s) were you experiencing at the time? What did you need in order

to overcome that emotion? How could you have gotten what you needed to manage that emotion and more productively engage the conflict?

2) Reflecting on the same conflict, do you have insights into what emotions the other party was experiencing at the time? How did the other party's emotions influence how the conflict was handled? Is there anything you could have done to help them get what they needed to manage their emotion and more productively engage the conflict?

Source: Jameson, J. K. et al., 2006 / John Wiley & Sons.

Chapter Summary

This chapter supports the point that conflict is a complex phenomenon and the dynamics related to power, identity, and emotion described in this chapter are all interrelated, making engaging conflict especially challenging. The way that organizational members communicate on a daily basis constructs a culture that either supports or impedes the active engagement of conflict. This is why organizational leaders should be intentional and mindful about how they model listening and communication that demonstrate the value of all employee voices.

Research that involves talking to organizational members about their experiences of conflict across workplaces as diverse as corporations, healthcare institutions, and nonprofit organizations suggests that there are strong norms against engaging in open conflict. This chapter described two common narratives found in employee descriptions of organizational conflict: conflict as political maneuvering and conflict as mission impossible. These stories reveal the perception that only those with power will prevail in conflict and it is not worth the risk to engage in conflict unless you have connections or powerful allies. The second theme reinforces research on organizational voice and silence, which has found that employees often do not believe they have *voice efficacy*, defined as the extent to which one's voice will result in positive change (Morrison et al., 2011). The overwhelming sense of the futility of engaging conflict was found in the stories describing conflict as mission impossible.

In addition to the obstacle of power and hierarchy, the challenges associated with identity were described. When the desire to protect one's identity results in conflict avoidance, employees become disengaged and consequences can include relational damage; increased stress; decreased health and well-being; loss of morale; increased theft, absenteeism, and turnover; and an overall decrease in organizational citizenship behavior.

Conflict is also accompanied by emotion, and this fact creates another series of impediments for organizational members. Fear of negative repercussions for the individual or relationship prevents people from communicating when they feel wronged or disagree with actions being taken. Anger can cause people to attribute blame more easily and respond with adversarial tactics. The combination of anger and fear may create an even more insidious response to conflict, in which an employee remains silent on the issue but engages in indirect or subversive tactics to get revenge on those who have wronged them.

The remaining chapters of this book integrate a variety of studies to provide insights on the characteristics of engaging conflict. Importantly, the emphasis on socially constructed expectations and behavioral norms suggests that to change the way people communicate during conflict, individuals, groups, and organizations must also change the way they orient to and talk about conflict. Transforming existing patterns of communication is contingent upon changing what I will call the "rules of engagement." These rules of engagement are the topic of Chapter 5.

For Reflection and Discussion:

1) Think about a time you had a conflict with someone of higher power, authority, or status. This could be a boss or a teacher. Did you engage the conflict? Why or why not? How did either the other person or the organizational environment affect your decision to engage?
2) If you did engage the conflict and it went well, think about what you did specifically that helped the interaction go smoothly. If it did not go well, what happened? What could you (or the other person) have done differently to make the conflict interaction more engaging?

Activity

Work with a partner to develop a conflict scenario that you might experience at this stage of your life. Your instructor may also provide one for you. Each student will randomly select one of the five conflict styles without telling their partner which one they have chosen. You will then role-play negotiating (trying to resolve) that conflict using the style you have chosen. When you have either resolved the conflict or reached an impasse, discuss what happened. Were you successful? How did the style each student chose impact how the negotiation (or discussion) unfolded? Can you point to specific moments where communication (conflict style) choices had a direct impact on what happened next? As time permits, try resolving the conflict using different combinations of styles to see what happens and how you feel afterward.

References

Blake, R., & Mouton, J. (1964). *The managerial grid: The key to leadership excellence.* Houston, TX: Gulf Publishing.

Eichenwald, K., & Henriques, D. B. (2002, February 10). Enron buffed image to a shine even as it rotted from within. *New York Times*, pp. 26–27. Retrieved January 1, 2023, from https://www.nytimes.com/2002/02/10/business/enron-s-many-strands-company-unravels-enron-buffed-image-shine-even-it-rotted.html

Ellingson, L. L. (2005). *Communicating in the clinic: Negotiating frontstage and backstage teamwork.* Cresskill, NJ: Hampton Press.

Friedman, R. A., Tidd, S. A., Currall, S. C., & Tsai, J. C. (2000). What goes around comes around: The impact of personal conflict style on work conflict and stress. *The International Journal of Conflict Management, 11*: 32–55. https://doi.org/10.1108/eb022834.

Gayle, B. M., & Preiss, R. W. (1998). Assessing emotionality in organizational conflicts. *Management Communication Quarterly, 12*: 280–302.

Gross, M. A., & Guerrero L. K. (2000). Managing conflict appropriately and effectively: An application of the competence model to Rahim's organizational conflict styles. *The International Journal of Conflict Management, 11*: 200–226. https://doi.org/10.1108/eb022840.

Harress, C., & Caulderwood, K. (2013, September 13). The death of Lehman Brothers: What went wrong, who paid the price and who remained unscathed through the eyes of former Vice-President. *International Business Times*. Retrieved January 1, 2023, from https://www.ibtimes.com/death-lehman-brothers-what-went-wrong-who-paid-price-who-remained-unscathed-through-eyes-former-vice

Heider, F. (1958). *The Psychology of Interpersonal Relations.* New York: Wiley.

Infante, D. A., & Wigley, C. J. (1986). Verbal aggressiveness: An interpersonal model and measure. *Communication Monographs, 53*(1): 61–69.

Jameson, J. K. (1999). Toward a comprehensive model for the assessment and management of intraorganizational conflict. *International Journal of Conflict Management, 10*(3): 268–294.

Jameson, J. K. (2001). Employee perceptions of the availability and use of interests-, rights-, and power-based conflict management strategies. *Conflict Resolution Quarterly, 19*(2): 163–196.

Jameson, J. K. (2007, November). *Respectful interaction among nonprofit boards of directors.* Paper presented to the Organizational Communication Division at the Annual Meeting of the National Communication Association, Chicago, IL.

Jameson, J. K., Bodtker, A. M., & Jones, T. S. (2006). Like talking to a brick wall: Implications of emotion metaphors for mediation practice. *Negotiation Journal, 22*(2): 199–207.

Jones, E. E., & Harris, V. A. (1967). The attribution of attitudes. *Journal of Experimental Social Psychology*, *3*(1): 1–24. https://doi.org/10.1016/0022-1031(67) 90034-0.

Kerwin, S., Doherty, A., & Harman, A. (2011). "It's not conflict, it's differences of opinion": An in-depth examination of conflict in nonprofit boards. *Small Group Research*, *42*(5): 562–594.

Kim, J., & Meyers, R. A. (2012). Cultural differences in conflict management styles in east and west organizations. *Journal of Intercultural Communication*, *29*(32): 1.

Lacayo, R., & Ripley, A. (2002). Persons of the year 2002: The Whistleblowers, Sherron Watkins of Enron, Coleen Rowley of the FBI, Cynthia Cooper of WorldCom. *Time*, *160*(27): 30–34.

Leslie, M. B. (2010). The wisdom of crowds? Groupthink and nonprofit governance. *Florida Law Review*. Retrieved January 1, 2023, from http://www.floridalawreview.com/2010/melanie-b-leslie-the-wisdom-of-crowds-groupthink-and-nonprofit-governance/

Long, D., Iedema, R., & Lee, B. (2007). Corridor conversations: Clinical communication in casual spaces. In R. Iedema (Ed.), *The discourse of hospital communication: Tracing complexities in contemporary health care organizations* (pp. 182–199). Basingstoke and New York: Palgrave.

Losada, M. (1999). The complex dynamics of high performance teams. *Mathematical and Computer Modeling*, *30*: 179–192.

Lovelace, K., Shapiro, D. L., & Weingart, L. R. (2001). Maximizing cross-functional new product teams' innovativeness and constraint adherence: A conflict communications perspective. *Academy of Management Journal*, *44*(4): 779–793.

Metelsky, B. A., & Jameson, J. K. (2013). Generative communication: Fostering generative governance through diverse perspectives. In T. Tempkin (Ed.), *You and your nonprofit board: Advice and tips from the field's top practitioners, researchers, and provocateurs* (pp. 54–61). Rancho Santa Margarita, CA: CharityChannel Press.

Morrison, E. W. (2011). Employee voice behavior: Integration and directions for future research. *The Academy of Management Annals*, *5*(1): 373–412.

Morrison, E. W., & Milliken, F. J. (2000). Organizational silence: A barrier to change and development in a pluralistic world. *The Academy of Management Review*, *25*(4): 706–725.

Morrison, E. W., & Rothman, N. B. (2009). Silence and the dynamics of power. In J. Greenberg & M. S. Edwards (Eds.), *Voice and silence in organizations* (pp. 111–133). Bingley, UK: Emerald Group Publishing.

Morrison, E. W., Wheeler-Smith, S. L., & Kamdar, D. (2011). Speaking up in groups: A cross-level study of group voice climate and voice. *Journal of Applied Psychology*, *96*(1): 183–191.

Pruitt, D. G. (1995). Flexibility in conflict episodes. *Annals of the American Academy of Political and Social Science*, *542*(1): 100–115. https://doi.org/10.1177/0002716295542001007.

Rahim, M. A. (1983). A measure of styles of handling interpersonal conflict. *Academy of Management Journal, 26*: 368–376.

Rahim, M. A. (2011). *Managing conflict in organizations* (4th ed.). Westport, CT: Quorum Books.

Ross, L. (1977). The intuitive psychologist and his shortcomings: Distortions in the attribution process. In L. Berkowitz (Ed.), *Advances in experimental social psychology* (pp. 173–220). New York: Academic Press.

Stohl, C., & Cheney, G. (2001). Participatory processes/Paradoxical practices: Communication and the dilemmas of organizational democracy. *Management Communication Quarterly, 14*: 349–407. https://doi.org/10.1177/0893318901143001.

Tannen, D. (1986). *That's not what I meant! How conversational style makes or breaks your relations with others.* New York: Morrow.

Thomas, K. W., & Kilmann, R. H. (1974). *Thomas-Kilmann conflict MODE instrument.* Tuxedo, NY: Xicom.

Ting-Toomey, S. (1988). Intercultural communication styles: A face-negotiation theory. In Y. Y. Kim & W. B. Gudykunst (Eds.), *Theories in intercultural communication* (pp. 213–235). Thousand Oaks, CA: Sage.

Trudel, J., & Reio, Jr., T. G. (2011). Managing workplace incivility: The role of conflict management styles. *Human Resource Development Quarterly, 22*: 395–423. https://doi.org/10.1002/hrdq.20081.

Ury, W. L., Brett, J. M., & Goldberg, S. B. (1988). *Getting disputes resolved.* San Francisco, CA: Jossey-Bass.

Watzlawick, P., Bavelas, J. B., & Jackson, D. D. (1967). *Pragmatics of human communication: A study of interactional patterns, pathologies, and paradoxes.* New York: W. W. Norton.

Yan, S. (2014, April 9). Toyota recalls 6.4 million cars worldwide. *CNNMoney.* Retrieved January 1, 2023, from http://money.cnn.com/2014/04/09/autos/toyota-recall/

5

Changing the Rules of Engagement

Peace is not absence of conflict, it is the ability to handle conflict by peaceful means.
> Ronald Reagan (1911–2004, 40th President of the United States)

Great leaders make it clear that they welcome challenges, criticism, and viewpoints other than their own. They know that an environment where people are afraid to speak up, offer insight, and ask good questions is destined for failure.
> Travis Bradberry (author and cofounder of TalentSmart®)

Chapter 4 presented the argument that people often avoid conflict, especially in the workplace; and while sometimes it is prudent to avoid, change cannot happen if we do not face the conflict. Further, as noted in the above quote from Ronald Reagan (40th President of the United States), the absence of conflict does not equal a peaceful environment, as conflict is often simmering below the surface and contributing to an uncomfortable – sometimes toxic – workplace. Our goal is to focus on engaging conflict constructively and collaboratively to successfully manage it while maintaining a peaceful – or at least collaborative – environment. The goal of this chapter is to consider specific communication strategies and behaviors that help us "change the rules of engagement" in the workplace. Given the dynamics of power, identity, and emotion and popular perceptions of conflict as adversarial, this is clearly no easy task. Nevertheless, if individual employees, group members, and organizational leaders change the way they think about, talk about, and approach conflict management, the structure of expectations described in Rummel's (1976) model (see Chapter 1) can be incrementally changed, hence altering the rules of conflict engagement. In the first part of this chapter, I return to the focus group study discussed in Chapter 4 to describe the third, less prevalent conflict narrative of *conflict as a collaborative process* (in contrast to the earlier

Communication for Constructive Workplace Conflict, First Edition. Jessica Katz Jameson.
© 2023 John Wiley & Sons, Inc. Published 2023 by John Wiley & Sons, Inc.

described narratives of conflict management as either *political maneuvering* or *mission impossible*). This narrative offers a vision for changing the rules of engagement. Then I will present specific strategies for engaging conflict in peaceful, collaborative ways, drawing from research on organizational dissent, communication tools of reframing and inquiry, and the process of mediation.

Conflict as Collaborative Problem Solving

Although they represented the minority viewpoint of the focus group participants, stories emerged from the 12 focus groups described in Chapter 4 that were much more positive about organizational conflict management. They described the behaviors of individuals who effectively managed conflict, employees who saw conflict as an opportunity to problem solve, and stories of managers or human resources (HR) professionals who acted as effective third parties.

Consistent with the dominant belief that it is best to resolve conflict on your own, focus group participants indicated that the most successful conflict management occurred when individuals and groups managed conflict without assistance of any third party:

> *In my type of environment you need to take care of business now, so usually the way we approach a resolution is that you understand you will put in a lot more than you will expect at this point in time, however next week, next time, you will be more than compensated for attempting to reach the resolution.*

This quote is interesting in that it describes an organization with a high level of citizenship and a norm of *generalized reciprocity* (in which members reciprocate acts of kindness). Employees in this environment recognize a process of give and take, where, if they do whatever is needed to get the job done now, someone else will do the same for them in the future. Another example describes an office ritual that led to productive conflict engagement:

> *Every two weeks we used to have organizational staff meetings; they were to lay everything out on the table in terms of tasks and get that out of the way and then what's going on between each other, like so and so leaves the coffee on and stuff like that. Interpersonal problems or personality conflicts . . . It was effective, it was really good.*

Participants also described what they perceived as appropriate steps for managing conflict: taking the time to examine all of the information and giving all parties equal consideration. In one specific example, upper management told employees they could not give salary increases that year, and employees were very unhappy and dissatisfied. The focus group participant (an HR officer) took the initiative to conduct her own study of comparable salaries in their industry, and when she presented the report to her superiors, they ended up giving raises and increasing employee morale. It is possible that in this case, even if the salary increases had not come through, employee morale *may* have been increased by the fact that the HR officer made the effort to investigate competitive salaries. While this is not always enough to keep good employees, it sends an important message that organizational members' interests will be given consideration. Previous research has concluded that employees are more likely to perceive organizational decisions as fair when they believe they have been heard and their concerns have been considered (McFarlin & Sweeney, 1996; Shapiro & Brett, 1993).

Another example of the benefits of investigating conflict issues came from a focus group participant who worked at a dry cleaning store. This participant described being confronted by an angry customer who claimed a lost jacket was worth $200. While the store owner wanted to tell the customer the store was not responsible, the focus group participant decided to call local stores to find out how much the jacket would cost. He learned a similar jacket was for sale for $30, and the owner agreed to compensate the customer accordingly. In this example the customer had taken a highly competitive and adversarial stance, yet, importantly, an employee chose to investigate and problem solve rather than reciprocate in an adversarial manner. The solution met each party's underlying interests: the customer received reimbursement for the lost item and the store maintained positive public relations. Note that in this case the dry cleaner acknowledged the customer's interests while not agreeing or blindly accommodating. This validating behavior clearly makes a difference in whether unfolding conflict communication remains adversarial or becomes more engaging and it will be discussed further in Unit Three in the *acknowledge* section of the LEARN framework.

While the focus group participants' stories mostly affirmed the common perception that individuals should try to manage conflict on their own, there were a few stories in which third parties were described as successfully managing conflict. One participant indicated that going to a third party is appropriate "when things get personal and too emotionally intense," while another recollected that "the mediator was there to tell people when they were making stuff up, to say things like 'hey, what are you talking about?' and kind of bring everybody back to earth so that it couldn't become too one-sided." One story of a specific mediation described a situation in which:

> *The mediator's role here was to get them to stop screaming and get them to listen to each other, and then they were able to say "it's not that bad, we can*

> *work it out so that it doesn't have to be where I have everything and you have nothing."*

These stories point out that when conflict is escalated to a point where there is heightened emotion, it is especially helpful to bring in a third party.

Two stories also stood out because they disconfirmed the common perception that managers and HR departments did not have effective conflict management skills. These quotes demonstrate positive experiences:

> *My manager is good . . . she has a graduate degree and was a former education counselor; she has those skills, I would go to her before I would go to HR.*
>
> *I was highly encouraged to go right to human resources so that there was an objective third party to help mediate . . . HR in the company was well respected, well established . . . Employees always saw front line managers go to HR for consultation or help on this issue or that issue, so it must have made very logical sense, when you had a problem, you went to HR, and they would bring disputants together to have them agree on the problem and develop solutions for resolving it.*

One additional participant described a time when her organization hired an interim HR director after the previous director was terminated. The interim director was a contract employee and did not spend time with other organizational members. The participant explained that the interim director did not establish open relationships with management and, because he was not a permanent employee, organizational members felt comfortable going to him for help with conflict management. This story reveals the distrust that is often inherent in the relationship between HR departments and management. The story confirms research that has found employees are more willing to seek conflict assistance when there is greater distance between the third party and management (Blancero & Dyer, 1996). The stories that comprise the narrative of *conflict as collaborative problem solving* demonstrate that specific organizational members can be effective conflict resources when they are perceived as neutral and have a reputation for having conflict management skills.

The focus group interviews revealed that some organizational members experience conflict as a process of collaborative problem solving, but this was the least common of the three narratives of organizational conflict. Based on the three underlying themes within this focus group narrative, in the remaining sections of this chapter I discuss effective ways of engaging conflict through *prosocial dissent strategies*, *inquiry and reframing*, and *use of mediators or the skills taught in mediation*.

Organizational Dissent

It is not uncommon for employees to disagree with a decision made by their supervisor or a specific organizational policy or practice. Organizational dissent involves the articulation of such divergent views about organizational practices, operations, or policies (Kassing, 2011). The expression of dissent is especially risky for employees because it challenges the legitimacy of authority (Berg, 2011; Shahinpoor & Matt, 2007). As described in Chapter 4, perceptions of power and one's place in the hierarchy are major impediments to engaging in conflict, and hence expressing dissent. Dissent scholars confirm that the most common reasons for not voicing dissent are loss of status, embarrassment, damage to reputation, feelings of futility, concerns about negative impact on others, fears of damaging a relationship, and receiving low job performance evaluations (Milliken, Morrison, & Hewlin, 2003; Kennedy-Lightsey, 2007; Sprague & Rudd, 1988). Employees who engage in dissent may also become victims of organizational shunning and be ostracized by other members of the organization (Anderson, 2009). Factors that have been found to increase the likelihood of expressing dissent include high satisfaction and high quality relationships with supervisors (Kassing, 1998, 2000). Creating a workplace environment where employees feel safe and satisfied and trust their supervisors leads to greater likelihood of employees dissenting in constructive ways – in other words, promoting employee voice.

Kassing (2011) suggests that people express dissent when their expectations are violated beyond their level of tolerance. Specific events likely to trigger dissent include employee treatment, organizational change, changes in roles or responsibilities, resource distribution, ethics, performance evaluations, preventing harm, supervisor inaction, supervisor performance, and supervisor indiscretion (Kassing, 2011; Kassing & Armstrong, 2002). This is consistent with Rummel's (1976) social conflict helix (see Chapter 1), which describes the cycle of conflict as an ongoing balance of power caused by disruptions in the structure of expectations.

Due to the risks inherent in upward dissent, employees often use *latent dissent*, such as complaining to coworkers (Kassing, 2000), or covert strategies, such as showing up late to meetings or other antisocial behaviors (Goodboy, Chory, & Dunleavy, 2008) to express their dissatisfaction. Organizational members may also use a strategy called *displaced dissent*, in which they express dissent to individuals outside the organization such as friends and family. How organizational members dissent, and management responses to dissent, are critical factors in the development of climates that either support or discourage voice and, by association, willingness to engage conflict (Morrison, 2011). The problem with latent and displaced dissent is that while they may offer employees a chance to "blow off steam" and receive social support, they do not usually lead to productive problem solving because they do not directly engage the conflict. Upward dissent, which involves speaking directly to a supervisor or other levels of management, is arguably the most direct and constructive way to voice concerns. The next section describes the most common dissent strategies, highlighting *prosocial* dissent. Prosocial communication refers to the willingness to go out of one's way to do something for the other (Chartrand & Bargh, 1999). It is not surprising that prosocial dissent has been shown to have the most positive impacts on getting problems resolved and maintaining effective relationships and a constructive workplace climate.

Upward Dissent Strategies

Kassing (2002) discovered five predominant strategies organizational members use when they communicate their dissent to a supervisor or someone else of higher status. These strategies are solution presentation, direct-factual appeal, repetition, circumvention, and threatening to resign. *Solution presentation*, as the name implies, involves voicing dissent while simultaneously offering a possible solution to the problem. This was illustrated in the above story of the employee who investigated salary standards in her industry and provided a report to her supervisors to advocate for reconsideration of a recent decision to deny salary increases. The dry cleaning employee who investigated the cost of the lost jacket and took that to the owner is a second example. Solution presentation has been found to be the most effective and appropriate upward dissent strategy (Garner, 2012; Kassing, 2011).

Along with solution presentation, Kassing refers to the *direct-factual appeal* as a second prosocial strategy. In the direct-factual appeal, employees provide evidence to support their concerns with organizational decisions. Both of these strategies are intuitive choices for voicing upward dissent. If I am going to complain to my boss, and I am concerned about my reputation and being perceived as a troublemaker, then I would want to be as prepared as possible. Presenting facts and evidence to support my claims and even offering potential solutions are consistent with expectations of logic and rationality that are the norm in most professional organizations. A study comparing the use of conflict management styles and upward dissent strategies confirms that solution presentation and direct-factual appeals are highly correlated with use of the collaborative conflict style (Redmond, Jameson, & Binder, 2016).

The appropriateness of a strategy does not necessarily mean it will achieve the desired result, however. Organizational members use the strategy of *repetition* to continue to voice their concerns in an effort to influence supervisors to take action on an issue that has been ignored. At least one study found that repetition can be an effective strategy, although it may not be perceived as appropriate (Garner, 2012). One possible explanation for this is that repetition tactics may become increasingly adversarial. Kassing (2002) found that dissenters may start with prosocial tactics, but communication becomes more face threatening over time. This suggests that repetitive dissent may shift from more collaborative to more adversarial communication.

Circumvention consists of dissenting to someone other than one's immediate supervisor, typically going over their head to express dissent. Not surprisingly, this strategy is most often used when the problem concerns the actions of one's supervisor (Kassing, 2009). Circumvention often results in damage to the relationship between the employee and supervisor, although it has been found to be perceived as conversationally effective (Garner, 2012) and to produce satisfactory outcomes when concerns are related to policy or sanctioning supervisors (Kassing, 2007).

Threatening to resign is the least common and most risky upward dissent strategy. Kassing (2002, 2005) refers to this strategy as a last resort that is used when employees feel a threat to their integrity. It is not perceived as appropriate or effective. Redmond et al.'s (2016) study of conflict management styles and upward dissent strategies found a negative correlation between both circumvention and threatening to resign and the collaborative conflict style. Both of these strategies are more adversarial and are likely to reflect an environment that is not conducive to engaging conflict productively. In the ideal organization, there would be a channel for expressing one's concerns that would be organizationally appropriate. Examples include an ombudsman[1] or well-trained HR professionals such as described by the focus group participants above. Unfortunately, research has found that these venues are often not available or don't produce the desired results (Katz & Flynn, 2013). In a culture that does not support open conflict, employees are more likely to express their discontent to coworkers or people outside the organization. Constructing an atmosphere of openness to employee concerns encourages prosocial tactics, which is one way to support collaborative conflict management. When conflict starts off in an adversarial manner, however, another strategy is to change the rules of engagement by reframing the nature of the interaction.

---

[1] The word ombudsman comes from the Swedish parliament. In the early 1800s, the office was created to provide citizens a means to pursue grievances against the government. According to Howard Gadlin, ombudsman for the National Institutes of Health, it is the most misunderstood model of dispute resolution (Gadlin, 2000). Modern ombuds (the more politically correct term) offices are found in government, academia, journalism, and corporate settings. Ombuds roles include listening to and helping disputants consider their options, investigating concerns, and possibly coaching or mediating. Ombuds offices will be discussed in more detail in Chapter 6.

Reframing and Inquiry

Gregory Bateson (1972) defined a frame as a psychological concept that delimits how we understand a set of messages and, thus, what counts as a meaningful response or action. You have likely heard the term *frame of reference*, which describes how we make sense of communication based on our life experiences and cultural expectations. Our background serves as a lens through which we frame, or interpret, what we see and hear. For example, imagine an employee tells her supervisor, "I have a Doctor's appointment later today," which is interpreted by the supervisor as a request for the afternoon off. When the supervisor responds with "as long as your work is completed that is no problem," the employee says, "it may be more complicated than that." This follow-up response suggests the employee may be looking for a longer conversation about serious health issues. The supervisor may therefore *reframe* the interaction and, rather than hearing it as "a request for time off," may now frame this as "a need for social support." The point here is that frames, or our interpretations of the communication, are negotiated through ongoing interaction.

Framing may also refer to how a relationship is framed. In the above example, the employee will approach the supervisor differently depending on the nature of the relationship (more formal or informal; more professional or friendly, as examples). An employee who frames a relationship with a coworker as a friendship may start a Monday morning conversation by recounting their weekend activities. If the coworker reciprocates, it sends a message that they share the friendship frame. On the other hand, the coworker might quickly change the subject to work or exit the interaction, which suggests a reframe of the relationship as coworkers, but not friends. Supervisors bear the responsibility of framing or reframing the kind of relationship they would like to have with their employees. For example, if employees insist on using titles, such as Dr. Jameson, and a supervisor wants to create a more egalitarian workplace to support trust and openness, the supervisor might say, "please call me Jessica since I use your first name when I speak to you." This subtle reframing can make a big difference in how employees perceive their relationships and workplace climate. Conflict scholars have discussed reframing as an important mechanism for reaching conflict transformation (Donohue, Rogan & Kaufman, 2011), and Box 5.1 uses excerpts from recordings of nonprofit board meetings to demonstrate different types of framing and reframing and how they can be used to successfully engage conflict and negotiate new understanding (Jameson & Metelsky, 2011).

Box 5.1 illustrates that an important strategy in reframing is inquiry. These board meeting conversations included frequent questions about what members' concerns were, how this issue was handled in other organizations, and what people perceived as differences between a newsletter and a website. The questions

---

Box 5.1   Nonprofit Board Meeting Communication and Reframing

---

Two examples from a nonprofit board meeting help illustrate the role of framing and reframing in engaging conflict. In the first example, there was internal controversy over whether the nonprofit should participate in a statewide walk-a-thon. Some board members believed it would compete with a local walk event and did not wish to ask sponsors for donations twice in one year. The following interaction is between a board member (Cathy, a pseudonym) who opposes participation in the statewide walk and a visiting state representative who is promoting the walk (Joann, a pseudonym):

CATHY: I would like to go on record that that's a very bad policy for the affiliates because we can appeal to people to sponsor teams or come up with a team of walkers, and they would do it because they think they were helping [us]. But if they realize it doesn't help [us] specifically, well, we got [our other walk].

JOANN: I'd like to believe that we're all working toward the same goal, and I'm hoping that, even though the money from the teams doesn't go back to the county, we really are all working together, we are working for the same thing. It does help [your affiliate], maybe not directly . . .

In this case, the representative's attempt to reframe the organizations as working together rather than competing for donors is not successful. The board chair (Monica), however, secures the group's agreement to participate by *reframing* the purpose of the event as advocacy rather than fundraising:

MONICA: The timing of the walk is very intentional for that reason, for the publicity that it generates. And I think it's important. We need to get that publicity because there will be people from [surrounding areas] who participate because it's at [location] to get some high profile attention . . .

Shortly following this statement the group makes a motion to support both walks, with the understanding that their fundraising priority is for the local walk. They agree to encourage members and volunteers to participate in both walks in order to increase visibility for their organization and cause. This reminds the board that creating public awareness for their cause is as important as fundraising.

   In the next excerpt from the same board the chair, Monica, raises the issue of creating a policy on whether to promote programs from other agencies that may serve their same clients. Several board members are engaged in this discussion, and it is clear that they frame the issue differently based on their professional backgrounds, previous experiences, and values. This discussion is initially raised as an administrative issue, asking the group how the chair should respond when other agencies request to advertise in their newsletter:

> MONICA: I think we need to have a policy about how we're going to publicize groups like this. My initial thought was that we could have a listing on the website.

Another member reframes this as a legal issue. There is concern that if they promote other groups they will be seen as endorsing them:

> MAURICE: I mean, obviously, if we did something like that we'd have language in there that we're not endorsing it, but I think people will still see it as an endorsement … If it's in the newsletter, it's an endorsement.

Another board member contests this legal frame. Aaron claims part of this organization's mission is to provide resources for their members:

> AARON: I don't agree with that. I think you can [say] these are [our] support groups and say "other support groups available" and you can list them . . . It's a way of communicating things that wouldn't be communicated otherwise.

The invocation of the legal and mission frames serves to sustain discussion on this issue for approximately 35 minutes of a 90-minute meeting. While on one hand this was a source of frustration for Monica (who thought this would be a quick agenda item), the example reveals the importance of listening to multiple voices and considering multiple perspectives during decision making. Important issues that surfaced included: the mission and identity of the organization, stakeholder needs, connecting to other programs in their community, legal and ethical responsibilities, and the purpose of the website and newsletter as communication tools. These are all important governance topics, and this was one of the few conversations over the course of a year of meetings in which nearly all of the board members were engaged in the conversation. This was also one of the few episodes from board meeting transcripts that provided a clear example of conflict. The tension created by the use of both the legal frame and the mission frame reinforced the conflict, and the use of acknowledging the previous speaker's point and explicit requests for participation supported an engaging climate (to be discussed in more detail in Unit Three). Unfortunately the board was not able to come to a decision during this meeting, but the discussion helped members gain clarity on the organization's identity and provided information for important future discussions of the organization's role and purpose.

For Reflection and Discussion:

Discuss with a partner or small group.

1) Have you been a participant in a group project (at school or at work) in which you disagreed with others in the group? Consider a time when you *did* speak up and contrast that with a time you *did not* say anything. Can you identify the differences in those two situations to pinpoint specific obstacles to participation and facilitators of participation?
2) Based on the response to question 1, come up with three things you can do as a group member to facilitate participation from all group members to make sure you have discussed the issue or task thoroughly and are making wise decisions.
3) Try to think of one example where you reframed a problem or a conversation in order to make the conversation more productive or to turn the group's attention to an important issue that was not being considered.

---

helped members to gauge where they were coming from (how they framed the issues) and then get ideas from outside the organization that reframed the underlying concern and how it might be handled. The importance of inquiry was discussed in Chapter 3, and here I revisit asking questions as a valuable strategy for changing the rules of engagement in conflict interaction.

There is a long history of research on group communication to support that asking questions promotes listening and inclusive participation. Early systems theory studies of group interaction identified the importance of balancing the amount of information provided with the seeking of information (Bales, 1950). Peter Senge (1990), a well-known organizational development scholar who has detailed the important characteristics of the learning organization, emphasized the need for constant pursuit of new knowledge for organizational effectiveness. Following the work of Bales and Senge, Losada's (1999) study of high performance teams using a computer program to code group interaction found that the communication of more productive groups emphasized inquiry over advocacy, included a balance of internal and external information, and was dominated by positive interaction. In other words, effective groups actively seek information and engage with external others rather than relying only on members' information and ideas. Groups in Losada's study felt free to question each other and responded to differences in positive rather than negative ways. Losada characterized the high performance teams as having "expansive emotional spaces" described as:

> an atmosphere of buoyancy that lasted during the whole meeting. By showing appreciation and encouragement to other members in the team, they created emotional spaces that were expansive and opened possibilities for

action and creativity. They were also fun to watch and there was rarely a dull moment during their meetings. In addition, they accomplished their tasks with ease and grace. In stark contrast, low performance teams struggled with their tasks, operated in very restrictive emotional spaces created by lack of mutual support and enthusiasm, often in an atmosphere charged with distrust and cynicism. (p. 181)

Nancy Axelrod (2007) parallels Losada's findings in her call on nonprofit leaders to build a *culture of inquiry*. Specifically working in the context of nonprofit boards of directors, Axelrod describes a culture of inquiry as consisting of four key elements: trust, information sharing, teamwork, and dialogue. She also outlines several important roles group members perform in order to develop a culture of inquiry, such as the "healthy skeptic," "caller," and "reframer" (p. 33). Her definition of the reframer is consistent with the discussion above, as she describes this as the person who is "skilled in recasting a divisive or complex issue in a new light, ferreting out and reframing the real challenge at hand, and opening up new possibilities to shift attention to fertile new ground for realistic options" (p. 33). The *healthy skeptic* role is similar to what is more popularly known as the "devil's advocate." This is the group member who raises questions about group assumptions and considers possible flaws or unanticipated consequences of group decisions. This is an important role for ensuring critical thinking and preventing premature consensus or groupthink, which occurs when lower status members accommodate those perceived as having more power in a group.

One challenge to creating a culture of inquiry is that the healthy skeptic may be a cause of frustration or irritation to other members, who are often anxious to move on to the next agenda item. Imagine you are attending a class (or in a meeting) and the instructor or facilitator asks, "does anyone have any questions?" How many times have you said to yourself, "please no one ask a question" or glared at the person who did? It is not necessarily that we do not care about the issue at hand, but we often feel pressure to move on to the next part of our day or the next task on our list rather than remaining engaged in the present moment. This is where the work of the *caller* is especially beneficial. The caller is someone who is "[c]ourageous, sensitive, and skillful in calling individuals on questionable or inappropriate actions or disrespectful behaviors, the board's desired norms of behavior, or the welfare of the organization" (Axelrod, 2007, p. 33). It is undoubtedly useful to have someone in the group who is willing to speak up when someone attacks the healthy skeptic or otherwise attempts to influence the group through shutting down healthy discussion and conflict. The conundrum is creating a supportive environment in which someone can safely serve the role of the caller.

Examples from the board meetings we observed provide helpful illustrations of these various roles and the value of inquiry as a method to promote engaging conflict. The excerpts in Box 5.2 demonstrate how inquiry is used (i) to create shared meaning by revealing unstated assumptions, (ii) to reframe underlying issues, and (iii) to prevent premature closure of an important topic.

Box 5.2   The Value of Inquiry in Engaging Conflict

These examples come from a different nonprofit organization than the excerpts in Box 5.1. Below, inquiry is used to get clarity on the meaning of "board participation." The topic arises in a discussion of board development. The board chair (Denise) has just told the group that they need to have "100% board participation" (all names are pseudonyms):

EDWIN: What does that mean? Does that mean money?
SARAH (executive director):   Yeah.
DENISE (chair):   Yes.
EDWIN: A hundred percent participation means you contribute money?
DENISE: Um hmm.
EDWIN: That's so funny. I mean I don't think that's bad. It's just I don't consider, I mean, I think you can be a total work horse and not contribute money.

The use of inquiry is important because this group needs to have a collective sense of what they mean when they ask their board members for 100% participation. This conversation occurs in the context of revising their board member handbook, so the implications are critical to setting expectations for current and future board members.

The importance of the issue under discussion is reflected in the interaction below when a new participant joins the discussion (Maria):

MONICA: Well would this be out of order then to ask you, Edwin, are you bringing this up as an action item? We've got definitely more on the agenda. Would you like to submit this?
EDWIN: Yes. I want to make a motion that we vote to adopt these responsibilities.
MARIA: Can we go back to that fundraising piece? So when we talk to people we would still be giving them a rough concept of a dollar amount. Like when we generally know the people that we're talking to, their socioeconomic situation, are we – I mean, it would still be nice to have an idea of what we are asking them to donate.

Maria's inquiry serves several functions in the above turn. It prevents the group from making a decision without coming to agreement on a dollar amount for board member donations, and it requires the group to engage in a conversation about what kind of board they are: Will they only include members who will contribute thousands of dollars or will they allow donations based on what board members can comfortably afford? This is also an important *reframing* of the issue. It is not just about what it means to participate, it is also about how inclusive the board is willing to be, because by requiring a certain level of donation from board members, they will exclude people from participating. This is a highly sensitive topic that Maria continues to press in the follow-up statement below:

MARIA: So I mean is it worthwhile for us to kind of acknowledge that we still need to include a dollar amount in the document?

MONICA: That's a good point. The two prospective board members that I'm going to nominate, I told them two hundred dollars.

EDWIN: Well I think the standard was sort of established last year for me personally when you said, "I expect everybody to sponsor for two hundred and fifty dollars." We could say that we encourage everyone to come in at a sponsorship level of two hundred and fifty dollars but that's optional ... I mean do you think that would be helpful?

MARIA: Yeah. I just think it's helpful to have some kind of concept. I know Denise mentioned it to me when I came on board. I'm sure most of you all had the same discussion and that was helpful. Because if she had said you need to give two grand a year, I'd be like "okay it was a great conversation" but you know ... I mean you don't want to be picking a figure out of the air, but I think there needs to be something stated about that because I think if you tell people a hundred it's going to be hundred.

Note that the excerpts above include asking questions and soliciting other opinions, such as "do you think that would be helpful?" Maria also makes it clear that she does not see this as an exclusive board that would expect members to contribute thousands of dollars. This is supported by others who have stated that board members should be asked to contribute $200 or $250. Through this communication, the board ultimately agrees that they would like to ask for $250, but in order to be as inclusive as possible, they will not put a number in the document so that they can tell prospective board members that they only expect a contribution at the level they can afford.

In this case, not providing a specific donation amount allows the nonprofit to demonstrate their commitment to having a diverse board. Because this organization works with an underserved and marginalized population, this is an important part of their identity. On the other hand, they do need board members to play a large role in fundraising, and they expect board members to make as significant a donation as they can reasonably afford. If Maria had not raised the question of fundraising after the motion was called for, the board would likely have closed the conversation before reaching consensus on the expectations of their board members. All too often, this kind of premature closure occurs because groups privilege meeting efficiency and group harmony over engaging in difficult conversations. In fact, I could provide several examples from the board meeting transcripts of both organizations in which board chairs referred to the need to move on to the next agenda item as a reason to make a decision or table an issue. This behavior serves to avoid, rather than engage, conflict.

For Reflection and Discussion:

These could also be used to role-play with a partner.

1) Imagine that your boss is giving you feedback on your work and she says that your tone needs to be more professional. What does this mean to you? Do you know if your boss has the same definition of professional as you do? Practice what you might say to your boss to get clarity on this feedback to make sure you are meeting expectations. You also want to make sure you protect your boss's face when you ask the question. What might you say?

2) You are working with your project team and everyone seems to agree with the dominant member of the group (the one who speaks most often and seems to have been appointed group leader). This is frustrating to you because you do not think this dominant member is always correct. What might you do or say to alter this dynamic, again, protecting the face of the "leader" and other group members, while encouraging more thought and discussion of key issues?

While only one episode is used in Box 5.2 to illustrate inquiry, the larger systematic study of board meeting interaction supports a pattern in which the use of inquiry raises important topics and helps group members develop shared understanding. There are risks to the use of inquiry, however. I once co-facilitated a leadership workshop for banking executives and my co-facilitator specifically warned the group that they should "never ask why." The reasoning was that "why" questions make people defensive. However, further support for the value of being inquisitive is found in Cooperrider and Srivastva's (1987) call for *appreciative inquiry*. Appreciative inquiry was originally conceived as a tool to improve organizational dynamics by focusing on positive experiences. Appreciative inquiry suggests observing successful organizations and posing the question: What are they doing right? According to Bushe (2012), the overriding goal of appreciative inquiry is to help organizations bring people and ideas together to generate innovation and change. Asking questions is seen as pivotal to this task. Directly connected to conflict is the point that innovation and change challenge the status quo and there are always some organizational members who will resist calls for change. It seems clear that asking questions is a critical part of group and organizational life. While questions will not always lead to conflict, they may be a trigger for crucial conversations that lead to important organizational change.

The issue of how questions are asked (or framed) is paramount. Tone of voice, facial expressions, body posture, and word choice all serve to frame a question as either a challenge or a sincere request for additional information or a new perspective. There is a difference between a nurse asking a physician, "Why would you induce anesthesia when you know the patient has eaten in the last 30 minutes?" as opposed to, "I understand that the surgeon has a very busy schedule today, but is everyone aware that the patient has eaten within the last 30 minutes?" The first example is evaluative in tone and contributes to an adversarial framing, while the second example protects the doctor's face and raises the question as a shared problem to be resolved collaboratively. Conflict scholars have found that we often default to an adversarial approach to conflict. In the final section of this chapter we describe the adversarial narrative and then describe key features that mediators (neutral third parties who facilitate communication among disputing parties) use to change the "rules" to move parties to a more cooperative stance.

Changing the Rules of Engagement from Adversarial to Collaborative

In their book on narrative construction in mediation, Stewart and Maxwell (2010) refer to a common pattern called the "bilateral adversarial narrative." In this interaction, one party explains the events leading to the conflict by placing the blame on the other party. The second party counters with his or her version, defending that position and placing the blame on the other party. This probably sounds familiar as the way playground conflicts often sound: "he pushed me off the slide," "she started it by moving so slowly." While this may be a mundane example, it is important because many of us learn this "script" on the playground and continue to follow it even as we get older and conflicts become more complex. When conflict communication maintains the bilateral adversarial narrative, parties get more and more entrenched in their positions, leading to escalation and possible intractability as each party continues to blame the other. While Stewart and Maxwell (2010) confirmed the prevalence of the adversarial narrative, they also found evidence of other patterns. In one of the mediations in their book, only one party maintained the adversarial stance, while the second party was more collaborative. Ultimately, this enabled the parties to co-construct a new version of events that met both parties' needs. In a second example, one party used the adversarial frame to maintain power, while the second party chose not to actively engage. Although this mediation sounds like it might advantage the person with more power, the fact that the second party refused to engage in the adversarial "script" enabled the mediator to help the parties construct a more collaborative interaction that led to agreement.

In a study of simulated mediations, my co-authors and I observed the bilateral adversarial narrative at the beginning of the majority of the mediation sessions (Jameson, Sohan, & Hodge, 2014). We also found exceptions to this rule, however, and found that mediators were able to help disputants hear new information, change their perceptions of each other, and transition to more collaborative interactional patterns. While not all conflicts require a third party (and sometimes there is no third party available), there are some strategies we have seen in mediation – coming either from the mediator or the parties themselves – that provide insights on how we can make the rules more collaborative in the midst of conflict. I have already covered reframing and asking questions (also important mediator strategies), so below I highlight four additional tools used by mediators: *paraphrasing*, focusing on *common ground*, focusing on *emotion*, and focusing on *problem solving*. These communication strategies often help the disputing parties engage in more collaborative interaction, including *perspective-taking* and *accepting one's share of responsibility for the conflict*.

Strategy 1: Paraphrasing

Paraphrasing is often associated with active listening, as discussed in Unit One, as it involves repeating what a speaker said in the listener's own words. Repeating what the speaker has said serves a few important functions for engaging conflict: (i) it shows the speaker that the listener is truly engaged in the conversation, and (ii) it provides the speaker an opportunity to clarify what they were saying if the paraphrase is incorrect. The importance of this should not be underestimated, because many times in conversation, and perhaps especially in times of conflict, the listener does not correctly interpret the other person, which can lead to continued misunderstanding, frustration, and conflict escalation. A third feature of paraphrasing that is especially useful in mediation is that it enables the mediator to *reframe* what one party says to make it easier for the second party to hear.

This is worth repeating: When a mediator restates what one party said in front of the second party in a slightly different way, the second party may actually *hear* what is said differently. Think about a time you have been really angry at or frustrated with someone. You blame them for something they did that felt disrespectful, for example. In that situation you may make a dispositional attribution, as described in Chapter 4. When we have it in our mind that someone is mean, uncaring, or disrespectful, and that is part of their "personality," we interpret everything they say through that evaluative filter (the opposite of non-evaluative listening, discussed in Unit One). When a mediator asks us to describe the conflict, we might say, "She is impossible, she criticizes everything I do, and nothing I do is ever right!" A mediator might paraphrase this by saying, "I understand you feel frustrated when she gives you feedback because you don't think you hear anything positive, is that correct?" Note how in this reframing the mediator removes the evaluative language of "she is impossible," which would likely make the other party defensive and unwilling to listen. The mediator also focuses on a specific action – providing only negative and not any positive feedback. By focusing on something specific, the other party can reflect on their behavior and whether that may be accurate, which gives the parties something specific to talk about. This can lead to an improved ability to see things from the other's perspective. In our study, we found many examples of statements of increased understanding that directly followed a mediator's paraphrase in our simulated mediations. Box 5.3 revisits the Roberta and Margaret mediation from Chapter 2 (see Box 2.1) to show how the mediator's paraphrase helped Margaret and Roberta better understand each other and the perceptions that were underlying their communication.

Box 5.3   Revisiting Margaret and Roberta: "Familiarity Breeds Contempt"

Remember that Margaret is upset because she is relatively new to the department, and she feels Roberta gets upset with her when she asks questions. Imagine the following conversation happens in mediation with Margaret and Roberta together in the room with the mediator.

MARGARET: Well, we work together in a very small space and it is difficult when we are both there at the same time. I have a bad back and I need to have my chair pushed away from my desk a bit to be able to put my legs on a stool to relieve some pain. I know this annoys Roberta. But I wish she would not take it out on me by getting upset when I have a question about something. Roberta has been here a lot longer than I have and sometimes I really need to learn from her, but she gets very frustrated and snaps at me.

MEDIATOR: It sounds like you feel badly that you are taking up a lot of space in a small office due to your back problem, is that right?

MARGARET: Yes. That is exactly right. But I can't help it.

MEDIATOR: Have you ever talked directly to Roberta about your need to put your feet up under the desk?

MARGARET: No. I'm too uncomfortable because we don't talk about personal things.

MEDIATOR: So Roberta, you've heard that Margaret believes your conflict stems from the small office, do you agree that is the source of the problem?

ROBERTA: Well actually no. For me the source of the problems is that I thought Margaret was lazy. But after hearing this I now understand that she has back pain, and I understand that because I suffer from arthritis. The reason I get frustrated with her questions is that I thought she was not trying to learn, but now I better understand.

For Reflection and Discussion:

1) How does the mediator's paraphrase change the nature of the conflict between Margaret and Roberta?
2) What other examples of mediation strategies discussed in this chapter do you see at play in this brief excerpt?

Strategy 2: Focusing on Common Ground

Often when we are in conflict with someone, we focus on all the ways in which we differ and see things differently. In fact, negotiation research has discovered that most conflicts include mixed motives: There are incentives to compete (increasing one's personal gain, for example), but also reasons to cooperate (maintaining a positive relationship with the other party). Mediators can help the parties move from competing to cooperating by reminding them of what they have in common. Hearing each other talk may cause parties to see things more similarly than they realized, or the mediator might remind them that they share a common goal. In the case of Roberta and Margaret, realizing that they both suffer from physical pain provided some common ground that came up in the mediation session. When helping them come to an agreement, the mediator might remind them that they need to work together to get the job done since they are supervisors of the same facilities crew. Nearly all conflict participants have some common ground, whether it is as specific as a task that needs to be accomplished or higher-level needs such as wanting to have better work–life balance or protecting their jobs.

Focusing on what parties have in common can shift the nature of the conversation from adversarial to cooperative.

Strategy 3: Focusing on Emotion

We are often taught that we should take the emotion out of our conflicts, especially in the workplace. However, there is research to support the claim that emotion accompanies conflict and also morally frames it for us (Jones, 2005). This means we have to address the underlying emotion if we are to successfully shift from adversarial to more cooperative interaction. In the Margaret and Roberta example, the mediator focused on emotion when she paraphrased Margaret by saying, "It sounds like you feel badly that you are taking up a lot of space in a small office due to your back problem, is that right?" Here the mediator is checking the interpretation that Margaret is feeling badly or feels some "guilt," and, importantly, when Margaret confirms this, Roberta is able to hear how Margaret feels. We get the sense from Roberta's next statement that this has changed her attribution that Margaret is lazy. By understanding that Margaret feels badly – that she knows she creates an inconvenience for Roberta – Roberta is able to see Margaret differently. This is a subtle but powerful impact of raising emotion to the surface. It should be noted that when we are engaged in direct conflict with another, we often do not discuss the emotions we are feeling. There are a variety of reasons for this, including (i) we don't want to show weakness or vulnerability, (ii) we don't want to be judged for being "emotional" at work, and (iii), as Margaret expressed, we may not believe we have the kind of relationship with the other party where we discuss our feelings or personal issues (such as our health). This creates a challenge to the notion that employees should be able to handle conflicts on their own (one of the focus group narratives discussed in Chapter 4). It is also a reason why having a third-party mediator can be valuable in helping parties become more collaborative and reach agreement. In fact, a study comparing the discussion of emotion in negotiated and mediated conflict interactions found parties were much more likely to discuss emotion in mediation and that they were more likely to include issues related to their ongoing relationship in mediated agreements as opposed to negotiated agreements (Jameson et al., 2009). Because how we both experience and express emotion is complicated, especially in conflict, this will be discussed further in Unit Four: Rapport (Building).

Strategy 4: Focusing on Problem Solving

A final mediator strategy that helps move disputing parties toward cooperation is to turn their attention away from the past (i.e., who did what and why), and move them toward identifying the source of the problem and possible solutions. In the case of Margaret and Roberta, they had to do some work to identify the source of the problem, which turned out to be Margaret's attribution of Roberta as lazy and her resulting reluctance to help her. Once Margaret had a new understanding, the mediator was able to ask both parties, "Now that you know more about each other and each other's intentions and motivations, what do you need to work better together?" This shifted the conversation to specific things they could do, such as Roberta agreeing to help Margaret learn the processes and answer her questions. Examples of how mediators turn parties in conflict directly toward problem solving include statements such as, "What is it that you would really want to satisfy your need?" "What would be a perfect situation for you?" or "Now that you both understand you have deadline concerns, what can you do to help each other out with that?" (Jameson et al., 2014). The important point here is that the parties must do the hard work of listening to each other and engaging in perspective-taking before moving to problem solving too quickly. This leads to the discussion of two additional strategies parties in conflict can use to shift the rules from adversarial to cooperative: perspective-taking and accepting one's own responsibility for conflict.

Strategy 5: Perspective-Taking

Roberta communicates that she understands Margaret's perspective when she admits she did not know she had a bad back. This statement acknowledged that she understood Margaret in a new way and that changed her opinion of her. We found many examples in our data in which a statement of perspective-taking shifted a mediation from adversarial to cooperative. Two examples from two different role-played mediations follow:

> *Perspective-Taking Example 1*: I have misinterpreted her actions as being lazy. I just feel that if I was always there to help you, you would never help yourself. Now, these things that I didn't understand, like where you come from, probably would have helped, but to know that you need more orientation, I didn't know that.
> *Perspective-Taking Example 2*: I do understand you also have things to do and your own goals and I do not want to step into them or keep you away from them.

When disputants engage in perspective-taking and are willing to state what they have learned out loud, the other party typically responds with appreciation and often a statement of reciprocal understanding that not only moves the parties toward an agreement, but also may repair a harmed relationship. This may also be directly related to each party's willingness to accept responsibility.

Strategy 6: Accepting Responsibility

Mediation and negotiation scholar Jean Poitras has found that accepting responsibility is an important step in the emergence of cooperation in mediation (2005). As with expressing emotion, he also has found that accepting responsibility is more challenging for parties in a negotiation setting because it makes one party more vulnerable (Poitras, 2007). In our study of simulated mediations, we found several examples of parties expressing their own responsibility for a conflict situation, and these statements almost always moved the discussion to a more cooperative stance. Examples include statements such as, "I'm sorry that I misinterpreted you and I wasn't aware of your job goals" and "I didn't know about the bad situation . . . we don't have to have this blame game going on like 'he did this to me and I did this to him' and things like that."

Importantly, in both of these final examples, perspective-taking and accepting responsibility, the speaker is acknowledging something important: either new understanding of the other party or that their own behavior could have been different or better. This is a great way to transition to the next unit, which covers the A in LEARN: *Acknowledge*.

Chapter Summary

The goal of this chapter was to highlight ways we can communicate that help others engage in rather than avoid conflict by making it more collaborative. I started by sharing a third set of narratives employees use to talk about conflict in their workplace, conflict as collaborative problem solving, to point out that not all workplaces experience conflict as "political maneuvering" or "mission impossible," as described by the narratives in Chapter 4. We then reviewed several ways to change the nature of conflict interaction or the "rules of engagement" to make conflict more engaging. These ideas come from research on organizational dissent, reframing and inquiry, and mediation.

Literature on organizational dissent was presented to demonstrate two ways employees can communicate disagreement with workplace policies or practices: solution presentation and direct-factual appeal. Yet we are also reminded that employees must have supportive and trusting relationships with supervisors and a supportive voice climate to use these strategies. When these conditions are not present, employees are likely to use less prosocial tactics, such as circumvention or threatening to quit. Dissatisfied employees may also use lateral or displaced dissent tactics, which do not directly engage the conflict and can have negative consequences for the individual and the organization. Venting to family and friends at home or via social media, while playing an important social support role, was shown to be detrimental to effective conflict management.

Reframing was presented as an important way to increase collaborative communication by helping parties negotiate the underlying problem they are trying to solve or identify the nature of the relationship. As shown in the third section on mediator strategies, paraphrasing is a good way to reframe by clarifying what the speaker said and possibly stating it in a more specific and positive way that can help the parties move toward more collaborative problem solving. Asking questions was also discussed as an important way to avoid making assumptions and create shared meaning among parties in a conflict.

In the final section we turned to mediation practice to understand some specific communication strategies or techniques we can use to move conflict interaction from adversarial to collaborative. In addition to paraphrasing, these strategies include focusing on common ground, focusing on emotion, focusing on problem solving, perspective-taking, and taking responsibility for one's own role in the conflict. When people in conflict gain a new understanding of the causes or motivations behind another's behavior, it often changes our attributions from dispositional to situational, removes the blame, and paves the way for constructive conflict management.

Activity: Reframing Practice

Look back at the specific examples of reframing provided in this chapter. Practice reframing the following statements by paraphrasing the speaker. If it helps, you can use the formula: I understand you feel _____ when s/he says/does _____ because you need/would like _____.

1) He is so arrogant! He acts as though he always has all the answers and never allows anyone else to talk.
2) She drives me crazy when she brings the subject back to her every time I'm trying to explain a problem I am having.
3) My boss is completely unreasonable. She expects me to work all weekend even though I have kids at home.
4) That guy is nuts! How can he expect me to get my part of the report done on time when he never gives me the information I need?

References

Anderson, J. W. (2009). Organizational shunning: The disciplinary functions of "non-sense." *Atlantic Journal of Communication, 17*: 36–50. https://doi.org/10.1080/15456870802506140.

Axelrod, N. R. (2007). *Culture of inquiry: Healthy debate in the boardroom.* Washington, DC: BoardSource.

Bales, R. F. (1950). *Interaction process analysis: A method for the study of small groups.* Cambridge, MA: Addison-Wesley Press.

Bateson, G. (1972). *Steps to an ecology of mind.* New York: Ballantine Books.

Berg, D. N. (2011). Dissent: An intergroup perspective. *Consulting Psychology Journal: Practice and Research, 63*(1): 50–65. https://doi.org/10.1037/a0023052.

Blancero, D., & Dyer, L. (1996). Due process for non-union employees: The influence of system characteristics on fairness perceptions. *Human Resource Management, 35*(3): 343–359.

Bushe, G. R. (2012). Appreciative inquiry: Theory and critique. In D. Boje, B. Burnes, & J. Hassard (Eds.), *The Routledge companion to organizational change* (pp. 87–103). Oxford: Routledge.

Chartrand, T. L., & Bargh, J. A. (1999). The chameleon effect: The perception–behavior link and social interaction. *Journal of Personality and Social Psychology, 76*: 893–910. https://doi.org/10.1037//0022-3514.76.6.893.

Cooperrider, D. L., & Srivastva, S. (1987). Appreciative inquiry in organizational life. In R. W. Woodman & W.A. Pasmore (Eds.), *Research in Organizational Change and Development, Vol. 1* (pp. 129–169). Stamford, CT: JAI Press.

Donohue, W. A., Rogan, R. G., & Kaufman, S. (Eds.). (2011). *Framing matters. Perspectives on negotiation research and practice in communication.* New York: Peter Lang Publishing.

Gadlin, H. (2000). The ombudsmen: What's in a name? *Negotiation Journal, 16*(1): 37–48. https://doi.org/10.1111/j.1571-9979.2000.tb00201.x.

Garner, J. T. (2012). Making waves at work: Perceived effectiveness and appropriateness of organizational dissent messages. *Management Communication Quarterly, 26*(2): 224–240. https://doi.org/10.1177/0893318911431803.

Goodboy, A. K., Chory, R. M., & Dunleavy, K. N. (2008). Organizational dissent as a function of organizational justice. *Communication Research Reports, 25*: 255–265.

Jameson, J. K., Bodtker, A. M., Porch, D., & Jordan, W. (2009). Exploring the role of emotion in conflict transformation. *Conflict Resolution Quarterly, 27*(2): 167–192.

Jameson, J. K., & Metelsky, B. A. (2011, May). *The role of framing in the social construction of nonprofit governance.* Paper presented at the Annual Meeting of the International Communication Association, Boston, MA.

Jameson, J. K., Sohan, D., & Hodge, J. (2014). Turning points and conflict transformation in mediation. *Negotiation Journal, 30*(2): 125–237.

Jones, T. S. (2005). Emotion in mediation: Implications, applications, opportunities and challenges. In M. Herrman (Ed.), *Blackwell handbook of mediation: Theory and practice* (pp. 277–306). New York: Blackwell.

Kassing, J. W. (1998). Development and validation of the Organizational Dissent Scale. *Management Communication Quarterly, 12*: 183–229.

Kassing, J. W. (2000). Investigating the relationship between superior-subordinate relationship quality and employee dissent. *Communication Research Reports, 17*: 58–70.

Kassing, J. W. (2002). Speaking up: Identifying employees' upward dissent strategies. *Management Communication Quarterly, 16*(4): 187–209. https://doi.org/10.1177/089331802237234.

Kassing, J. W. (2005). Speaking up completely: A comparison of perceived competence in upward dissent strategies. *Communication Research Reports, 22*: 227–234. https://doi.org/10.1080/00036810500230651.

Kassing, J. W. (2007). Going around the boss: Exploring the consequences of circumvention. *Management Communication Quarterly, 21*: 55–75. https://doi.org/10.1177/0893318907302020.

Kassing, J. W. (2009). In case you didn't hear me the first time: An examination of repetitious upward dissent. *Management Communication Quarterly, 22*: 416–436. https://doi.org/10.1177/0893318908327008.

Kassing, J. W. (2011). *Dissent in organizations.* Malden, MA: Polity Press.

Kassing, J. W., & Armstrong, T. A. (2002). Someone's going to hear about this: Examining the association between dissent-triggering events and employees' dissent expression. *Management Communication Quarterly, 16*: 39–65.

Katz, N. H., & Flynn, L. T. (2013). Understanding conflict management systems and strategies in the workplace: A pilot study. *Conflict Resolution Quarterly, 30*(4): 393–410. https://doi.org/10.1002/crq.21070.

Kennedy-Lightsey, C. (2007, November). *Dissent and whistle blowing: A conceptual Consideration.* Paper presented to the Organizational Communication Division of the National Communication Association Annual Convention, Chicago, IL.

Losada, M. (1999). The complex dynamics of high performance teams. *Mathematical and Computer Modeling, 30*: 179–192.

McFarlin, D. B., & Sweeney, P. D. (1996). Does having a say matter only if you get your way? Instrumental and value-expressive effects of employee voice. *Basic and Applied Social Psychology, 18*(3): 289–303. https://doi.org/10.1207/s15324834basp1803_3.

Milliken, F. J., Morrison, E. W., & Hewlin, P. (2003). An exploratory study of employee silence: Issues that employees don't communicate upward and why. *Journal of Management Studies, 40*: 1453–1476.

Morrison, E. W. (2011). Employee voice behavior: Integration and directions for future research. *The Academy of Management Annals, 5*(1): 373–412.

Poitras, J. (2005). A study of the emergence of cooperation in mediation. *Negotiation Journal, 21*(2): 281–300.

Poitras, J. (2007). The paradox of accepting one's share of responsibility in mediation. *Negotiation Journal, 23*(3): 267–282.

Redmond, V., Jameson, J. K., & Binder, A. R. (2016). How superior–subordinate relationship quality and conflict management styles influence an employee's use of upward dissent tactics. *Negotiation and Conflict Management Research,* *9*(2): 164–172.

Rummel, R. J. (1976). *Understanding conflict and war, Volume 2.* New York: John Wiley & Sons.

Senge, P. M. (1990). *The fifth discipline: The art & practice of the learning organization.* New York: Doubleday.

Shahinpoor, N., & Matt, B. F. (2007). The power of one: Dissent and organizational life. *Journal of Business Ethics, 74*: 37–48. https://doi.org/10.1007/s10551-006-9218-y.

Shapiro, D. L., & Brett, J. M. (1993). Comparing three processes underlying judgments of procedural justice: A field study of mediation and arbitration. *Journal of Personality and Social Psychology, 65*(6): 1167–1177. https://doi.org/10.1037/0022-3514.65.6.1167.

Sprague, J., & Rudd, G. L. (1988). Boat-rocking in the high-technology culture. *American Behavioral Scientist, 32*: 169–193.

Stewart, K. A., & Maxwell, M. M. (2010). *Storied conflict talk: Narrative construction in mediation.* Philadelphia, PA: John Benjamins.

Unit Three

Acknowledge

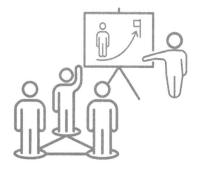

6

The Importance of Belonging and Recognition

The deepest principle in human nature is the craving to be appreciated.

William James (1842–1910, American philosopher)

If you are familiar with Maslow's (1943) hierarchy, you may recall that our basic needs are physiological – air, food, water – followed by security needs, such as protection from the elements through adequate clothing and having a safe place to live. Once these basic needs are met, we want to feel we belong to a community and we crave (in James's words above) appreciation from others, which gives us a sense that others value us and our contributions (see Figure 6.1). Our desire for belonging and recognition complements the notion of face, discussed in Chapter 2. Scholars describe face as how we want to be seen by others, and they note that people have competing needs to be included (called positive face), but also to be seen as autonomous and independent (negative face) and valued for making an important contribution (Brown & Levinson, 1987). As described in Chapter 1, conflict is often triggered when someone feels a threat to their face or identity or when they perceive they are not being valued. The various ways in which we acknowledge others can actually protect both positive and negative face, and this chapter and the next focus on the A in LEARN: *Acknowledge*.

In this chapter I will overview theories from interpersonal communication, linguistics, and mediation to demonstrate how scholars have discussed the importance of communication that confirms others (Cissna & Sieburg, 1981; Sieburg, 1973), saves face (Brown & Levinson, 1987), and provides both empowerment and recognition (Bush & Folger, 1994). I will draw from my research on communication between doctors and nurses to illustrate the value of confirmation, face-saving communication, and recognition. Then, in Chapter 7, I will talk about acknowledgment in the group context using examples from nonprofit board meetings and interdisciplinary research teams to further illustrate how different

Communication for Constructive Workplace Conflict, First Edition. Jessica Katz Jameson.
© 2023 John Wiley & Sons, Inc. Published 2023 by John Wiley & Sons, Inc.

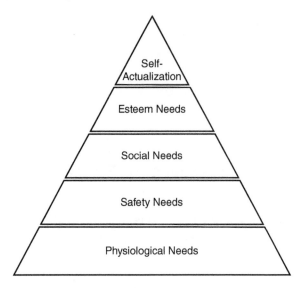

Figure 6.1 Maslow's Hierarchy of Needs.

forms of acknowledgment improve the team and organizational environment and promote constructive conflict communication where everyone feels valued.

Confirming and Disconfirming Communication

The roots of this interpersonal communication theory come from the fields of philosophy and psychology. The basic idea is that humans require communication that confirms or validates their existence. An example of *confirming* communication can be as simple as when someone says "good morning" and you say "good morning" in response. But you may also imagine a time when you said "good morning" to someone and they did not respond. When we feel ignored, it sends a subtle (or not-so-subtle) message that we are not important, recognized, or valued, and this is considered *disconfirming*. Over time, if we are the targets of many disconfirming messages it will have detrimental consequences on our self-esteem, sense of belonging, and possibly our mental health (Watzlawick, Bavelis, & Jackson, 1967).

Communication scholars have defined specific types of communication that are confirming or disconfirming (Cissna & Sieburg, 1981; Sieburg, 1973). Confirming responses include recognition, acknowledgment, and endorsement, while disconfirming responses include indifference, imperviousness, and disqualification.

Table 6.1 Confirming and disconfirming responses.

Confirming responses	Definition	Examples
Recognition	Communication recognizes the other exists	Saying "good morning" in response to another or smiling at another person.
Acknowledgment	Communication shows the person was heard	Repeating what someone said or asking a question in response. "That's an interesting idea; what do others think about it?"
Endorsement	Communication shows agreement with the speaker	"That is an interesting idea; let's brainstorm how we could make that happen."
Disconfirming responses	**Definition**	**Examples**
Indifference	Verbally or nonverbally suggests the other does not exist	Not responding to a "good morning"; ignoring someone's idea in a meeting; verbally interrupting someone who is speaking.
Imperviousness	Denies the other's experience, emotions, or perceptions	Responding to someone's statement by saying, "you do not really believe that," or "you can't be upset about this."
Disqualification	Confuses the speaker through evasive communication that cannot be easily interpreted as the words are either irrelevant, tangential, unclear, ambiguous, or contradictory	Someone asks, "What did you think of my report?" and the response is, "We have so many reports, it is frustrating," or "Yeah I glanced at it but, no, I haven't had a chance and I'm sure I'll get to it." [Often followed by a subject change!]

Table 6.1 provides examples of communication that illustrates each of these responses. A contemporary and all-too-common example of disconfirming messages is illustrated by what has come to be known as a *microaggression*. Microaggressions target specific underrepresented identity groups and are grounded in implicit bias (Sue et al., 2007). Consider the example of a Latina woman who made a suggestion in a meeting and it was completely ignored, yet a week later she learned by accident that another group member (a White woman) had been tasked with starting a project to execute the exact idea she had offered during the meeting. This is an example of a microaggression, and it is also a disconfirming message of *indifference*. Other examples of microaggressions occur

when a team leader cannot remember the names of their Black team members, confuses one person from a minority group with another, or makes comments such as, "Wow, you are so articulate," which suggests surprise that someone from a minority identity group would be a good communicator. What all of these examples have in common is that they send the message that an individual's ideas do not deserve further discussion, that an individual is not important enough to be remembered, or that an individual was not expected to be capable. Even though microaggressions might be unintentional (i.e., implicit), this communication sustains systemic privilege and marginalization, and we must recognize and eradicate this type of communication if we are committed to creating an equal, inclusive workplace that fosters collaboration and constructive conflict management. As will be illustrated more in the next section, communication that confirms others through acknowledgment is especially powerful because it both reinforces the individual's importance and recognizes their participation even when others may not agree with them. This is an especially valuable way to communicate during conflict to keep the conversation collaborative and respectful rather than shutting someone down or suggesting that their opinions, perceptions, or ideas do not deserve consideration. This brings us back to the discussion of protecting individuals' feelings of self-worth through attention to face-saving behavior, which is further explained by politeness theory (Brown & Levinson, 1987).

Politeness Theory

A theory from the field of linguistics provides more insights into why acknowledgment is important and describes specific examples of communication that is both confirming and validating. The theory of politeness (Brown & Levinson, 1987) was developed to illustrate how people use communication strategies that either support or threaten an individual's identity or *face*. Erving Goffman (1967) originally coined the term "face" to describe how we want to be seen by others, and likely you have heard and even used the phrase "saving face." We save face when we communicate to protect our own image and/or to support someone else's image. One example of when we need to save another's face is when we need to provide feedback to an employee who has made a mistake or did not meet expectations on an assignment. The most effective feedback will be clear and direct about the problem and its impact, but will also protect the employee's desire to be seen as a competent and valued member of the team. When face is threatened, people become defensive and they often stop listening, as described in Chapter 2. Most people respond to a face threat by focusing all their effort on trying to engage in face repair, and when an individual's communication is solely devoted to face saving, this promotes competitive interaction and conflict escalation rather than collaborative interaction (Oetzel & Ting-Toomey, 2003; Wilmot & Hocker, 2010). Practicing communication that is face supportive is therefore critical to developing an environment that facilitates constructive conflict management.

Brown and Levinson's (1987) theory of politeness differentiates positive and negative face. Positive face is defined as the desire to be accepted by others (i.e., to maintain connection), while negative face is the desire not to be imposed upon by others (i.e., to maintain autonomy). When communication threatens either the need for connection or the need for autonomy, it is considered a *face-threatening act*. An additional layer of complexity comes from the fact that people have multiple face concerns in any interaction (Oetzel & Ting-Toomey, 2003). *Self face* refers to protecting one's own autonomy and/or connection needs while *other face* is the desire to protect the other party's needs for autonomy and/or connection. When we are communicating at work, we are often simultaneously protecting autonomy while threatening connection or vice versa. For example, when I reach out to a coworker to ask for help on a project, I am supporting my positive face by indicating we are a team, but I am threatening my negative face by admitting that I need help and cannot complete the project on my own. Further, by reaching out for help I am supporting the other's positive face by indicating I value our partnership/collaboration, but I am threatening their negative face because I am imposing on their autonomy by (at least potentially) giving them more work. Depending on how the request is worded (and, indeed, whether it is a request versus a demand), and how the other person responds, we may have a more or less cooperative interaction. It is likely to go most smoothly if I am attending to face saving in my communication. *Mutual face* is the term used to describe the need to protect the relationship by attending to both autonomy and connection for both self and other. The most effective and collaborative communication will manage both aspects of face for the self and other concurrently. The complexity of this interaction is illustrated in Table 6.2.

Box 6.1 provides an example of communication challenges that emerged from a study of doctors and nurses and includes examples of face-saving communication that were found to improve relationships and collaboration (Jameson, 2004). Since the desire to save and support face is experienced by all members in all kinds of organizations, these examples have implications for effective conflict communication that are transferable to other contexts.

The case of anesthesiologists and CRNAs provides a clear and compelling example of the relationship between how individuals communicate over time and how that impacts not only relationship development, but the overall climate. As described in Box 6.1, several anesthesiologists described that when they first started working with CRNAs they were very directive. This was partially due to anxieties about moving from being a resident to a full-fledged physician, and all the responsibility and accountability that this role entails. It is not surprising that

Table 6.2 Complexity of face negotiation.

	Face saving (protecting autonomy)	Face supporting (protecting connection)	Face threatening (threatens autonomy or connection)
Self face	Communication protects speaker's need for autonomy; emphasizes expertise or ability	Communication protects speaker's need for connection; shows desire for cooperation	Communication imposes on speaker's needs for autonomy and/or connection
Other face	Communication protects the target's need for autonomy; attempts to justify or minimize imposition	Communication protects the target's need for connection; shows cooperation and respect	Communication imposes on target's needs for autonomy and/or connection
Mutual face	Communication protects the relational need for autonomy	Communication protects the relational need for connection	Communication imposes on relational needs for autonomy and/or connection

---

Box 6.1   Face-Saving Communication among Doctors and Nurses

One unique workplace partnership that is found in nearly all hospitals is that between anesthesiologists and certified registered nurse anesthetists (CRNAs). While anesthesia practice models vary according to hospital size, location, and available resources (i.e., rural versus urban hospitals), typically the doctor and nurse must work together in a relationship in which CRNAs stay with the patient throughout surgery and anesthesiologists supervise multiple patients at one time, making themselves available for support if complications arise. This relationship creates built-in opportunities for face-threatening communication, as doctors often want to demonstrate the need for their supervision, while nurses often feel their autonomy is being threatened. In both cases, each group may feel disrespected by the other. In a study based on in-depth interviews with CRNAs and anesthesiologists, I learned that members of both groups wanted to demonstrate their individual contributions to the anesthesia process while also earning each other's respect. The study revealed a variety of approaches to communication, some of which exacerbated defensiveness and conflict, and others that created trusting, collegial relationships and fostered an overall positive, collaborative environment. Below I share a few examples of face-threatening communication that had a negative impact on relationships and the overall climate, followed by examples of face-saving communication. (In order to clarify the role of each speaker while minimizing status differences, anesthesiologists are referred to as "Dr." followed by a first name and CRNAs are referred to by first name, all of which are pseudonyms).

Face-Threatening Communication

One important category of face-threatening communication is micromanaging, described by Jill: "Some of the anesthesiologists want to tell you every single thing to do, okay, like 'turn this on, use that, do this, do that.'" This clearly threatens one's autonomy or desire to be seen as competent.

A second, related example of micromanaging is described by Dr. Mitch as being most likely when doctors are new to the hospital, so the connection with nurses has not yet been created: "When you are supervising you are already anxious because you are so new and now someone is between you and the patient ... you have to somehow acclimate yourself to the new system. Now that may involve being in the room the whole time, and especially when you have a CRNA who has experience, that may be a little grating for them, you know?"

A third example of face-threatening communication is also a good example of a microaggression, as Dr. Terry recounted a time when a doctor used language that was disrespectful of the nurse as it described the difference between anesthesiologist and CRNA as similar to the difference between the skills of a pilot those of someone whose primary role is to serve drinks and make customers comfortable:

"The anesthesiologist was explaining the process to the patient and said 'it is like being on a flight and I'm the pilot on the airplane and this would be the flight attendant.'" Using this analogy to explain the CRNA to the patient did not acknowledge or validate the CRNA's skills and expertise.

It is important to note that nurses in this study were also guilty of using face-threatening communication. For example, Jenny explained that "If you have a know-it-all attitude and don't communicate with your anesthesiologist and just make decisions without letting them know what's going on, that will cause a conflict." Sarah recalled a specific incident where a CRNA said to an anesthesiologist, "you do the case yourself if you don't like how I'm doing it." Dr. Terry described a few types of CRNA behavior that were considered face-threatening, such as "monosyllabic answers where you weren't really sure she followed you" or when "There was always some excuse and hostility ... or some kind of crack about the ologist ... I hate being called an ologist." In this example there are two types of face threat, the former in the form of not listening, and the latter in the form of using a disrespectful term to describe the anesthesiologist.

Whether used by the doctors or the nurses, all of these examples threaten the face of the other by demeaning them in some way rather than emphasizing and acknowledging their necessity and value to the surgery, the patient, and the overall organization. When this type of communication happened, the interviewees said that many of the doctors and nurses could no longer work together. Not only does this make it more difficult to schedule surgeries, it also disrupts the workplace climate in an occupation that is already highly stressful and requires a high degree of reliable collaboration.

Face-Saving and Supporting Politeness Strategies

In contrast, there were five specific types of communication that were found to be face saving and supporting, leading to relational growth, mutual respect, and positive climates (see Table 6.3). One of the most common strategies discussed by both CRNAs and anesthesiologists was simply *emphasizing respect* for and acknowledging the competence of the other, a simultaneously face-saving and face-supporting strategy. Dr. Bob noted, "None of us like to be belittled. Some of these CRNAs are quite senior … you have to be sensitive to their feelings, to their self-esteem." Likewise, Sarah reported, "It all comes down to the theme of mutual respect and recognizing that each brings to the table legitimate knowledge; and one is not necessarily better than the other one."

Table 6.3 Politeness strategies and outcomes for self, other, and mutual face.

Strategy	Speaker (self face)	Hearer (other face)	Mutual face
Emphasize respect	Face supporting	Face saving and face supporting	Protects relational needs for connection and respect
Emphasize solidarity	Face supporting; *but* may threaten autonomy	Face supporting; *but* may be perceived as threat to autonomy	Protects relational need for connection and acceptance
Provide explanation	Face saving and face supporting	Face saving and face supporting	Emphasizes relational equality and minimizes social distance
Show deference	Face supporting; *but* threatens autonomy	Face saving and face supporting	Emphasizes desire for collaboration *but* may increase social distance
Discuss in private after the fact	Face supporting; *but* threatens autonomy	Face saving and face supporting (although potentially face threatening)	Emphasizes respect and desire for collaboration

A related face-supportive strategy is to *emphasize solidarity* as well as respect. Dr. Mitch explained: "I go about it by saying 'hey we're a team, I want to know what you have to say', and I try to be as friendly as possible, and that is 90% of it." Dr. Terry recounted a specific relationship with a nurse in which "I could understand her technique and allowed her as much autonomy as possible . . . I recognized that she had real talent, and she realized that I could teach her stuff as well . . . We had a certain commonality; we were both from Pennsylvania."

Both anesthesiologists and CRNAs also offered face support by *providing an explanation*. As Dr. Aaron explained: "My way of approaching it is to sit down and explain my reasoning and tell 'em why I think it would be better. Also with the understanding that it could be done the other way, but sort of presenting my side of the argument." Dr. Bill concurred, saying that "I'll suggest [a certain drug], and I'll just give the reasoning for it, and it's generally accepted." Larry described his approach to working with the anesthesiologists: "I would give my opinion and listen to what they have to say, and whoever can sort of justify or give their reasons, it usually works out where it is not a problem." Tim also described how he approaches the doctors in a face-saving way, specifically stating: "Without confronting them, you don't want to do that. You might begin to talk about the situation, you may have seen some similar problems and how they were made better, make suggestions. You don't point fingers or say 'wrong' or anything like that."

One anesthesiologist recommended that CRNAs use a strategy that *shows deference* to the anesthesiologists' knowledge and therefore addresses their needs for autonomy and connection. Dr. Terry suggested: "I would approach the anesthesiologist and say "here's the plan I'm thinking of, here's why. Is there anything I should know about this surgeon or anything else I should consider?" Amy shared how she handles differences of opinion using this strategy by saying, "I really do think she needs more anesthesia; can I try that first?"

Giving deference may threaten the autonomy of CRNAs, however, in that it emphasizes power distance by suggesting the CRNA must ask the anesthesiologist for permission before continuing the anesthesia plan.

Giving deference is also used by anesthesiologists, although many admit they did not start out that way, as Dr. Terry explained: "When we go over the pre-op together, I'll say 'here are the things I think are important; how do you want to do the case?' I didn't start off this way . . . I used to be very directive." This last example is face saving for the speaker and hearer because the anesthesiologist is sharing knowledge while also asking for the CRNA's opinion. Because the anesthesiologist has higher status, his or her use of deference signals respect for the CRNA and a desire to cooperate.

A final face-supportive approach used by both doctors and nurses was *having a conversation at a later time, usually in private.* Sarah described a situation in which another CRNA asked, "are you working late today?" The anesthesiologist said yes, and she said, "so am I, and I am composing a list of things I want to discuss with you before I leave today." And so before the day was over she took the list to him of all the things he had done that offended her ... and it ended up that he took her list home and then he came back and discussed it at a later time. Amy indicated that she "might bring it up at a later time, not bring it up in front of other people ... If we inquire what they do and why, the more we show them we really do care. Everybody wants to feel they are making a contribution." Frank similarly said, "I always counsel them to go to the person afterwards and ask, but always give that person the opportunity to save face ... put it in terms of what [you] didn't understand, but make a point or two of your own."

These strategies show concern for respecting the other in that they provide reasons rather than simply telling the other what to do (especially in the case of the anesthesiologist, who often has more formal status and authority). These strategies also show the speakers' concerns for their own face by demonstrating special knowledge or experience, so they simultaneously protect self face and other face, which supports mutual face (see Table 6.2). All these strategies minimize the face threat by indicating the speaker has additional experience or information that the hearer needs, justifying the speaker's imposition on the other's autonomy.

For Reflection and Discussion:

Discuss with a partner or small group.

1) Based on your knowledge or assumptions of the medical profession, what are the environmental or organizational influences that might add to the face or identity concerns for doctors and nurses? Discuss how this complicates everyday communication and collaboration.
2) Consider environmental or organizational influences in other kinds of professions (such as those you and your classmates are interested in). How can you use the examples described in this case (and in Table 6.3) to prepare for and practice responding to face-threatening situations without getting defensive and to protect self, other, and mutual face?
3) What ideas do you have for organizational leaders about structures, procedures, or policies they might put in place to promote face-supportive communication?

doctors would be anxious given that (i) they are responsible for patients' lives, and (ii) if anything goes wrong, they are the most likely to be charged in a malpractice lawsuit. What we learned is that when they explained their "excessive supervision," nurses were more likely to accept it without getting defensive. Over time, a relationship of trust develops and the doctors give the nurses more autonomy, resulting in a combination of collegial relationships, improved organizational performance, and a collaborative climate. This relationship between empowering others and recognizing their unique concerns and interests, skills, and expertise has been shown to be an effective approach to conflict management in the context of mediation, the final subject of this chapter.

Insights from Transformative Mediation on Empowerment and Recognition

At the end of Chapter 5 I pointed out that an important turning point in mediation practice that can move parties from adversarial to collaborative communication is when one party openly recognizes a difficulty or situation the other has experienced. A specific approach to mediation that provides a theoretical explanation for this relationship and supports the value of acknowledgment is called transformative mediation (Bush & Folger, 1994, 2005). For context, it is helpful to contrast the transformative approach with what is commonly called either a facilitative or a problem-solving mediation style.[1] The final section of this chapter will contrast these two styles of mediation, describe the concepts of empowerment and recognition and why they are so powerful, and identify what we can learn from this about the value of acknowledging others in our everyday communication.

As defined in Chapter 5, mediators are neutral third parties who facilitate communication among disputing parties. The underlying premise of mediation is that parties will be more satisfied with the outcome of the conflict management process if they (i) have an opportunity to voice their concerns, complaints, and interests and (ii) have agency (are empowered) to develop the final agreement. There

---

[1] There are actually many more styles of mediation than problem-solving and transformative, such as evaluative mediation and narrative mediation. At least one study has found that in practice, many mediators use a combination of styles as they choose mediation strategies that are most likely to help the parties reach their goals (see Charkoudian et al., 2009). Because the majority of mediations are done in court-mandated situations where the primary goal is to reach agreement and avoid going to court, many mediators take the more directive approaches of problem-solving and evaluative mediation.

is an abundance of research on approaches to workplace conflict that have found that parties are more satisfied with both the process and the outcome of conflict management when they feel heard and not judged (think back to non-evaluative listening; see Jameson, 1999, for a review). One common comparison is made between mediation, an interest-based approach, and arbitration, a rights-based approach (Costantino & Merchant, 1996; Jameson, 2001; Lipsky, Seeber, & Fincher, 2003). In arbitration, a third party acts as a judge. Depending on whether parties speak for themselves or have an attorney speak for them, arbitration may give parties voice to make their "case," but it remains an adversarial process as the third party (arbiter) will ultimately decide the outcome. Note that while arbitration is usually a more formal dispute resolution process, managers are more likely to act as arbitrators than mediators when they get involved in conflicts among coworkers (Karambayya & Brett, 1989).

Now that we have a better understanding of mediation, we can contrast two approaches to mediation: the problem-solving style and the transformative style. Problem-solving mediation, arguably the more common approach, emphasizes getting the parties to agreement. When mediators are trained in a problem-solving (also called facilitative) style, they learn a series of steps or stages that typically include (i) introduction, (ii) hearing from each party, (iii) agenda-setting, (iv) brainstorming, and (v) writing the agreement. The introduction involves explaining the process and providing some ground rules. The explanation reminds parties that the mediator is neutral – they are not there to hear "evidence" and make a ruling, but instead mediation is a collaborative process in which the mediator hopes to help the parties listen to each other and develop their own agreement. Ground rules often include statements such as: no interrupting (if you have a thought, write it down so you can remember to say it when it is your turn) and maintaining civility (no name calling or cursing, for example). In problem-solving mediation, there may also be a ground rule that parties speak to the mediator rather than to each other (although if things go well, this rule is often relaxed at later stages of the mediation).

After the introduction and a commitment from both parties to continue the process, the mediator will ask one party to describe why they are there. Usually this is the party who brought the concern to the attention of management (sometimes referred to as "the grievant" in more formal dispute resolution systems). The party will be allowed to speak without interruption and the mediator will ask questions using many of the techniques of effective, nonjudgmental listening described in Chapter 3. The mediator's goals in this stage are at least two-fold: (i) to identify the underlying interests or concerns of the party (while parties come to mediation wanting a specific outcome, such as more money or a promotion, the mediator wants to know what needs underlie those stated goals), and (ii) for the *other* party to hear directly how their co-disputant is describing the conflict. Often in this early phase of the conflict, the two parties will disagree with how the other is describing the events that led to the conflict. When the mediator asks questions, it is important that the other party is listening to those answers, as by listening (and not being allowed to interrupt) they might hear something new and learn something about the other party they did not know. Note how having a third party facilitate the conversation disrupts our natural patterns in conflict, in which one party says what they are upset about, and the other party interrupts, gets defensive, and may challenge what is said or simply leave the interaction. Since mediation does not allow either of those typical responses, there is greater chance for listening and new understanding to occur (although to be clear, it does not always work that way).

Once both parties have had a chance to explain the conflict in their own terms, and the mediator and parties agree that all underlying interests have been identified, they move onto step three, which may be referred to as "agenda-setting." Here the mediator and the parties review the interests they just identified and look for areas of common ground, interests that are common to both parties. For example, common interests may include the desire to be treated with respect, the desire for recognition, and the desire for job security (if these sound like they are related to Maslow's hierarchy and face concerns, this is not a coincidence). Whether the interests are in common or unique to each party, the mediator will ask the parties to help set the agenda for the next phase of the mediation process by prioritizing the interests that need to be discussed and addressed in order to reach an agreement. If we think back to Roberta and Margaret's mediation described in Box 2.1, the initial set of interests after stage two of the mediation might have included the following items to be addressed:

- Getting Margaret's questions answered
- Respecting each other's space (chair and telephone placement) [common ground]
- Respectful communication (not snapping at each other) [common ground]
- Concern for each other's personal health (Margaret's and Roberta's back/ neck pain)

In the agenda-setting phase, the parties may agree to start with the areas of common ground: how to better respect each other's space and how to be more respectful in their communication, and then they may move on to making sure Margaret has the proper training, concern for her back pain, and (hopefully) concern for each other on a more personal level.

Once the agenda has been agreed upon, the mediator moves the parties into brainstorming, and each item on the agenda is discussed as parties are asked to come up with ideas on how to solve them. If the mediation is going well and the parties are engaged and positive, the mediator may actually have the parties talk directly to each other at this stage. Once the parties have brainstormed ideas and agreed on those that are most feasible and realistic, they move into the final stage of mediation and write down the agreement.

There are many advantages to a mediated outcome, as described above. It is a very logical approach and, if an agreement is reached, the parties should be committed to it because they wrote it. There are, however, a couple of limitations to the problem-solving approach to mediation. One is that the parties may feel pressure to come to an agreement (for example, to be viewed positively by a supervisor who suggested to them or required them to go to mediation). In this case, they may come to agreement but not really be committed to it due to continued animosity toward the other party. Mediators similarly may feel pressure to reach an agreement because they may be evaluated based on the percentage of mediations that reach agreement. If the mediator is paid or is concerned about being hired again in the future, they may take a more active role in suggesting solutions, and this may increase the chances that parties sign a final agreement that they are not 100% committed to. Another limitation of problem-solving mediation is that mediators often focus on the "facts" provided by the parties, and they may be less likely to probe into the emotions parties are feeling. As we found in the mediation study described in Chapter 5, mediation sessions in which parties felt all issues were resolved tended to include attention to emotion, and in fact several studies have supported the value of addressing emotion in conflict management (Gayle & Preiss, 1998; Jameson et al., 2009; Jameson, Sohan, & Hodge, 2014; Jones, 2005).

This brings us to an alternative approach, transformative mediation. Transformative mediation is grounded in the counter-intuitive idea that reaching agreement is not the primary goal of mediation. Robert A. Baruch Bush and Joseph Folger, who introduced the idea in their 1994 book, suggest that transforming relationships should be the goal of mediation. They emphasize that mediators have a unique opportunity to transform relationships through a focus on empowerment and recognition. Empowerment is defined in this context as being able to deliberate and/or make decisions in conflict interaction (Della Noce, Bush, & Folger, 2002). While empowerment is a natural part of mediation in that parties are in control of the final agreement rather than having a third party control the final decision, transformative mediators look for all opportunities to empower the parties. For example, while ground rules are imposed on the parties in problem-solving mediation, a transformative mediator will ask the parties what will make them feel safe or comfortable participating in the mediation and allow the parties to generate the rules. Rather than indicating who should speak first, a transformative mediator will ask the parties who wants to speak first. As Bush and Folger describe, if you can get the parties to agree on these small issues from the very start of the mediation, the parties are more empowered and may gain confidence to fully and authentically participate in the process. In addition to giving parties more freedom to determine what they want to talk about throughout the process, transformative mediators also continuously seek opportunities for recognition. Recognition is described as the ability to hear the other party and their perspective during the conflict interaction (Della Noce et al., 2002). While this is an important goal of any type of mediation, transformative mediators are likely to keep the parties in the same room as much as possible,[2] and a hallmark of transformative mediation is patience. Transformative mediators believe parties should be empowered to hear the other, engage in perspective-taking, and, if possible, express recognition of the other on their own without direction from the mediator. For an easy comparison, imagine how you would feel if your mother said, "tell your sister you are sorry," versus if you genuinely felt badly about what you did and told your sister you were sorry without your mom's interference. In the workplace, this could be the difference between a supervisor saying, "you two need to figure out how to work together," versus coming to a new understanding of each other's experience and seeing each other in a new way. In the former scenario, employees are likely to keep the conflict hidden to avoid future attention from the boss, but they have not resolved underlying issues and there is often lingering emotion and resentment (toward both the coworker and the boss). When coworkers are able to engage in perspective-taking and see each other differently, this can lead to compassion that transforms the working relationship and creates a more collaborative and productive atmosphere.

Calling attention to transformative mediation is relevant to this chapter because of the central role of acknowledgment in this approach. The steps of problem-solving mediation, which emphasize a path to agreement, can encourage mediators to move too quickly to brainstorming solutions, often at the expense of listening fully to what parties have to say. Having practiced both styles of mediation, I can say first-hand that the problem-solving style is especially likely when parties are resistant to the process and their goal is to get out of the mediation as quickly as possible. I have experienced mediation when I was more directive than I intended; and even if the parties came to agreement, I did not feel confident that the agreement would last. This is why those who are committed to transformative mediation emphasize small steps, patience, and allowing the parties to drive the process and share (or not share) as they are comfortable (Della Noce et al., 2002). While the process may take longer, and ultimately may not end with agreement,

---

[2] In problem-solving mediation, a caucus is often used to separate the parties if the mediator believes they are unwilling to be fully open in front of each other. In court-based mediation, mediators may act more like facilitators who keep parties in separate rooms and carry information between them. These practices are in opposition to the underlying values of transformative mediation.

this approach is shown to have long-term benefits for relationships and organizational culture. This has been demonstrated in several studies of a mediation program institutionalized in the US Postal Service, which was based on transformative mediation because the organizational leaders knew they needed to create a more understanding and collaborative culture (Nabatchi & Bingham, 2010; Nabatchi, Bingham, & Moon, 2010; this mediation program is described in more detail in Chapter 10).

My own research has also found significant differences in role-played mediation agreements when parties in mediation expressed acknowledgment (or recognition). The mediation study described in Chapter 5 reported differences across the final agreements of the 10 mediation role-plays examined. While all 10 of these simulated mediations achieved agreement, there was a qualitative difference between those that reached resolution and those that showed evidence of transformative outcomes. The five mediation simulations that were found to have transformative elements all included examples of acknowledgment among the disputants. The five mediation simulations that came to resolution without evidence of conflict transformation did *not* have examples of recognition and were characterized by mediators who were more directive, reducing the parties' sense of empowerment (Jameson et al., 2014). These examples have important implications for workplace conflict, even though mediation may not be a common practice. Managers and supervisors often are called upon to intervene in employee conflicts, and from these examples they can learn the value of taking a more facilitative role that encourages parties to communicate, listen, and engage in perspective-taking that leads to understanding and, hopefully, acknowledgment of each other's needs, struggles, and circumstances. Just as I found in the communication among doctors and nurses, engaging in face-supportive communication that respects each party's expertise and value goes a long way to improving interaction and relationships and supporting an organizational environment that promotes collaboration and constructive conflict management.

Chapter Summary

Chapter 6 introduced the significance of acknowledging others in our daily interactions, from something as simple as returning a greeting to the ability to engage in perspective-taking when we perceive someone has harmed us in some way. Three theoretical approaches to acknowledgment were discussed. First, we examined the interpersonal communication theory of confirming and disconfirming responses. This reminds us of the damage we can do to others when we respond in ways that, even indirectly, suggest they are unimportant and their opinions and perspectives are not valued. Confirming responses include recognition, acknowledgment, and endorsement, while disconfirming responses include indifference, imperviousness, or disqualification. Confirming interaction tells the other that they are important, valued human beings and contributors to the team and organization, and this type of communication is necessary to foster an inclusive workplace in which employees perceive they have voice.

We then looked at politeness theory, coming from the field of linguistics, which indicates that individuals want to protect their face, or their image, in the eyes of others. We need to protect both positive face – the desire for connection with others – as well as negative face – the desire to be autonomous and not be imposed upon by others. Further, our interpersonal communication is complex as we negotiate face saving for ourselves, to support others' face, and to support mutual face, which protects our definition of the relationship. The study of communication between anesthesiologists and certified registered nurse anesthetists provided a case study that illustrated how communication that is face saving for oneself and face supporting for others not only allows for more direct and effective communication, but also promotes long-term relationships that facilitate listening and engagement (not to mention rapport-building and nurturing, the final two parts of the LEARN acronym to be discussed later).

You may have already picked up on a connection between politeness theory and the transformative theory of mediation – autonomy sounds a lot like empowerment and connection to others is supported by statements of recognition. I therefore spent some time in this chapter contrasting problem-solving mediation with transformative mediation, both to underscore the value of acknowledging others (in this case, through recognition) and also to demonstrate how this act of acknowledging can transform relationships. As the founders of transformative mediation have espoused, a relational focus highlights people as the foundation of communities, and by emphasizing the value of understanding what others are experiencing and their unique circumstances, we have the potential to not only improve conflict management, but transform our relationships, our workplaces, and our world (Bush & Folger, 1994). While this may seem like an extreme and ambitious goal, it is one worth striving for, and it starts with listening and understanding to help construct climates for collaborative conflict management.

Activity: Practicing Face-Saving and Supportive Communication

1) Work with a partner or small group to generate examples of interaction in which you need to give a coworker or an employee negative feedback. Practice providing the feedback in a direct but face-supportive manner. What do you say?
2) You have been working hard with your team to meet a deadline at work, and there is a meeting with the client that overlaps with an important and unique

opportunity for professional development that you have been looking forward to. How do you ask your team if you can miss the client meeting in a way that protects your positive face and supports the team's negative face?

3) A coworker has come to you asking for your help with a project, and this is not the first time they have come to you at the last minute. You sincerely believe this is a pattern of bad planning on their part, and you do not want to set a precedent that you will bail them out every time. How might you use any of the face-saving and supporting strategies discussed in Chapter 6 to save face for yourself and your coworker while also directly addressing the concern?

References

Brown, P., & Levinson, S. C. (1987). *Politeness: Some universals in language usage.* Cambridge, MA: Cambridge University Press.

Bush, R. A. B., & Folger, J. P. (1994). *The promise of mediation: Responding to conflict through empowerment and recognition.* San Francisco, CA: Jossey-Bass.

Bush, R. A. B., & Folger, J. P. (2005). *The promise of mediation: The transformative approach to conflict.* San Francisco, CA: Jossey-Bass.

Charkoudian, L., De Ritis, C., Buck, R., & Wilson, C. L. (2009). Mediation by any other name would smell as sweet – or would it? The struggle to define mediation and its various approaches. *Conflict Resolution Quarterly, 26*: 293–316.

Cissna, K. N. L., & Sieburg, E. (1981). Patterns of confirmation and disconfirmation. In C. Wilder-Mott & J. H. Weakland (Eds.), *Rigor and imagination: Essays from the Legacy of Gregory Bateson* (pp. 253–282). New York: Praeger.

Costantino, C. A., & Merchant, C. S. (1996). *Designing conflict management systems.* San Francisco, CA: Jossey-Bass.

Della Noce, D. J., Bush, R. A. B., & Folger, J. P. (2002). Clarifying the theoretical underpinnings of mediation: Implications for practice and policy. *Pepperdine Dispute Resolution Law Journal, 3*(1): 39–65.

Gayle, B. M., & Preiss, R. W. (1998). Assessing emotionality in organizational conflicts. *Management Communication Quarterly, 12*: 280–302.

Goffman, E. (1967). *Interaction ritual: Essays on face-to-face behavior.* New York: Random House.

Jameson, J. K. (1999). Toward a comprehensive model for the assessment and management of intraorganizational conflict. *International Journal of Conflict Management, 10*(3): 268–294.

Jameson, J. K. (2001). Employee perceptions of the availability and use of interests-, rights-, and power-based conflict management strategies. *Conflict Resolution Quarterly, 19*(2): 163–196.

Jameson, J. K. (2004). Negotiating autonomy and connection through politeness: A dialectical approach to organizational conflict management. *Western Journal of Communication, 68*(3): 257–277.

Jameson, J. K., Bodtker, A. M., Porch, D., & Jordan, W. (2009). Exploring the role of emotion in conflict transformation. *Conflict Resolution Quarterly, 27*(2): 167–192.

Jameson, J. K., Sohan, D., & Hodge, J. (2014). Turning points and conflict transformation in mediation. *Negotiation Journal, 30*(2): 125–237.

Jones, T. S. (2005). Emotion in mediation: Implications, applications, opportunities, and challenges. In M. Herrman (Ed.), *Blackwell handbook of mediation: Theory and practice* (pp. 277–306). New York: Blackwell.

Karambayya, R., & Brett, J. M. (1989). Managers handling disputes: Third-party roles and perceptions of fairness. *Academy of Management Journal, 32*(4): 687–704. http://www.jstor.org/stable/256564.

Lipsky, D. B., Seeber, R. L., & Fincher, R. D. (2003). *Emerging systems for managing workplace conflict: Lessons from American corporations for managers and dispute resolution professionals.* San Francisco, CA: Jossey-Bass.

Maslow, A. H. (1943). A theory of human motivation. *Psychological Review, 50*: 370–396. https://doi.org/10.1037/h0054346.

Nabatchi, T., & Bingham, L. B. (2010). From postal to peaceful: Dispute systems design in the USPS REDRESS® program. *Review of Public Personnel Administration, 30*: 211–234.

Nabatchi, T., Bingham, L. B., & Moon, Y. (2010). Evaluating transformative practice in the U.S. Postal Service REDRESS program. *Conflict Resolution Quarterly, 27*: 257–289.

Oetzel, J. G., & Ting-Toomey, S. (2003). Face concerns in interpersonal conflict: A cross-cultural empirical test of the Face Negotiation Theory. *Communication Research, 30*(6): 599–624.

Sieburg, E. (1973, April). Interpersonal confirmation: A paradigm for conceptualization and measurement. Paper presented at the Annual Meeting of the International Communication Association, Montreal, Quebec.

Sue, D. W., Capodilupo, C. M., Torino, G. C., Bucceri, J. M., Holder, A. M. B., Nadal, K. L., & Esquilin, M. (2007). Racial microaggressions in everyday life: Implications for clinical practice. *American Psychologist, 62*(4): 271–286. https://doi.org/10.1037/0003-066X.62.4.271.

Watzlawick, P., Bavelas, J. B., & Jackson, D. D. (1967). *Pragmatics of human communication: A study of interactional patterns, pathologies, and paradoxes.* New York: W. W. Norton.

Wilmot, W., & Hocker, J. (2010). *Interpersonal conflict* (8th ed.). New York: McGraw-Hill.

7

Acknowledging Team Member Contributions

A group becomes teammates when each member is sure enough of himself and his contribution to praise the skills of the others.

Norman Shidle (1895–1978, author)

From classrooms to nonprofit boardrooms to the executive suite of Fortune 500 companies, it is a key feature of organizational life that decisions get made and work gets done by groups and teams. While we often use these terms interchangeably, the quote that opens this chapter makes an important distinction in that teams share a cohesiveness, esprit de corps, or collegiality that not every group is fortunate enough to experience. There are decades of research on group dynamics demonstrating that group members often do not fully contribute to the process or the group's collective goal. Whether by choice, exclusion, or group influence, individuals often do not share relevant information or question ideas, even when they see faulty reasoning. This reality flies in the face of everything that was discussed in earlier chapters of this book, so how do we overcome group dynamics that include *not listening*, *disengaging*, or *disconfirming* and *face-threatening communication*? This chapter will describe the role of acknowledging the value and contributions of all team members as an essential element of building a team culture that supports constructive conflict management.

Group Conflict Communication Patterns

In Chapter 4 I introduced attribution theory and verbal aggressiveness theory to describe common interpersonal dynamics in groups as well as dyads, but there are also patterns more unique to groups and teams that impede constructive

Communication for Constructive Workplace Conflict, First Edition. Jessica Katz Jameson.
© 2023 John Wiley & Sons, Inc. Published 2023 by John Wiley & Sons, Inc.

conflict communication. Research on group influence and information sharing demonstrates how interpersonal dynamics create patterns of group interaction that must be changed in order to engage in productive conflict. There is also a robust literature on group conflict. Most of that research has concluded that conflict about tasks leads to greater group productivity and satisfaction while conflict rooted in relationships disrupts the group process (Amason & Schweiger, 1997; De Dreu & Weingart, 2003; Jehn, 1995; Murninghan & Conlon, 1991). These conclusions are not without merit, as to spend group energy and resources on what is often described as interpersonal differences (such as when two group members simply do not like each other) is often unwise and counterproductive. However, the focus group research I described in which organizational members discussed their workplace conflict experiences (see Chapter 4) demonstrated the negative individual, group, and organizational outcomes of ignoring relational conflict among coworkers. Managers who chose to avoid such conflicts were seen as less competent and often accused of treating employees unfairly by relocating or even promoting people who created problems in the workplace. The results of ignoring relational conflicts included decreased respect, lowered morale, and increased experiences of conflict in the workplace (Jameson, 1999). One of the problems with ignoring relational conflict is that team members will feel disrespected and excluded, leading to the disengagement and avoidance described in Chapter 4. When team members are listening and engaged in the conversation, they can foster inclusiveness by reminding the group of the value of each team member and acknowledging their contributions. When these activities become a normative part of group interaction, they can overcome, or at least mitigate, damage inflicted by underlying relational conflicts among some team members.

Another challenge is that conflicts over tasks, such as board member disagreements about how to spend money, can easily turn into relational conflicts. Such conflicts can lead to a pattern of disagreement that continues to disrupt the group process over time. Yet in the most successful groups, members will find productive ways to engage in conflict even when there are relational elements. In the next section, I briefly describe previous research that describes some of the challenges to constructive group communication, including *group influence and conformity* and *information sharing*. I then share research on collaborative group decision making, including *functional group communication theory* and the role of *elaboration* in innovative teams. The value of acknowledging and elaborating on diverse group member ideas is illustrated through a case study of discourse patterns during nonprofit board decision making. This field study supports previous research findings and carries implications for facilitating more constructive communication through acknowledgment.

Group Influence and Conformity

Early group research demonstrated the prevalence of norms that privilege conformity over divergent thinking (Schachter, 1951; Janis, 1982). Jack Gibb (1961) found that groups often create defensive climates in which new ideas are negatively evaluated. Further, a series of studies on group influence demonstrated that when individuals do raise unique ideas or opinions, group members aim substantial communication toward the deviant members to persuade them to conform (Schachter, 1951). Schachter's research revealed that when even one group member shows support for another with a different view, the member is more likely to sustain his or her position. Offering support for diverse opinions is characteristic of a positive voice climate (Morrison, 2011). In contrast, when only one member voices opposition, the pressure to conform is often overwhelming. Irving Janis's (1982) well-documented study of groupthink found that group members are especially likely to conform when one or more members have high status (consistent with the discussion of power and status in Chapter 4). The results of dismissing discrepant views should be obvious. The group fails to benefit from the knowledge and experience of all members, which, ironically, is the reason people work in groups to begin with. In previous chapters the importance of listening and creating a culture of inquiry have been described in some detail. Acknowledging others' ideas, concerns, or questions is an important antidote to groupthink, false consensus, and conformity and can help foster a culture of inquiry, inclusive communication, and constructive conflict management.

Information Sharing

Research on information sharing in groups provides another perspective on group dynamics that limit participation and effective communication. A rich area of research known as "hidden profiles" shows the group tendency to rely more heavily on shared rather than novel information (Stasser & Titus, 1985; Wittenbaum, Hollingshead, & Botero, 2004). The term hidden profiles refers to information that is unique to certain group members, or in other words, information that is not shared by the whole group. In the *hidden profile* task (performed in numerous laboratory settings), groups are given a problem that requires the pooling of information given to individual members. Numerous studies have found that very few groups come up with the optimal solution because members do not share unique information that is pertinent to the final decision (Bonito, 2007). Researchers agree that this phenomenon illustrates a bias toward information that members already share because, by definition, this information is more readily available and easier to remember. This line of research supports the finding that group members tend to avoid asking questions. Further, because individuals desire validation of their ideas, shared information is considered more credible than unique information (Wittenbaum et al., 2004). This dynamic is also consistent with confirmation bias and distortion, processes that explain that people tend to seek out information that supports what they currently believe to be true (Nickerson, 1998).

Because work teams are created for the purpose of solving complex problems that require diverse perspectives and expertise, members must work to overcome the dynamics described above by constructing a climate of inquiry and conflict engagement. Once again, an important component in fostering such a culture is validating individual members' contributions through acknowledging and confirming communication. Three areas of research provide insights on improving collaborative group processes and decision making.

The phenomena of group influence and information sharing are related to the tension between individual autonomy and interdependence described in Chapter 6. Group members often struggle to make meaningful individual contributions while also maintaining group cohesiveness. Social identity and perceptions of group acceptance play a dominant role in this process. If a group member believes that new information will be criticized or perceives themselves as different from the group majority (based on demographics such as sex, race, ability, nationality, or sexual orientation), the member may protect themselves by remaining silent. Members from underrepresented communities who serve on nonprofit boards, for example, often report frustration with either being expected to speak for a larger identity group and/or feeling invisible when they try to participate (Widmer, 1987). The importance of including diverse voices is underscored by voluminous research that confirms groups with more member variety and greater commitment to diversity create a climate for productive conflict (i.e., Ayub & Jehn, 2014; Hobman, Bordia, & Gallois, 2003). One interesting example of how a particular community constructs a collaborative and supportive culture is found among the Quakers[1] (see Box 7.1).

---

[1] I first learned about the Quakers from a presentation at the National Conference of Peacemaking and Conflict Resolution in Minneapolis, Minnesota, in 1995. I wish I could provide a reference here, but this was the first conference I ever attended, and I have not been able to locate a conference program on the Internet. I have confirmed much of what I remember from descriptions of the Quakers online and thank Joseph Folger for his insights given his experience with Quaker philosophy. This example has stayed with me for all these years and is too good not to share. For more on Quakers, see http://www.bbc.co.uk/religion/religions/christianity/subdivisions/quakers_1.shtml

---

Box 7.1   Unanimous Decision Making in the Quaker Community

While there is no central church and all Friends chapters are autonomous, Quakers are unified in the belief that all persons are equal, and they maintain a strong commitment to social justice. Their dedication to equality reinforces the use of consensual conflict management processes: no decisions are made until all members of a congregation come to complete agreement. Quakers also believe that God lives in and speaks through everyone, and thus the dominant conflict metaphor is that of a puzzle that can only be solved through collaboration as each individual member contributes their piece of the puzzle.

While trying to reach a unanimous decision would seem to require highly adversarial and contentious conflict, Quakers also have a norm of harmony and conflict avoidance. Like other collectivist cultures, the group is seen as more important than any one individual's needs. This is counter to the predominant assumptions of individualistic cultures, in which someone who opposes the group is often assumed to be acting in self-interest. Although Quakers are a small community and not representative of the larger culture in which they reside, this example is interesting because of the way it reframes the nature of group conflict. A puzzle is a collaborative game in which players work together to solve a problem. The implication of the Quaker orientation to group conflict is that the pattern of interaction can be changed if group members trust that everyone is authentically working toward the same goal and no single person has an alternative motive or hidden agenda.

For Reflection and Discussion:

What would it take to create a Quaker-like climate in a team on which you participate? Consider how you respond to others, even when you disagree or believe their comments are irrelevant. How can you disagree or state your perception while also communicating that other team members are valued and their contributions are important?

Finding the balance between individual ideas and collective interests is clearly a major challenge for relationships, groups, and organizations. A very practical takeaway from this discussion is to reflect on your own thoughts and emotions as you participate in group discussions. When you make a contribution and another group member questions it, how do you feel? Do you feel personally attacked? Do you get defensive? How do you respond next? How each group member responds in those moments will collectively produce a group climate of either support, inclusivity, and vigilance (Janis, 1982) or one of defensiveness, conformity, and silence. It is critical to remember that questions and insights from others about our ideas, statements, or opinions are necessary to move the group forward. When someone asks us why we believe what we do, we must try to hear the question with a shared commitment to the problem at hand as opposed to experiencing it as a personal attack. (See discussions of the difference between argumentativeness and verbal aggressiveness from Chapter 4 for review of how our responses may be related to traits and communication style.) Responding in ways that acknowledge another's contribution, even when we disagree, is an important step toward a more collaborative group climate and becoming a team and is a central tenet of Gouran and Hirokawa's (1983, 1996, 2003) functional group communication theory.

Functional Group Communication Theory

Dennis Gouran and Randy Hirokawa introduced the functional theory of group decision making in 1983 as a prescriptive model of effective group communication during a decision-making process. The basic tenets of the theory are that effective groups should engage in four activities: (i) *Focus on the problem*, including an exploration of the type of problem (such as rooted in facts, values, or policy) and identifying underlying causes (preconditions) while distinguishing them from symptoms (events or incidents that coincide with the problem – for example, when one has the flu, one may also have a cough, but the cough is not the cause of the flu, it is a symptom); (ii) *Clarify the group goal*, in other words, what must happen in order for the problem to be solved? What are the criteria for a good decision?; (iii) *Develop a list of possible alternatives* for addressing the problem; brainstorming and coming up with as many ideas as possible are relevant here – which is why we focus on the importance of all group member contributions; (iv) *Critically evaluate the pros and cons of the possible decisions*. Note that this step of the process is separate from the development of possible solutions. This is intentional in order to be inclusive of as many ideas as possible and encourage both participation and creativity. It is not uncommon for one group member to propose an idea that seems crazy but inspires another member to contribute something new. By eliminating evaluation and judgment from the brainstorming process, members are free to express wild thoughts and build on each other's ideas. This process of *elaboration* is critical to innovation and effective collaboration, as will be discussed in the following section. Once the group has examined the positive and negative aspects of possible solutions and measured them against the criteria for a good decision, the most optimal decision should be clear.

It will not be surprising to hear that the functional theory has been criticized because it cannot account for all possible group contexts and issues that arise, as well as due to the challenge of defining *effectiveness* (Salazar, 2009; Stohl & Holmes, 1993). Gouran and Hirokawa have added elements to the theory over the years (1996, 2003). It is often referred to as *vigilant interaction theory*, drawing from Janis's work on groupthink and the need for group members to be vigilant in critically examining possible solutions before making a final decision. Additional recommendations for group decision making include: articulating the collective desire to arrive at the best decision, constructing ground rules to ensure inclusive participation (such as not evaluating ideas during brainstorming), and considering the obstacles to implementing various decisions, such as cost, time, other resources, and resistance (Salazar, 2009). In a field test of the decision-making approach using nine existing decision-making groups in an industrial setting, Hirokawa and Rost (1992) concluded that the group's willingness and ability to engage in the critical evaluation of a variety of solutions was related to effective group performance. In keeping with the theme of this chapter, it should be clear that ensuring all members are engaged in the problem-solving and decision-making process requires acknowledgment of all members' contributions to prevent individuals from feeling excluded or unheard. An effective brainstorming and problem-solving process requires that members are listening to each other and building on others' ideas. This is a process of elaboration that takes acknowledgment a step further and is discussed in more detail in the next section.

Elaboration

Vigilant interaction may also be described as *deliberation*, defined by the Merriam-Webster dictionary as "(1a) the act of thinking about or discussing something and deciding carefully" and "(1b) a discussion and consideration by a group of persons (such as a jury or legislature) of the reasons for and against a measure" (Merriam-Webster.com, 2021). In a study of group deliberation, Jennifer Stromer-Galley (2007) developed a content analysis coding system to capture communication during a political deliberation on the topic of public schools. A subset of her codes include *agreement/disagreement, solicitation* (when a speaker explicitly makes a request for participation or directs a question to another group member), *asking questions, acknowledgment* (of the previous statement), *elaboration* (of the previous statement), and *a topic change.* Elaboration, as described above, presumes listening and acknowledgment of what the previous speaker contributed by building on it. As Stromer-Galley notes:

> Elaboration can be in the form of further justification (as simple as: I'm for k-8, because I think it solves the problems we face), a definition, a reason for holding the opinion, an example, a story, a statistic, or fact, a hypothetical example, a solution to the problem, further explanation for why the problem is a problem, a definition, an analogy, a consequence to the problem or solution, a sign that something exists or does not exist, or any further attempt to say what they mean or why they have taken the position that they have. (p. 10)

In Stromer-Galley's (2007) study, she found that 84% of opinions expressed were elaborated on by the next speaker. The elaborations most often included a personal anecdote, reference to specific materials that had been assigned for group reading, something another participant said, or something reported in the media. Again, this is relevant as it illustrates one type of acknowledgment in group communication. Interestingly, and relevant to vigilant interaction more broadly, Stromer-Galley found a very low rate of disagreement in the group deliberation (5.6% of group statements) and few incidents of asking questions (8% of statements). This is concerning because a lack of disagreement could give way to groupthink, and previous chapters have described the importance of inquiry (see Chapters 3 and 5). In my own research, co-authors and I found similar trends in a study of nonprofit board deliberation and decision making (see Box 7.2).

Box 7.2   Discourse Patterns in Group Decision Making[2]

Given that nonprofit board members are volunteers who are committed to the organization's mission, one might speculate that members would be more focused on the collective goal (like the Quakers) rather than individual interests. Nonprofit board meetings, therefore, provide an interesting context for examining group communication during conflict. The study described below confirmed that open disagreement is hard to capture, yet provides concrete examples of patterns of discourse in group decision making that carry implications for productive conflict engagement (Leonardo, Jameson, & Metelsky, 2010).

As described earlier in Chapter 5 (Box 5.1), we observed group decision making during the meetings of two nonprofit boards of directors during a one-year period. The case described below was guided by the desire to identify features of group communication during decision-making episodes to examine features of collaborative and adversarial interaction.

We used discourse analysis so that we could make inferences based on actual communication rather than relying on participants' accounts of what they or others said. This is helpful when looking at communication during conflict or disagreements, when people's recollections of how they communicated are especially subject to attribution bias (because we see ourselves and want others to see us in the best light). In keeping with a point made earlier in this chapter, a key subject of interest in this study was how board members respond to disagreement.

---

[2] This case comes from research that was reported in an unpublished conference paper by Dr. Melinda Leonardo, me, and Dr. Barbara A. Metelsky. Reproduced with permission from Dr. Melinda Leonardo.

We purposefully selected a sample of eight decision-making episodes, four from each of two nonprofit organizations. COURAGE (a pseudonym) is a nonprofit health organization. It is an all-volunteer nonprofit and is the local affiliate of a state and national organization. COURAGE's mission focuses on support, education, and advocacy for people who live with a specific health diagnosis. The board consisted of 12 members at the time data were collected. The second organization, CHANGE (also a pseudonym), is a larger nonprofit organization with an executive director and salaried staff. CHANGE supports the social and professional needs of a targeted group of community members. The all-volunteer board included 14 members at the time of data collection.

The following section describes a subset of the categories we used to analyze and describe the boards' communication. These categories ultimately helped us compare and contrast disagreements that led to a stalemate with disagreements that characterized collaborative decision making.

Modeling the work of Stromer-Galley, we coded each turn of talk in terms of its function in relation to the previous speaker. This enabled us to examine patterns of unfolding interaction. For example, when a speaker explicitly made a request for participation or directed a question to another group member, this was coded as a *solicitation* (Stromer-Galley, 2007). One of the most important goals of this study was to determine how often board members expressed agreement or disagreement with each other. Each turn of talk was coded for its *valence*, defined as whether the speaker agreed or disagreed with the previous speaker (or neither). The intent was to identify patterns of agreement or disagreement that might impact participation and provide evidence of a group's comfort with conflict. Since speakers do not always explicitly agree or disagree, the next category examined the content of the response. Types of content were coded as either *elaboration* of the previous statement, an *acknowledgment* of the previous statement, *a topic change*, or none of these options (Stromer-Galley, 2007).

As described in Chapter 6, acknowledgment was defined as an explicit validation of another's statement or idea. This might include a statement of recognition or understanding, but not necessarily agreement with the idea. Based on the importance of disagreement during effective deliberation, we wanted to see whether acknowledgment might be used in conjunction with disagreement in order to help others save face and maintain a collaborative climate. Topic change was also coded to determine whether group members changed the topic to avoid conflict or differences of opinion.

The final category in our coding scheme was *interruption*, defined as an incomplete statement or exchange. This was included in order to determine whether there would be a relationship between interruptions and disagreement

(Stromer-Galley, 2007). Interruptions might indicate emotional intensity and escalating conflict (Ayoko, Hartel, & Callan, 2002), or they can signal high rapport and engagement (Tannen, 1986). We were, therefore, interested in whether we would see patterns of interruption during times of agreement or disagreement.

Results

Coding of the eight decision-making episodes revealed several patterns of group communication during decision making that are relevant to conflict interaction. Four of the eight episodes dealt with policy or governance issues, such as whether to hire a director of development and what topics should be included during the board retreat. The other four decisions were related to organizational operations, such as how to reimburse volunteers for workshop materials they photocopied, where to advertise support groups, and who would bring various refreshments to a volunteer event.

To illustrate the results, Table 7.1 illustrates the percentage of speaking turns that fell into each coding category across all eight episodes.

An important finding was that there were very few solicitations, or requests for participation, which accounted for only 6.93% of all speaking turns in our sample. Given that nonprofit boards are volunteers and members are often recruited due to specific skills or knowledge they possess, we expected there to be a high level of solicitation for involvement. Instead we found that certain members frequently dominated conversations while others remained silent. Given the tendency for lower status or newer group members to remain silent (as discussed in Chapter 2), the lack of requests for participation is concerning. It is not necessarily surprising, however, and is consistent with Stromer-Galley's (2007) findings. The objective for many people during

Table 7.1   Percentage of speaking turns per coding category across decision-making episodes.

Coding category	% of all speaking turns
Solicitation	06.93
Agreement	29.58
Disagreement	08.32
Elaboration	20.68
Acknowledgment	31.02
Topic change	12.04
Interruption	25.77

meetings is to get through the agenda and end the meeting on time. Since soliciting ideas or opinions takes time and is likely to uncover areas of disagreement, the fact that this did not happen frequently in our sample is consistent with previous research on group communication and nonprofit board interaction. When a small group of members dominate meetings, they may consciously or unconsciously suppress conflict by not soliciting opinions from others. Unfortunately, this prevents the kind of communication that will contribute to an inclusive climate and more collaborative conflict management.

In accordance with our expectations, patterns of agreement were prevalent (29.58% of all exchanges), with far fewer instances of direct disagreement (8.32%). Also consistent with our expectation that board members would use face-saving discourse, the content of responses most often included acknowledgments (31.02%), with elaborations (20.68%) following second. Interruptions occurred in 25.77% of exchanges, while topic changes (12.04%) were somewhat infrequent, although more common than direct disagreement or requests for participation. This is consistent with more global patterns found in the larger study of board communication, which included two additional nonprofit organizations and concluded that communication was largely characterized by politeness (Jameson, 2007). Board members were more likely to communicate agreement than disagreement, either through direct agreement or indirectly through acknowledging or elaborating on others' statements. This is also consistent with Stromer-Galley's findings, which included low rates of disagreement and high rates of acknowledgment and elaboration. While interruptions were noted in over a quarter of exchanges and are often thought to be impolite, there was no relationship between the amount of interruption during agreement or disagreement. Interruptions were likely more closely related to rapport and engagement (Tannen, 1986) than conflict escalation in this study.

Since we were most interested in patterns of conflict interaction, we examined the episodes with the highest rates of disagreement in each organization more closely. Table 7.2 provides a comparison of coding on key categories among all eight episodes. Because of our focus on conflict, below I highlight the episodes that had the highest individual rate of disagreement in each nonprofit: In CHANGE 8 the board discussed whether to hire a director of development (18.28% of turns coded as disagreement), and in COURAGE 5 the board discussed whether the nonprofit should maintain a list of providers and physicians on their website (7.96% of turns coded as disagreement).

CHANGE 8 had by far the highest amount of disagreement in our sample. This is not surprising as the board was discussing a proposal to hire a director of development, which would require significant fundraising and alter the leadership structure of an organization with a relatively small staff. While the board members agreed with the proposal in principle, there were dissenting

Table 7.2 Comparison of episodes with the highest percentage of disagreement.

Episode	Agree	Disagree	Acknowledge	Topic Change	Interrupt
COURAGE 1	36.17	4.26	30.43	8.70	36.96
CHANGE 2	26.53	4.00	30.61	12.24	18.37
COURAGE 3	16.42	7.46	13.43	13.43	14.93
CHANGE 4	29.23	9.23	26.15	7.69	30.77
COURAGE 5	**38.05**	**7.96**	**40.18**	**10.71**	**26.13**
CHANGE 6	33.33	3.17	38.71	9.68	18
COURAGE 7	22.37	7.24	29.87	14.29	35
CHANGE 8	**36.56**	**18.28**	**33.33**	**15.05**	**20**

Note: All numbers are reported as a percentage of all exchanges in the episode.

opinions about the details, such as whether to hire a staff person or consult-ant, whether the position should be full- or part-time, and details of the job description. Two other patterns are especially interesting in this episode: CHANGE 8 included the highest amount of topic change and a high level of acknowledgment. We had speculated that changing the topic would be used as a conflict avoidance strategy when group communication became tense. In contrast, we found that speaking turns coded as topic changes were often used to provide context for newer board members or additional details needed to make a good decision. This brief exchange is illustrative:

SPEAKER	TURN	CODE
Speaker A	In the meantime do we have money to think about someone in terms of a consultant part time or somebody who . . .	Topic change
Speaker B	I know somebody that might be interested part time.	Interruption
Speaker A	. . . even someone that could maybe work with a couple of board members.	(Continuation of above turn)
Speaker C	Well we are in a good position right now if we're . . .	Elaboration
Speaker D (chair)	Let me, before we go into the detail. Is there any kind of disagreement that this is kind of where we need to go?	Topic change

This excerpt includes two topic changes in this conversation. The first one followed a discussion of timing: how long did the board think it would take to raise enough money to hire a director of development? Speaker A changes the subject to a discussion of what to do to meet the organization's needs now. The topic change moved the group from a future focus (an important governance function) to an immediate solution. Speaker B interrupts the first speaker but supports the topic change with a relevant response about someone who might be interested in consulting on a part-time basis. The second topic change was used by the board chair to ensure there was group agreement on the overall plan before drilling into the details of implementation. This example is consistent with other patterns of topic change throughout this episode. The group moved back and forth from the higher-level discussion of proposal acceptance to specific implementation details. Changes of topic were used to keep all members engaged in the conversation by making sure everyone was on the same page in terms of relevant information. Counter to our expectations, we only found one episode in which a topic change was used when an interaction became tense due to disagreement (described further below).

Another feature of CHANGE 8 that functioned to maintain a collaborative climate was the frequent use of acknowledgment. Building on the discussion in Chapter 6, note that acknowledgment captures three types of *confirming messages*: recognition, validation, and endorsement (Cissna & Sieburg, 1981). Recognition is a verbal or nonverbal signal that the listener is paying attention; it can be as simple as making eye contact and nodding. Validation is typically a verbal strategy and is a slightly stronger statement that one is listening and sees the other person's ideas as valid, even if the listener does not agree. Endorsement is the strongest type of confirmation, as this response not only acknowledges the speaker but also supports what they are saying or feeling. The use of confirming messages throughout the CHANGE 8 episode demonstrates respectful disagreement and deliberation about an issue. The episode ended with a decision that integrated almost everyone's concerns. They agreed to pursue a relationship with a volunteer consultant who would help the board develop the job description and generate a fundraising plan to help them find the best person they could afford to grow the organization.

The episode with highest disagreement for COURAGE (COURAGE 5) involved deciding whether it was appropriate for the organization to maintain a list of local physicians and providers to assist newcomers to the community. The conflict centered on the legal and ethical implications (e.g., Who would or would not be on the list? Would they be liable if they recommended a provider and someone had a bad experience?). These concerns were held in tension with the nonprofit's mission to provide information and resources for community members. This discussion also included a high proportion of turns coded as acknowledgment. The following excerpt demonstrates one member's concern about liability and another member's disagreement:

SPEAKER	TURN	CODE
Speaker A	I think you're getting into dangerous territory if you're going to rate a doctor . . .	Disagreement
Speaker B	Yeah.	Acknowledgment
Speaker A	Because you might get liability and problems from that perspective and also from the family members. I do want to be helpful. I think that's a great idea, but I do have reservations about keeping up a list.	Disagreement (cont'd from previous turn)
Speaker C	I don't believe that at all.	Disagreement
Speaker A	You don't agree?	Disagreement
Speaker C	No. I think there are a number of . . .	Disagreement
Speaker A	Well, that's just my opinion.	Interruption
Speaker C	Yeah. There are a number of ways to be sure that that doesn't happen, and we're not saying that the doctor is incompetent.	Elaboration
Speaker B	Yeah.	Acknowledgment
Speaker C	We're sharing with people that want to know who we would say we had good experiences with.	Elaboration

This excerpt from COURAGE 5 demonstrates strong opinions being shared. Note that the speakers do make use of acknowledging messages, such as Speaker A's statement that "I do want to be helpful. I think that's a great idea," as well as Speaker B's use of "Yeah" in two cases to recognize the points of both speakers A and C. Despite these affirming messages, the ensuing communication makes it clear that at least some board members are uncomfortable with the disagreement. While not shown in the excerpt above, the next line in this transcript is a new speaker commenting that it is raining outside. This is coded as a topic change, yet, if this tactic was intended to help the group avoid conflict, it was not successful. One of the most interesting aspects of this episode is how reframing the problem (see Chapter 5) was used to bring the adversaries to common ground. The excerpt below shows how Speaker C persuades Speaker A by reframing the issue from a legal problem to an important part of the organization's mission:

SPEAKER	TURN	CODE
Speaker C	Yeah. But I think if you come into an area and there's an organization like a support group, [and you are thinking] "who do I go to, my son needs a doctor." At least you can see where you could start.	Elaboration
Speaker A	Um hmm.	Acknowledgment
Speaker C	Why can't we help? Why can't we as an organization help?	Elaboration
Speaker A	I see your point.	Agreement

After Speaker A's agreement, another board member elaborates on Speaker C's turn by pointing out that other agencies maintain such lists, and they should find out how they deal with the liability issue. One board member volunteers to get that information, and the group agrees to return to this issue at the next meeting when they have more information. It is noteworthy that in both of these episodes, disagreement was used to successfully raise important points, yet the boards also managed their conflict by delaying resolution for a future meeting. While on one hand this makes sense as they needed external information to make a final decision, there was a larger pattern in the data demonstrating the tabling or postponing of more contentious decisions. This pattern may reinforce the claim that group members are uncomfortable with conflict.

For Reflection and Discussion:

1) Why don't people ask more questions during group interaction? Discuss the obstacles to asking questions and how groups might create ground rules to create a culture of inquiry (see Chapter 5).
2) Consider the function of a topic change or a decision to table a conversation when there is disagreement in groups. How might you "call out" this behavior to keep the group focused on the discussion even when it is uncomfortable? Further, how can you do this while still acknowledging how group members are feeling to avoid alienating, invalidating, or excluding individuals in the group?

In a study of multi-sector collaboration, elaboration has also been shown to be critical to successful group performance and innovative decision making (Tyler, Appleyard, & Carruthers, 2014). Management scholar Beverly Tyler and her team proposed a theoretical model of factors that contribute to collaborative, innovative team output. They predicted that elaboration on each other's ideas would lead to "team knowledge meshing," defined as "recombining existing knowledge into new patterns to co-create innovative outputs" (Tyler & Jameson, 2020, p. 76). In a study of perceptions of team collaboration among government, academic, and industry partners, Tyler and Jameson found that elaboration was a strong predictor of team member perceptions that their group was innovative. In focus group interviews with members of this collaboration, participants often commented on the value of elaboration in team meetings.

The remainder of this chapter presents an extensive case study that analyzed excerpts from two nonprofit boards to examine discourse patterns in group decision making to determine the prevalence of disagreement, acknowledgment, and elaboration. The primary goal of the study was to examine the features of constructive conflict management in team settings. Our coding scheme was heavily influenced by Stromer-Galley's (2007) work in deliberation, as described above.

Using Acknowledgment to Improve Group Interaction Patterns

The most interesting results from our discourse analysis of group decision making were the low frequencies of disagreement and solicitations, suggesting that these groups did not often seek differences of opinion or invite conflict. Our observations and interviews with board members (as part of a larger study) confirmed our suspicion that those who dominated meetings had higher status (due to longer tenure on the board), while those who spoke less were typically newer members and those from underrepresented populations (as discussed in Chapter 4). In order to change this pattern and create more inclusive communication, board chairs and other group members need to be cognizant of the value of multiple perspectives and work to construct a climate that encourages participation.

Our study suggests specific types of communication that engage group members and contribute to a supportive climate. As illustrated most explicitly in the CHANGE 8 episode, topic changes can be used effectively to make sure everyone has the background information necessary to make a good decision. This is one mechanism for ensuring more inclusive communication. Open communication is also reinforced through the use of confirming messages that validate the speaker. Some of the more effective discourse patterns found in this study were when acknowledgment was used in conjunction with disagreement. The use of confirming messages, whether as minimal as "yeah" or as explicit as "I see what you mean," sends a message that the speaker is a valued member of the group. Confirming messages also serve as a face-supportive device because validating allows one speaker to respond to another with an alternative view or idea while minimizing the chances of defensiveness. Acknowledgments also communicate to other group members (who are observing the interaction) that their contributions will be welcomed rather than shot down or ignored. The use of acknowledgment, therefore, appears to be an important contributor to creating a supportive climate where group members feel valued and are willing to share information, ideas, and opinions.

Chapter Summary

This chapter focused on the importance of acknowledging individual contributions in group and team settings. Three important group dynamics were discussed: group influence, groupthink, and hidden profiles or tendencies to withhold information. This was followed by presentation of the functional theory of group decision making, also called vigilant interaction theory, as a prescription for engaging in brainstorming and critical evaluation of possible solutions before making a final decision to prevent false consensus and faulty decision making. In order to illustrate how acknowledgment functions in group deliberation, I also presented the idea of elaboration and how it has been examined in three group contexts: political deliberation, interdisciplinary research teams, and nonprofit boards of directors. In the latter case, this chapter included a detailed discourse analysis of nonprofit board meetings to illustrate how a lack of acknowledgment can be an impediment to deliberation and problem solving and, conversely, how validation and elaboration of ideas help lead groups to productive and collaborative decision making.

Activity: Decision-Making Task

For this activity, you will need to work in a group. Imagine that you are the hiring committee for an airline that needs to hire a pilot for a new set of long-distance routes from the United States to Europe and the United Kingdom. Characteristics of each applicant can be found in the article by Schulz-Hardt and Mojzisch (2012) (Table 7.3). You will use the steps of functional theory of group decision making: (i) *Focus on the problem*; (ii) *Clarify the group goal, in this case, agree on the criteria you believe are most important for a good long-distance pilot*; (iii) *Develop a list of possible alternatives*; and (iv) *Critically evaluate the pros and cons of the possible decisions.*

1) Everyone in the group must participate.
2) The final decision should have unanimous agreement.

Table 7.3 Characteristics of four candidates for the pilot position.

Candidate A	Candidate B
• can anticipate dangerous situations • is able to see complex connections • has excellent spatial vision • has very good leadership qualities • is sometimes not good at taking criticism • can be unorganised • is regarded as a show-off • is regarded as being not open to new ideas • is unfriendly • eats unhealthily	• keeps calm in a crisis • known to be 100% reliable • good at assessing weather conditions • has excellent computer skills • can be grumpy • can be uncooperative • has a relatively weak memory for numbers • makes nasty remarks about his colleagues • is regarded as pretentious • sometimes adopts the wrong tone when communicating

Candidate C	Candidate D
• can make correct decisions quickly • handles stress very well • creates a positive atmosphere with his crew • is very conscientious • understands complicated technology • puts concern for others above everything • has excellent attention skills • has difficulty communicating ideas • is regarded as egocentric • is not very willing to further his education	• responds to unexpected events adequately • can concentrate very well • solves problems extremely well • takes responsibility seriously • is regarded as arrogant • has relatively weak leadership skills • is regarded as a "know-it-all" • has a hot temper • is considered moody • is regarded as a loner

Source: Schulz-Hardt, S., & Mojzisch, A. (2012).

After you have completed the activity, reflect on the following:

1) Did everyone in the group participate in the discussion? Did anyone take responsibility for inviting others to speak? Did anyone dominate the discussion? If so, why do you think that happened, and did anyone try to facilitate more equal participation?

2) How easy or hard was it to come to agreement on the criteria for a good long-distance pilot?

3) How did you know when you had reached a decision? Did you take a vote or were you able to achieve consensus? Did someone in the group help facilitate the final decision? What did they do?

References

Amason, A. C., & Schweiger, D. M. (1997). The effects of conflict on strategic decision making effectiveness and organizational performance. In C. K. W. De Dreu & E. Van De Vliert (Eds.), *Using conflict in organizations* (pp. 101–115). Thousand Oaks, CA: Sage.

Ayoko, O. B., Hartel, C. E. J., & Callan, V. J. (2002). Resolving the puzzle of productive and destructive conflict in culturally heterogeneous workgroups: A communication accommodation theory approach. *International Journal of Conflict Management, 13*(2): 165–195.

Ayub, N., & Jehn, K. (2014). When diversity helps performance: Effects of diversity on conflict and performance in workgroups. *International Journal of Conflict Management, 25*(2): 189–212. https://doi.org/10.1108/IJCMA-04-2013-0023.

Bonito, J. A. (2007). A local model of information sharing in small groups. *Communication Theory, 17*: 252–280. https://doi.org/10.1111/j.1468-2885.2007.00295.x.

Cissna, K. N. L., & Sieburg, E. (1981). Patterns of confirmation and disconfirmation. In C. Wilder-Mott & J. H. Weakland (Eds.), *Rigor and imagination: Essays from the Legacy of Gregory Bateson* (pp. 253–282). New York: Praeger.

De Dreu, C. K. W., & Weingart, L. R. (2003). Task versus relationship conflict, team performance, and team member satisfaction: A meta-analysis. *Journal of Applied Psychology, 88*(4), 741–749. https://doi.org/10.1037/0021-9010.88.4.741.

Deliberation. In *Merriam-Webster.com*. Retrieved June 5, 2021, from https://www.merriam-webster.com/dictionary/deliberation

Gibb, J. R. (1961). Defensive communication. *Journal of Communication, 11*(3): 141–148. https://doi.org/10.1111/j.1460-2466.1961.tb00344.x.

Gouran, D. S., & Hirokawa, R. Y. (1983). The role of communication in decision-making groups: A functional perspective. In M. S. Mander (Ed.), *Communications in transition* (pp. 168–185). New York: Praeger.

Gouran, D. S., & Hirokawa, R. Y. (1996). Functional theory and communication in decision-making and problem-solving groups: An expanded view. In R. Y. Hirokawa & M. S. Poole (Eds.), *Communication and group decision making* (2nd ed., pp. 55–80). Thousand Oaks, CA: Sage.

Gouran, D. S., & Hirokawa, R. Y. (2003). Effective decision making and problem solving in groups: A functional perspective. In R. Y. Hirokawa, R. S. Cathcart, L. A. Samovar, & L. D. Henman (Eds.), *Small group communication theory and practice: An anthology* (8th ed., pp. 27–38). New York: Oxford University Press.

Hirokawa, R.Y., & Rost, K. M. (1992). Effective group decision making in organizations: Field test of the Vigilant Interaction Theory. *Management Communication Quarterly, 5*(3): 267–288. https://doi.org/10.1177/0893318992005003001.

Hobman, E. V., Bordia, P., & Gallois, C. (2003). Perceived dissimilarity and work group involvement: The moderating effects of group openness to diversity. *Group & Organization Management, 29*(5): 560–587.

Jameson, J. K. (1999). Toward a comprehensive model for the assessment and management of intraorganizational conflict. *International Journal of Conflict Management, 10*(3): 268–294.

Jameson, J. K. (2007, November). *Respectful interaction among nonprofit boards of directors.* Paper presented to the Organizational Communication Division at the Annual Meeting of the National Communication Association, Chicago, IL.

Janis, I. L. (1982). *Groupthink: Psychological studies of policy decisions and fiascoes* (2nd ed.). New York: Houghton Mifflin.

Jehn, K. A. (1995). A multimethod examination of the benefits and detriments of intragroup conflict. *Administrative Science Quarterly, 40*: 256–282. https://doi.org/10.2307/2393638.

Leonardo, M., Jameson, J. K., & Metelsky, B. A. (2010, November). *Discourse patterns within small group decision-making.* Paper presented to the Small Group Division of the National Communication Association, San Francisco, CA.

Morrison, E. W. (2011). Employee voice behavior: Integration and directions for future research. *The Academy of Management Annals, 5*(1): 373–412.

Murninghan, J. K., & Conlon, D. E. (1991). The dynamics of intense work groups: A study of British string quartets. *Administrative Science Quarterly, 36*(2): 165–186.

Nickerson, R. S. (1998). Confirmation bias: A ubiquitous phenomenon in many guises. *Review of General Psychology, 2*(2): 175–220. https://doi.org/10.1037/1089-2680.2.2.175.

Salazar, A. (2009). Functional group communication theory. In S. W. Littlejohn & K. A. Foss (Eds.), *Encyclopedia of communication theory* (Vol. 1, pp. 417–420). Thousand Oaks, CA: Sage. https://www.doi.org/10.4135/9781412959384.n155.

Schachter, S. (1951). Deviation, rejection and communication. *Journal of Abnormal Social Psychology, 46*: 190–207.

Schulz-Hardt, S., & Mojzisch, A. (2012). How to achieve synergy in group decision making: Lessons to be learned from the hidden profile paradigm. *European Review of Social Psychology, 23*: 1, 305–343, DOI: 10.1080/10463283.2012.744440

Stasser, G., & Titus, W. (1985). Pooling of unshared information in group decision making: Biased information sampling during discussion. *Journal of Personality and Social Psychology, 48*: 1467–1478. https://doi.org/10.1037/0022-3514.48.6.1467.

Stohl, C., & Holmes, M. E. (1993). A functional perspective for bona fide groups. In S. A. Deetz (Ed.), *Communication yearbook 16* (pp. 601–614). Newbury Park, CA: Sage.

Stromer-Galley, J. (2007). Measuring deliberation's content: A coding scheme. *Journal of Public Deliberation, 3*: 1–37.

Tannen, D. (1986). *That's not what I meant! How conversational style makes or breaks your relations with others.* New York: Morrow.

Tyler, B. B., Appleyard, M. M., & Carruthers, J. (2014, July 18). *Developing individual and team knowledge fusion capabilities: Managing revolutionary interdisciplinary R&D project teams.* Paper presented at the INGRoup Conference, Raleigh, NC.

Tyler, B. B., & Jameson, J. K. (2020). Member perceptions of collaboration. In J. K. Jameson, B. B. Tyler, K. M. Vogel, and S. Joines (Eds.), *Facilitating interdisciplinary collaboration among the intelligence community, academy, and industry* (pp. 55–108). Newcastle upon Tyne, UK: Cambridge Scholars.

Widmer, C. (1987). Minority participation on boards of directors of nonprofit human services agencies: Some evidence and suggestions. *Nonprofit and Voluntary Sector Quarterly, 16*(4): 33–44.

Wittenbaum, G. M., Hollingshead, A. B., & Botero, I. C. (2004). From cooperative to motivated information sharing in groups: Moving beyond the hidden profile paradigm. *Communication Monographs, 71*(3): 286–310. https://doi.org/10.1080/0363452042000299894.

Unit Four

Rapport (Building)

8

Building Relationships and Trust

Rapport: a friendly, harmonious relationship; *especially*: a relationship characterized by agreement, mutual understanding, or empathy that makes communication possible or easy.

Merriam-Webster Dictionary

As a graduate student I began working on a conflict management model that would help managers and other organizational members choose the most optimal approach for a given conflict. While the idea turned out to be overly ambitious, parts of the model make a lot of sense, such as the intuitive idea that the relationship history of the parties to a conflict would be an important consideration in how the conflict should be managed (Jameson, 1999). Certainly, the types of interactions we have had with others in the past will make us either more or less comfortable engaging in conflict in the future. The importance of building *rapport* with others was first introduced to me by the work of Deborah Tannen in her 1986 book *That's Not What I Meant! How Conversational Style Makes or Breaks Relationships*. Her work is integral to communication because she uses a linguistic, rather than psychological, perspective to examine and describe how the way we say what we say impacts our relationships.

As Tannen describes, establishing rapport involves an emphasis on finding connection and negotiating relationships. In earlier chapters, I mentioned the tension between our interdependence with others (connection) and our need for independence or autonomy. Rapport involves a focus on interdependence, which may be perceived to conflict with the desire to prove one's unique contributions to the workplace and impress the boss. As the Merriam-Webster definition suggests, however, good rapport "makes communication possible or easy," and by extension, conversations that can be especially difficult – those in which conflict is perceived – are easier to have when rapport has been established. A lot of the

Communication for Constructive Workplace Conflict, First Edition. Jessica Katz Jameson.
© 2023 John Wiley & Sons, Inc. Published 2023 by John Wiley & Sons, Inc.

specific communication techniques that build rapport were covered in earlier chapters of this book. For example, Unit One on *Listening* (Chapters 2 and 3) included ideas about listening without judgment, listening to understand, and asking questions to improve understanding and empathy. Clearly these are ways to build rapport. Many of these recommendations were repeated in different ways in Chapters 4 through 7, including concepts such as being aware of implicit biases and attribution bias, asking questions to avoid relying on assumptions, and creating collaborative as opposed to adversarial patterns. This chapter will emphasize additional approaches to rapport-building by talking about trust, nonverbal communication, and rapport in intercultural relationships. Chapter 9 will continue the focus on rapport by discussing the roles of emotion, taking personal responsibility, and apologies in fostering collaborative conflict management.

Communicating to Build Trust

Trust is one of those words that we understand on a basic level, but can be hard to define. We all know people we trust and people we don't, but we may be hard-pressed to put into words why we trust one person or another. Merriam-Webster defines trust as "firm belief in the reliability, truth, ability, or strength of someone or something" (Merriam-Webster.com, 2023). The trust we have in another has a direct impact on our own behavior, as illustrated in Lewicki and Weithoff's (2000) definition of trust as "an individual's belief in, and willingness to act on the basis of, the words, actions, and decisions of another" (p. 87). To further unpack the concept, other scholars have identified three dimensions of trust: benevolence, ability, and integrity (Levine & Schweitzer, 2015; Mayer, Davis, & Schoorman, 1995). *Benevolence* refers to whether someone has concern for another's interests. With respect to conflict behavior, we might think of this as whether we expect someone to be more collaborative or more competitive in a conflict interaction (See Chapter 4 for a review of conflict styles). *Ability* refers to whether we are confident that another has the knowledge, expertise, or skill to perform in a given circumstance. *Integrity* emphasizes one's reputation for honesty or ethical behavior. Mayer et al. (1995) point out that trust is different from similar concepts such as confidence or predictability, in that trust is inherently a feature of a relationship. As they describe, one only needs to trust when one person is reliant on the other for something and therefore allows themselves to be vulnerable to the other. Consider the difference between seeing your manager as *predictable* versus *trustworthy*. You might be able to predict your manager will be more likely to communicate criticism rather than praise based on the history of your relationship. That predictability is likely to lead you to take fewer risks and to "play it safe" to avoid criticism (or punishment). In this example, your confidence in how your boss will act leads to a *lack of* trust. It is useful to note that trust may not be reciprocal in a relationship. While, in this example, you may not trust your manager, your manager may actually trust your ability, and their tendency to provide critique rather than praise may be due to a perception that you are very good at your job and you only need information that helps you develop even further. The fact that you do not know how to interpret your boss's communication suggests a lack of rapport. In this example, the manager would be advised to communicate acknowledgment and recognition of the employee's strengths (per Chapters 6 and 7) in order to demonstrate trust and respect, which might then build trust and rapport.

Adding to the complexity of the phenomenon of *trust*, it is possible for the same person to be perceived as more or less trustworthy on different dimensions. In the previous example, you may not be confident that your manager is *benevolent* (due to some lack of interpersonal communication skills) or feel certain about their *integrity*, while you may have high trust in their *ability* due to their performance with the company. This suggests that the overall level of trust we have in another person is dependent on all three dimensions of trust, and it is the amalgamation of a series of interactions and events over time that will either increase or decrease trust. The three dimensions of trust give us a possible formula for thinking about how to communicate in ways that foster trust in the workplace (and other relationships): demonstrate authentic concern for others, do your job to the best of your ability (and seek help if and when needed), and act in ways that are honest and ethical. While that sounds relatively straightforward, we also know that there are times when one person's interests are more pressing than others', when people have different levels of ability, and when we have different perceptions of what is ethical. Further, sometimes deception for the sake of protecting another's feelings, referred to as either "white lies" or benevolent deception, does not harm perceptions of trust (Levine & Schweitzer, 2015). Again, we see that human interaction is complicated! Below we take a look at each of the three dimensions of trust in a bit more detail.

Benevolence

How do we communicate benevolence? The first, and perhaps most obvious, element here is that we have to authentically feel benevolence toward the other. Too often, especially in organizational settings, people in higher status positions want to appear as though they care, but their actions demonstrate otherwise. An example would be the supervisor who says they have an open-door policy, but who can never be found in their office. Or perhaps worse, when employees do seek them out, the supervisor continues to look at the computer screen or other distractions rather than actively listening to what the employee has to say. In management theory, Rensis Likert described four management systems, including one called the "consultative style" of decision making (Papa, Daniels, & Spiker, 2008). This style is often characterized by a manager who asks employees for their input but retains the "right" to make the final decision and may or may not take that input into consideration. While there are some potential advantages to this approach in providing employee participation in decision making, this manager may lose the trust and respect of colleagues and coworkers if they do not believe their input will be truly considered in the final decision. Benevolence is communicated – and trust is gained – when we demonstrate true empathy and concern for others through listening, following through on what we say we will do, and aligning our actions with our words. This is connected to taking a supportive and collaborative, or interest-based, stance in conflict management, in which we seek to meet both our own as well as others' interests simultaneously.

While taking an interest-based approach to conflict management might sound idealistic, this is an important place to note the difference between interests and positions. A position is a preferred stance or outcome of a conflict – it is what someone wants to happen. For example, an employee's position in a conflict, and a popular one in the wake of the COVID-19 pandemic, might be that they want to work remotely rather than returning to work at the office every day. The manager's position might be that they want their employees to be co-located in the office. The *interests* are the needs, wants, and desires that underlie those positions. Table 8.1 provides an example of interests that might underlie this hypothetical conflict in the positions of an employee versus a manager.

This example shows that positions are often mutually exclusive and, therefore, are the manifestation of conflict. Yet when we look at the underlying interests, we often find that there are creative ways to get both (or all) parties' needs met. For example, many organizations learned during the COVID-19 lockdown in 2020–2021 that their employees could be productive when working at home, and

Table 8.1 Hypothetical example of positions versus underlying interests.

	Employee	Manager
Position	I want to work remotely	I want you to work in the office
Interests	• Reduced travel time • Reduced stress • Safety (reduced risk of infection) • Reduced cost (gasoline/auto repair) • Balancing of work–home tasks	• Ease of connection with employees • Fostering climate of collaboration and teamwork • Spontaneous conversations leading to increased efficiency and innovation • Availability to customers/clients

many new software tools have been developed that support remote work while maintaining interpersonal connections (including meeting spaces such as Zoom and Microsoft Teams, as well as team project management platforms such as Slack). As a result, organizations are more open to flexible work arrangements, and we are likely to see more hybrid models of work that meet the needs of management and employees such as flex time, greater use of virtual meetings, and adoption of online project management tools. Importantly, such creative and collaborative solutions are only found when both parties have a commitment to taking the time to investigate all parties' interests and seek solutions for mutual gain – and this is the basis of benevolent trust as described here. Nadler (2004) describes that this desire for mutual benefit is a central condition of interpersonal rapport. It is hard to say which comes first, trust or rapport, but it should be clear that they are mutually reinforcing, in that good rapport builds trust and the establishment (and maintenance) of trust will produce a relationship characterized by good rapport. It may go without saying, but when you have good rapport, you tend to give people the benefit of the doubt, which means assuming good intentions and making situational, rather than dispositional, attributions (see Chapter 4), which will lead to more collaborative interactions even when conflict arises.

Ability

Mayer et al. (1995) describe ability as "that group of skills, competencies, and characteristics that enable a party to have influence within some specific domain" (p. 717). A good example of research that supports ability as an important dimension of trust is a study of National Collegiate Athletic Association (NCAA) basketball players' trust in their coaches (Dirks, 2000). The study specifically examined the relationship between trust in a leader and level of performance. Basketball provides a good case study for this research because there are relatively straightforward measures of ability (a coach's number of years of experience and career record, for example) and performance success (a team's percentage of wins). In this study, trust in the leader was largely based on the players' perceptions of the coach's ability (and, tangential to the point here, high trust had a significant effect on team performance). Ironically, Dirks's study inadvertently hints at a potential negative ramification of placing too much trust in another based on their track record. Consider this quote from an interview participant:

> . . . once we developed trust in Coach, the progress we made increased tremendously because *we were no longer asking questions or were apprehensive.* Instead, we were buying in and believing that if we worked our hardest, we were going to get there. (p. 1009, emphasis added)

While this quote illustrates the organizational benefit of trusting a leader and not questioning their intentions, motives, or requests, too much success or trust may lead to blind loyalty or the unwillingness to ask questions. As described in earlier chapters, the ability to ask questions is an important part of constructive conflict management in which everyone feels heard and able to participate. When organizational members feel unable to ask questions, they tend to avoid conflict, which can reduce understanding and impede development of a culture that fosters collaboration. Perhaps more concerning, if a leader is seen as very successful, organizational members may engage in practices even when they question the ethics of the leader's actions. Ashforth and Anand (2003) describe this dynamic in a theory of the "normalization" of corruption in organizations. As they describe, unethical practices can become embedded in an organizational culture if these actions lead to typical organizational measures of success. For example, imagine a college football team in which the coaches look the other way when an alumnus buys a recruit an expensive item to encourage them to join the team. This practice may be seen as "the way things are," and organizational members may make excuses such as "everyone does it" and "it is how teams get the players to win." When no one questions leadership due to trust in their ability and success, it can lead to disaster, as many college football teams have discovered when they have had sanctions placed against them or, in extreme cases, have had their football program shut down.

This example also highlights the important relationship between trust and rapport. If we have good rapport, I am more likely to feel comfortable pointing out a behavior of concern or questioning a practice that feels wrong, even when I trust your ability. This also highlights the importance of the third dimension – integrity – on trust.

Integrity

Integrity may be the most difficult dimension of trust to operationalize as it is generally thought of as adhering to a certain set of values or acting congruently with one's words (Mayer et al., 1995). This definition underscores the point that trust may either be strengthened or lost over time. We are constantly communicating with our leaders and colleagues, and we are often acutely aware when people act in ways that are seen as a betrayal of trust or an integrity violation. Our perception of another's integrity is also related to perceptions of benevolence: if I believe another person has my best interests at heart, I will be more likely to interpret their behavior in a positive way. For example, let's say that there are rumors of an organizational merger with a competitor. I am likely to be concerned about job security, how leadership will change, and other potential impacts of this decision, yet leadership may not be saying much, if anything. If I believe my supervisor is benevolent, I might assume the best of intentions: perhaps my boss is not saying anything because there are many details to be worked out, and my job is not in danger. My perception of benevolence may also make me more comfortable asking if there are any updates as I will have confidence in my supervisor's response. On the other hand, if I don't trust that my boss is benevolent, I may interpret the silence as bad news and perceive a lack of integrity because my boss is not sharing information about the future. In this environment, I may start looking for a new job rather than focusing on my work. If many organizational members feel this way, people may leave, and this may result in a loss of confidence in leadership that harms the organizational culture for those who stay. Situations like this, where leaders are limited in what information they can share at a given time, are not uncommon in organizations, so acting with benevolence and integrity is crucial to establishing trusting relationships with employees and partners that will build rapport and help construct a collaborative environment (see Box 8.1 for a more in-depth discussion of the impact of rapport on relationships, groups, and organizations).

Box 8.1 How Do You Know When You Have Good Rapport?

As described in the opening definition of rapport, we know we have good rapport when communication with others is easy. We know what they mean, even when they don't express themselves as clearly as they could. We are concerned for their well-being and have empathy for them. This care and empathy make it easier to forgive infractions, such as when someone does or says something that violates an expectation. Dirks and Ferrin (2001) propose that trust acts as a moderator of behavior in that it "affects one's interpretation of another's past action or events relating to the past action: Under high levels of trust, one is more likely to respond favorably to a partner's action than under low levels of trust" (p. 459). To apply this idea, consider a time when a close friend or coworker said something that was hurtful. How did you initially react? You may have said to yourself, "Wow, she must be having a bad day." This is a perfect example of making an excuse for someone's behavior using a situational attribution. In this case, we trust that the person did not intend to hurt us, and when they apologize, we are quick to forgive the transgression. Compare this to a similar interaction with someone you either don't know or have had difficult interactions with in the past. In these situations, we don't have good rapport with the other and we are quicker to judge and more likely to make a dispositional attribution, such as this person is not very nice, is rude, or does not care about our feelings. As this brief description portrays, relationships characterized by good rapport bring a cooperative and collaborative stance to conflict interactions, making them easier to discuss and resolve (and often preventing them). In contrast, relationships with zero history or negative history (i.e., no or poor rapport) are likely to be more adversarial and escalate quickly. In this text box I share three examples from different workplace contexts in which the absence of good rapport escalated conflict. Each of these scenarios was characterized by a lack of trust and understanding that resulted in interactants questioning each other's intentions, making dispositional attributions, and generally assuming the worst about each other. As these examples demonstrate, relationships characterized by poor rapport make conflict interaction more difficult.

Scenario 1: Mediation Between a Manager and Her Executive Assistant

In this mediation the supervisor and assistant each described a difficult relationship that they did not know how to resolve. They did not come in with a clear understanding of the problem, just a general desire to improve their communication and working relationship. As with all mediation sessions I conduct, I had each party in the room with me, and I asked each one to start by telling me what brought them to mediation. The assistant described how much she liked her supervisor and her job, although there were times when the workload was very busy and she experienced high stress. It was her perception that this was when they had the most difficult interaction and seemed unable to communicate well. I then asked the supervisor to describe what brought them to mediation from her point of view. She also commented on how much she appreciated her assistant and believed she wanted to do her best. When her assistant would feel stressed, she often said, "I can't do this." The supervisor indicated that the statement "I can't" frustrated her, and when she heard that, she tried to help by taking the task away from the assistant and assigning it to someone else. While she found it annoying to have to do this, the supervisor became even more upset listening to her assistant say "I can't."

When it was the assistant's turn to speak again, she immediately responded to this statement. She described that she gets upset when the supervisor takes work away from her, because it is interpreted as a signal that the boss does not think she has the *ability* to do her job. She went on to explain that when she says, "I can't do this," it is her habitual way of expressing stress, but it does not mean that she "won't" do it, only that she needs some time to process the new task and figure out how to prioritize it. When the supervisor removed tasks and assigned them to someone else, she felt guilty and feared that her coworkers would think she was incompetent and not a good team player.

It became clear to all three of us in the mediation that the underlying source of the conflict was the differing interpretations of the statement "I can't do this." Every time the employee said that phrase, it triggered a conflict that escalated so much that the two could not speak to each other for days until each had time to calm down. They had not been able to identify that as the triggering event until we created a safe space in mediation to do so. With the source of the conflict identified, the three of us brainstormed how they could change the nature of the interaction that occurred when the workload got heavy. The two of them actually laughed about the situation and developed a new phrase, "I need help," that the assistant could use to signal that she needed her supervisor to help her prioritize the work and develop a strategy to tackle the tasks. This conversation successfully altered each party's perceptions of the other so that they could start to rebuild trust: for the manager, she now understood that when her assistant would say, "I need help," it was not because she was incompetent or did not have the ability (dispositional attribution) but due to a heavy workload and resulting stress (situational attribution). For the assistant, she was able to see that when the supervisor reassigned a task, the motivation was to alleviate her stress (show empathy and provide support), not a statement that she did not think the assistant was a competent employee. Note in this scenario that each party actually had trust in each other's ability, but good rapport was still lacking.

This is a great example of how our interpretation of the intent behind another's words can impact a relationship. It also reminds us of the value of asking questions. If either the supervisor or the employee had ever asked the other "Why would you say that?" or "Why would you do that?" they may have been able to solve this on their own. When there is not good rapport, we are afraid to ask questions because we are embarrassed or we are afraid to "cause" conflict. Ironically, it is *not* asking the question and the *avoidance* of conflict that serves to harm the relationship and escalate conflict.

Scenario 2: Conflict Expansion from the Operating Room to the Whole Unit

A certified registered nurse anesthetist (CRNA) we will call Nurse Smith (a pseudonym) complained that one of the anesthesiologists he worked with, Dr. Jones (a pseudonym), was a micromanager. Nurse Smith was offended that Dr. Jones "hovered" over him in the surgical suite and told him what to do next at every turn. This was offensive because Nurse Smith had graduated from his nursing program at the top of his class, and he had enough experience to know that there were many ways to provide anesthesia given the specific circumstances of the patient. Nurse Smith did not feel the need to be told what to do or be supervised so closely and perceived this behavior as a lack of trust in his ability, expertise, and knowledge. As a result of this perception, Nurse Smith often complained to others that Dr. Jones was a micromanager who did not believe CRNAs were competent. In this hospital, each anesthesiologist supervised four surgical patients at a time. The standard pre-surgery procedure was that Dr. Jones would review the anesthesia protocol with Nurse Smith and then leave the room to see another patient. To make the point that he was capable, one day Nurse Smith decided to provide anesthesia the way he thought best even though it differed from what he and Dr. Jones had agreed upon. When Dr. Jones returned and saw that Nurse Smith had not followed the agreed-upon protocol, she became angry and determined that she could not trust Nurse Smith. Dr. Jones then complained to other anesthesiologists and the CRNA manager that she could not work with Nurse Smith because he would not follow the agreed-upon anesthesia protocol. This created a challenging situation for the unit because it reduced trust among the CRNAs and anesthesiologists and disrupted the scheduling manager's process because Nurse Smith and Dr. Jones could not be scheduled for the same patients.

In my interview with another anesthesiologist at this hospital, he explained the challenges of the anesthesiologist's role and their responsibility for patient safety. As a supervisor of four patients at once, his job is to make sure the anesthesia plan is appropriate for the patient's unique circumstances and that the CRNA who stays with the patient throughout the surgery understands and agrees to the protocol. As this doctor described it to me, patients and the surgical team know that if anything goes wrong, "the buck stops" with the anesthesiologist, and they are ultimately responsible for whatever happens. This has implications for medical malpractice lawsuits as well as the hospital administration's view of the anesthesia team and gaining the trust of current and future patients. As a result, anesthesiologists take their supervisory role very seriously. When I asked for examples of conflict that may arise between CRNAs and anesthesiologists, the doctor described how CRNAs might perceive the doctor's supervision as micromanaging. He said he understood this perception, and described that especially the first time he works with a CRNA, he is likely to pay close attention to their work. Once he gets to know the CRNA, he gains trust in their ability, and he will back off to give them more autonomy. However, if in those initial encounters a CRNA does not follow the protocol they have agreed upon, there is no foundation for trust to develop, and the micromanaging is likely to persist. It is easy to see how these different expectations for the interaction and relationship between the CRNA and anesthesiologist can create the negative spiral described above, which started with Nurse Smith and Dr. Jones, but then spread throughout the anesthesia unit. Without an understanding of why the doctor was supervising so closely, the actions were misinterpreted and the seeds of a negative relationship and an adversarial climate were planted.

The anesthesiologist I interviewed explained that over time he learned to be very direct with CRNAs about his behavior and why he was doing it. Whenever he works with a new CRNA, he explicitly tells them he is going to be hovering a bit and, please, not to interpret this negatively, that once he gets to know them, he will allow them to be more independent. This kind of *meta-communication*, communication about our communication, has been recommended by Deborah Tannen (1986) and many other communication scholars. By directly explaining the motivations for our behavior, we prevent others' need to make assumptions (or attributions) about our intentions or benevolence. In the example described by Nurse Smith, he may not have felt the need to "prove himself" if he had understood that he needed to do his part to build a relationship with Dr. Jones, which would allow him to earn the trust that would provide more autonomy. This understanding would have prevented the negative relationship that evolved between Smith and Jones, as well as the climate of suspicion and scheduling challenges that developed. It is a great example of how the interaction between two people can impact an entire unit or workplace and underscores the importance of good rapport.

Scenario 3: Conflict in the Nonprofit Boardroom

In Chapter 7 you read about our research with a nonprofit organization we called COURAGE that included a discussion of whether the organization should maintain a list of local physicians and providers on their website as a resource for members. The discussion raised several questions about the legal and ethical implications of a list, such as: *Who would or would not be on the list? Would COURAGE be liable if they recommended a provider and someone had a bad experience? Was it part of the organizational mission to provide these resources?* Board members shared strong opinions during this conversation, asked important questions, and often expressed *acknowledgment* of others' views, all of which are signs of good rapport. Despite a robust deliberation, some board members were uncomfortable with the level of disagreement. This was illustrated initially when one board member tried to change the subject by commenting on the weather outside (as was described in Chapter 7). Yet this was followed in a more caustic manner when one board member blurted in frustration to another member's comment, "this is stupid." The unfortunate result was that the room went silent, and the board chair stepped in to suggest that they table the conversation, postponing further discussion until the next meeting.

This scenario provides an illustration of how a *lack of rapport* between two group members can impede group progress. The board needed to make a decision on this issue, and the group as a whole was engaging in a productive deliberation that came to a screeching halt because two members could not communicate well with each other. Like the executive assistant and her supervisor described in the first scenario above, these two board members communicated in ways that "pushed each other's buttons," which in this case harmed the larger group. Unlike the first scenario, we never had the opportunity to help these two members improve their communication. Instead, the board as a whole had to figure out how to work around the challenging relationship of these two, highly vocal members. Fortunately, in an ensuing meeting the board was able to focus on the mission of the organization and determine that it was appropriate for them to provide resources for their constituents. They resolved the conflict between achieving their mission and concerns for liability with a statement that the organization was not endorsing any particular provider or treatment, only making the resources available to their members. This solution met the interests of all board members' concerns and is another good example of the benefits of trust, rapport, and collaborative communication.

For Reflection and Discussion:

Discuss with a partner or small group.

1) How do you think power differences in each of these three scenarios may have impacted the development of rapport? Who has more responsibility for creating trust and rapport when parties have different levels of power or status in a relationship? If you have lower status in a relationship, what can you do to build rapport? If you have power and you see problems of rapport among team members, what might you do to help them build rapport?

2) Describe the different assumptions parties made about each other in each of these situations. What can you do when you feel yourself making assumptions about another person's motives or intentions? How does this change when you have more or less power? What would you recommend the parties in the above scenarios do instead of operating based on assumptions?

3) What can you do as a member of a work group when you observe a lack of rapport among your colleagues?

Nonverbal Communication and Rapport-Building

A lot of the communication that impacts rapport is nonverbal, as we often signal affinity and respect for others nonverbally. Nadler (2004) describes *proxemic cues* (how we use space) such as sitting in a circle, sitting next to someone, or directly facing the other without a barrier (such as a desk) in between as signs that we are giving another our full attention. Other nonverbal cues that signal focus, a positive attitude, and engagement include leaning forward in conversation, making eye contact, smiling, head nodding, and hand gestures. When people have good rapport, both (or all) parties are using these nonverbal cues and there is an authentic connection.

While in an ideal interaction these behaviors would be spontaneous, managers, leaders, and facilitators can set the stage for collaborative interaction by preparing a space in advance. For example, in mediation sessions, I try to find a room with a round table so that the mediator and the parties in conflict are all sitting side by side rather than directly facing each other at a square table. Sitting disputants on opposite sides of a table nonverbally and symbolically can reinforce an adversarial stance, while a round table signals cooperation.

A similar strategy for larger groups is to arrange chairs in a circle or around a table when leaders want participants to see, and engage in discussion with, each other. You may have experienced a classroom in which your instructor asked students to move their desks into a circle rather than sit "auditorium style." This contrasts with a typical classroom, where students are all looking at the instructor, who then becomes the focal point. The auditorium style impedes rapport among students as they may be engaging with the instructor but not with one another in discussion. You may have also experienced a workshop or training session in which participants are placed at small tables to encourage conversation and rapport. Such use of space encourages participants to get to know one another, find common ground, and build trust that is critical to sharing information, equal participation, and ultimately a climate of collaboration. This foundation breeds more willingness to voice differences of opinion or information and facilitates collaboration when conflict arises.

Nonverbal interaction is central to rapport because of the human tendency to mimic another's behavior to improve affiliation and understanding, which is explained by communication accommodation theory (Bernhold & Giles, 2020). Communication accommodation (Giles, 1973) occurs when a speaker adapts their communication to more closely resemble that of the person they are speaking to or to better meet their needs or expectations. While accommodation can extend beyond nonverbal communication (such as tailoring what you say for a specific audience), nonverbal examples include adopting the tone, pace, or volume of the hearer. Bernhold and Giles (2020) provide examples of specific accommodation situations, such as a politician adopting the local dialect of constituents or a young person speaking more loudly for an older family member who is hard of hearing. A college professor who adopts the vernacular or slang of the current students in a class might be another example of adapting one's communication in an effort to be more attractive to an audience and build rapport (the section below on intercultural rapport-building provides several more illustrations of this type of accommodation). Many years of research have supported the idea that communication accommodation leads to solidarity and other positive outcomes (see Soliz & Giles, 2014), although it is not without some risk. If the listener does not perceive the accommodation is authentic (in trust terms, that the speaker is benevolent), they might perceive it as condescending (such as speaking louder just because another person is older) or as trying too hard (a parent or teacher trying to act younger), which will undermine attempts to gain solidarity and build rapport.

In addition to accommodating others, coordination of communication may occur through mimicry, or mirroring another's behavior. Mimicry can be conscious or unconscious, but in either case, it has often been found to lead to greater liking, understanding, affiliation, rapport, and even increased prosocial behaviors (as described in Chapter 5). In a laboratory study, when participants were given a goal of increasing affiliation with a speaker who engaged in frequent face touching, the participant was more likely to touch their face during the observation (Lakin & Chartrand, 2003). In a follow-up experiment where the mimicry involved foot shaking, the same authors found that participants who failed to increase affiliation in the first interaction engaged in more mimicry in a second interaction in an attempt to improve their success. These studies suggest that mimicry will increase cooperation and coordination (Nadler, 2004).

Mimicry has also been studied specifically in the context of negotiation (Drolet & Morris, 2000). This study found that participants were more likely to reach impasse when seated side by side, and the explanation was that because they could not see each other's nonverbal cues they were less likely to mimic the other. This point is of interest as it stands in direct contrast to my earlier discussion of having parties in mediation sit side by side to enhance a collaborative over a competitive stance. It provides a strong argument that use of a round table where all parties can more easily see each other is most promising for facilitating cooperation and rapport, especially when difficult conversations are expected.

A final way that communication coordination might take place is through linguistic style matching (Niederhoffer & Pennebaker, 2002). While this is not entirely nonverbal, linguistic style matching is the phenomenon in which interactants influence each other's speech patterns and word choices in naturally occurring conversation to improve understanding and affiliation. Research by Niederhoffer and Pennebaker confirmed that speakers often choose similar words and match each other's rhythms, such as shorter or longer speaking turns, as well as positive or negative affect. In a study of linguistic style matching in the context of negotiation, Taylor and Thomas (2008) analyzed the police transcripts of successful and unsuccessful hostage negotiations. They found that successful negotiations involved greater coordination of turn-taking (nonverbal communication) and more reciprocation of positive affect (to be discussed in Chapter 9), and took a problem-solving orientation by staying in the present (rather than focusing on the past) and coming up with alternatives rather than maintaining a competitive frame. Given that hostage negotiations are arguably among the most escalated, emotional, and adversarial conflicts, these results suggest that coordinating communication, both nonverbally and verbally, bodes well for increasing rapport and creating an environment for more constructive conflict management.

The notion of coordinating our communication, whether through accommodation, mimicry, or linguistic style matching, is made more difficult in intercultural communication. The final section of this chapter takes a closer look at some of the additional challenges of building rapport in intercultural interactions, with some ideas for overcoming those obstacles to enhance communication and foster intercultural relationships.

Rapport and Intercultural Interactions

A discussion of rapport-building requires special consideration of intercultural relationships. It seems self-evident that building rapport is easier when interaction takes place among those who are more similar. In these situations, we most likely have the same "rules" or expectations for interaction. If you have ever worked somewhere for some time, you probably have grown comfortable communicating with your coworkers and supervisor because you have learned the norms and expectations of that organizational culture. You know, for example, when, and with whom, you can use humor, be more (or less) direct, and engage in social versus task-related communication. When we are new to an organization, we may be more cautious about how we communicate because we don't want to accidentally violate expectations and undermine our attempt to make a good impression and be seen as a competent employee. Now imagine the additional complication for someone who has a different background (i.e., ethnic, racial, regional, etc.) than the majority of employees in an organization. This individual needs to learn the organizational culture, but also may not share the underlying interaction norms or expectations of the majority culture. Consider the example of a new employee from the Philippines who joined a company in Hong Kong and struggled to engage in small talk in a way colleagues deemed appropriate (Mak & Chui, 2013; see Box 8.2).

Box 8.2 Challenge of Intercultural Rapport-Building

In their article "A cultural approach to small talk: a double-edged sword of sociocultural reality during socialization into the workplace," authors Bernie Chun Nam Mak and Hin Leung Chui (2013) describe their research on new-comer socialization into the workplace. They specifically examined small talk, an important way that organizational newcomers learn the social (as well as task-related) rules of the organization. They recorded several interactions between a newcomer (Anna) and her colleagues, and then the researchers took the extra step of interviewing the interactants to understand how the partici-pants interpreted what was going on during the interaction. The example below is a summary of an interaction described in their article that illustrates some of the extra challenges of building rapport when we interact with people from different countries of origin. Following the example, I present some of their recommendations for managing rapport in an intercultural relationship.

In this scenario, Anna, the new employee, has a conversation with Rebecca, a member of the senior management team, regarding a client they are having some problems with. Rebecca (the manager) starts the conversation with small talk by mentioning that Anna has been here three months and asking how it is going. Anna replies saying "no, [I've been here] already four months." Rebecca responds with laughter and an acknowledgment of her error, turning to the main question of "how it is going," to which Anna replies it is "too busy." Rebecca laughs and says "busy is good for business," and Anna responds by elaborating that there are too many things to follow, and this client is causing problems. This leads the two into the main topic and task for their meeting, which is to try to come up with a solution for the problem with this client.

Rebecca's expectation of how this interaction was supposed to unfold, as described in the authors' interview with her, is best characterized as *small talk*, generally defined as talk for primarily social purposes. Anna's responses violated the expectations of small talk, as she, a lower status employee, starts by correcting Rebecca's statement, which creates some embarrassment for Rebecca. When Rebecca tries to save face by laughing off her mistake and continuing the small talk, Anna goes directly into the challenges she is facing. Many of us may recognize that in a typical small talk interaction, an inquiry into how things are going is a courtesy. Even if there are problems, we typically start off by saying "things are fine" and, especially if we are a new employee, we might be likely to say something polite about how much we like working there. Once the conversation gets going, we might then move into the more complex details of the task at hand. As a result of this awkward interaction, Rebecca leaves the meeting with a negative impression of Anna. When Anna is interviewed about her reaction to the interaction, she explains she was nervous about being blamed for the problem with the client. The authors describe that in Anna's Filipino culture, there is a "propensity to feel shame" and a heightened "self-awareness of criticism" (p. 125). From Anna's perspective, she felt this conversation was very serious and was focused on the business aspects of the interaction and trying to save face. Unfortunately, by not knowing the "rules" of small talk as expected by Rebecca, there was a misunderstanding which will likely make it more difficult for Anna to build rapport with Rebecca and could impact her future with the organization.

There are at least two main takeaways from this intercultural workplace interaction.

1) Responsibility for learning the expectations of the dominant group in an organization should not fall exclusively on the employee from a minority group. In order to build an inclusive culture, all employees need to be open to the possibility of different rules and expectations for interaction, and be prepared to adapt or help others understand rather than assuming the worst about another (or we might say, using a dispositional rather than a situational attribution; see Chapter 4). There is mutual responsibility for effective communication, which involves learning to be a culturally competent communicator.

2) Workplace mentors can play a vital role in helping socialize new members into a group or organization. This may include providing new employees with insights on organizational expectations, meeting or greeting rituals, coworkers' communication styles, and other implicit or unwritten rules of interaction. Mentors can take the added step of asking newcomers about previous experiences or, if appropriate, some of their customs and expectations to improve their own understanding and help other colleagues accommodate the newcomer. As described in the introduction to this book, organizational culture is continuously co-constructed through the communication of organizational members, and the ongoing processes of assimilation (the newcomer adapting to the organization) and accommodation (the organization adapting to the newcomer) allow for the creation of an inclusive, collaborative organizational culture.

For Reflection and Discussion:

Discuss with a partner or small group.

1) Reflect on a time when you were either in a new group or workplace or met someone new who had a different background (however you want to define "different"). Can you recall any awkward moments in the interaction?

What did you do to reduce your uncertainty and/or try to build rapport with others in this situation?

2) Given that Anna and Rebecca have different levels of status and power in the case described above, do you think one of them bears greater responsibility for building rapport? Discuss the ways in which each party could take responsibility for building rapport as their relationship continues.

Source: Mak, B. C. N., & Chui, H. L. (2013) / Taylor & Francis.

As workplaces have become more global and diverse, we are all likely to work with people who are different from us, whether in terms of race, ethnicity, sexual orientation, religion, age, or ability, and we all have to make a commitment to intercultural competence. One of the leading authors in intercultural competence and rapport management, Helen Spencer-Oatey (2020), draws from the global competence framework developed by the Organization for Economic Co-operation and Development (OECD, 2018) to describe three criteria for intercultural competence: openness, appropriateness, and effectiveness. These are defined in the OECD report as follows:

> *Open* interactions mean relationships in which all participants demonstrate sensitivity towards, curiosity about and willingness to engage with others and their perspectives. *Appropriate* refers to interactions that respect the expected cultural norms of both parties. In *effective* communication, all participants are able to make themselves understood. (p. 10)

The important question becomes, *how do we improve our cultural competence in order to build rapport with all our coworkers and foster an inclusive and collaborative climate in our increasingly diverse workplaces?* This is hard work that requires commitment, willingness to take risks, and becoming comfortable with the uncomfortable (Pitts & Jameson, 2016; Spencer-Oatey, 2020). Perhaps the most obvious starting point is that we need to interact with others who are different from us and engage in an authentic desire to *learn* from and about others. Below I share a few more specific ideas for pursuing open, appropriate, and effective communication to gain cultural competence. As some of these ideas have been explored elsewhere in this book, I refer to other chapters as appropriate.

Openness

Open communication is nonjudgmental because the receiver does not make negative assumptions (or attributions) about the speaker's intent or motives. As described in Chapter 3, we bring mindfulness to our interactions when we pay attention to our impulses and engage in reflection before we respond. Openness also calls upon us to listen to understand, consider the speaker's frame of reference (Žegarac, Caley, & Bhatti, 2015), and ask questions to aid our understanding. Žegarac, Caley, and Bhatti provide an excellent example of how an English language learning instructor showed openness in a situation where rapport was threatened when students in her class began speaking Arabic and laughing during her class. Rather than responding in the moment, the instructor took time to reflect on what she was feeling and the most appropriate response. Realizing that she did not know what the students had said, she first used inquiry to find out, and confirmed that the students were, in fact, making fun of her. The next time the students did this she immediately shut it down using humor in the students' language (Arabic). While there was initial silence, the students laughed, and the student who had been making the comments treated her with respect from that point forward. While the use of humor can be risky (the students could have become offended and tension could have escalated), the authors suggest the strategy was successful because the instructor (i) used mindfulness to constrain her initial reaction rather than make assumptions about what was being said, (ii) communicated clearly that the behavior was not acceptable, and (iii) incorporated their language into her informal response to communicate respect for them as individuals. This example illustrates that cultural competence includes attention to the "individual, cultural-specific and universal aspects of social interaction" (Žegarac et al., 2015, p. 217). It is in fact all three of these areas that will inform the assessment of the appropriateness of communication in a given situation.

Appropriateness

Spencer-Oatey (2020) points out that determining the appropriateness of communication is especially challenging because what is considered appropriate is subjective and likely to be different across individuals, even those who share many cultural similarities. Spencer-Oatey's (2020) intercultural competencies for rapport management include the need to attend to the specific communication situation (i.e., a classroom), the expectations of the interactants (i.e., instructor and students), and the cultural appropriateness (awareness of one's own cultural expectations or biases and sensitivity to the other party's cultural expectations). Importantly, we often do not know whether another party has different cultural expectations, or what they are, but we can engage in appropriate communication by attending to face needs (i.e., desire to be seen as competent; see Chapter 6), respecting others' rights (i.e., to be treated with dignity and respect), and supporting others' goals (i.e., an employee's goal of completing their tasks and obtaining support, as illustrated in the case of Anna in Box 8.2).

Effectiveness

We should always strive for effectiveness in our interactions with others as we want to be heard and understood as intended. This is, of course, more complicated when interacting with someone new, someone we do not know well, or someone who does not share our frame of reference (i.e., background, organization, or cultural rituals). It is important to note that both parties in an interaction bear responsibility for ensuring effectiveness to the extent possible. For example, if we are being mindful and paying attention to the other party's nonverbal communication, we may see signs of confusion, and we might ask, "Am I making sense?" Similarly, if another person is sharing information with us and we are having trouble understanding, we could politely ask for clarification. Sometimes in intercultural interactions we fail to ask questions out of embarrassment, such as when we are having trouble understanding another because of their accent. This is a good example of an obstacle to rapport, because our difficulty in understanding combined with our discomfort may lead us to avoid interacting with this coworker. In group meetings, it may lead to implicit bias if other members also have difficulty understanding and do not ask for clarification, which may lead to important information or ideas being ignored. These challenges of effective communication will lead to marginalization and the opposite of an inclusive culture.

In a study of culturally diverse nurses who joined a hospital in Australia, Crawford, Roger, and Candlin (2016) provide an excellent case study of the challenges these nurses faced and how they engaged in communication accommodation to make their communication effective and develop rapport with patients. Effectiveness is vitally important in a patient care setting due to the goal of improving health outcomes, making this an especially relevant case for discussion of intercultural effectiveness. The nurses in Crawford et al.'s study were from various Asian countries and described four main challenges to their adjustment to Australia, including (i) accents, (ii) colloquialisms specific to the Australian language, (iii) nonverbal expectations of eye contact, and (iv) the directness of communication. Accents they encountered in their experience included patients and coworkers from India, the Middle East, Europe, and Australia. They also described that Australian English was different from the English they had learned at home, largely because of colloquialisms. Australians also tended to communicate with more directness than the nurses' home cultures, which was initially perceived as rude, although they adjusted to this over time and even recognized the value of directness in terms of efficiency and effectiveness. A related struggle occurred due to different cultural expectations of eye contact. In many Asian cultures, making direct eye contact is a sign of disrespect, especially when communicating with someone who is older. Australians, on the other hand, found it disrespectful when a nurse was not making eye contact with them, as it was interpreted as a sign of not paying attention.

The nurses used several strategies that have been discussed in this text, such as mindfulness and effective listening. To help with clarification they often repeated a question in a different way, used paraphrasing to make sure they understood, or saved the other party's face by blaming themselves for not understanding the other (i.e., "I'm sorry I'm a little slow today," Crawford et al. 2016, p. 270). The nurses also described how they reflected on their previous history when interacting with someone they knew in order to consider the communication that would be most effective. Nurses also gave examples of how they adapted their nonverbal communication, such as by making eye contact or smiling, to build rapport with patients. The authors make the important point that while the nurses took responsibility for adapting to the norms of the dominant culture, the organization should also provide mentoring and foster an inclusive culture for overall organizational effectiveness.

Chapter Summary

The goal of this chapter was to introduce the idea of rapport and demonstrate how good rapport makes interaction easier, which is especially important during difficult conversations, such as conflict. Relationships characterized as having good rapport often include all three dimensions of trust: benevolence, ability, and integrity (Mayer et al., 1995), because we believe the other has our best interests at heart, we believe they are capable, and we believe they will act with integrity. When we have trust and rapport, it is easier to ask questions that will help us clarify our understanding or confirm another's intentions or motives rather than relying on assumptions, and thus prevent conflict. This chapter also covered the importance of nonverbal communication in the development of rapport. Nonverbal cues such as where we sit in relation to others, smiling, nodding, and gesturing can all be signs of affiliation and respect as we show another we are paying attention (Nadler, 2004). Even the unintentional behaviors of communication accommodation (Giles, 1973), such as mimicry and linguistic style matching, have been shown to improve rapport and facilitate collaborative conflict management, even in difficult conflicts such as hostage negotiations (Taylor & Thomas, 2008).

Finally, this chapter discussed the challenges of rapport-building in intercultural interactions, which may be complicated by the use of different rules or expectations for interaction. Cultural competence requires that we interact with many different kinds of people and learn how to communicate openly, appropriately, and effectively. It is important that everyone take responsibility for building rapport and engaging in appropriate and effective communication using the tools described throughout this book (such as listening, engaging, and acknowledging, for example), and that means organizational leaders must also take care to facilitate effective and inclusive communication though orientation programs, mentoring, and modeling collaborative conflict management.

Activity

For reflection and sharing with a partner or small group:

1) Think about someone with whom you feel you have very good rapport. What are the characteristics of that relationship? How would you describe the features of the communication that make it easy to talk to that person? Can you recall whether your rapport developed over time or was always easy? Consider what makes it easier or harder to communicate with this person.

2) Now consider someone in your life you find it challenging to communicate with. What are the characteristics of that relationship? What happens when you communicate that makes it hard? Can you use the examples from your experience with positive rapport to consider any ways you could improve rapport in this situation? What are the obstacles to building rapport and how might they be overcome?

References

Ashforth, B. E., & Anand, V. (2003). The normalization of corruption in organizations. *Research in Organizational Behavior*, *25*(1): 1–52.

Bernhold, Q. S., & Giles, H. (2020). Vocal accommodation and mimicry. *Journal of Nonverbal Behavior*, *44*: 41–62. https://doi.org/10.1007/s10919-019-00317-y.

Crawford, T., Roger, P., & Candlin, S. (2016). "Are we on the same wavelength?" International nurses and the process of confronting and adjusting to clinical communication in Australia. *Communication & Medicine (Equinox Publishing Group)*, *13*(3): 263–275. https://doi.org/10.1558/cam.28953.

Dirks, K. T. (2000). Trust in leadership and team performance: Evidence from NCAA basketball. *Journal of Applied Psychology*, *85*(6): 1004–1012.

Dirks, K. T., & Ferrin, D. L. (2001). The role of trust in organizational settings. *Organization Science*, *12*(4): 450–467. https://doi.org/10.1287/orsc.12.4.450.10640.

Drolet, A. L., & Morris, M. W. (2000). Rapport in conflict resolution: Accounting for how face-to-face contact fosters mutual cooperation in mixed-motive conflicts. *Journal of Experimental Social Psychology*, *36*(1): 26–50. https://doi.org/10.1006/jesp.1999.1395.

Giles, H. (1973). Accent mobility: A model and some data. *Anthropological Linguistics*, *15*: 87–105.

Jameson, J. K. (1999). Toward a comprehensive model for the assessment and management of intraorganizational conflict. *International Journal of Conflict Management, 10*(3): 268–294.

Lakin, J. L., & Chartrand, T. L. (2003). Using nonconscious behavioral mimicry to create affiliation and rapport. *Psychological Science, 14*(4): 334–339.

Levine, E., & Schweitzer, M. E. (2015). Prosocial lies: When deception breeds trust. *Organizational Behavior and Human Decision Processes, 126*: 88–106. https://doi.org/ 10.1016/j.obhdp.2014.10.007.

Lewicki. R. J., & Wiethoff, C. (2000). Trust, trust development, and trust repair. In M. Deutsch & P. T. Coleman (Eds.), *The handbook of conflict resolution: Theory and practice* (pp. 86–107). San Francisco, CA: Jossey-Bass.

Mak, B. N., & Chui, H. (2013). A cultural approach to small talk: A double-edged sword of sociocultural reality during socialization into the workplace. *Journal of Multicultural Discourses, 8*(2): 118–133. https://doi.org/10.1080/17447143. 2012.753078.

Mayer, R. C., Davis, J. H., & Schoorman, F. D. (1995). An integrative model of organizational trust. *Academy of Management Review, 20*(3): 709–734.

Nadler, J. (2004). Rapport: Rapport in negotiation and conflict resolution. *Marquette Law Review, 87*(4): 875–882. Retrieved January 2, 2023, from https://scholarship. law.marquette.edu/cgi/viewcontent.cgi?article=1207&context=mulr

Niederhoffer, K. G., & Pennebaker, J. W. (2002). Linguistic style matching in social interaction. *Journal of Language and Social Psychology, 21*(4): 337–360. https:// doi.org/10.1177/026192702237953.

Organization for Economic Cooperation and Development (OECD). (2018). Preparing our youth for an inclusive and sustainable world: The OECD PISA global competence framework. Retrieved January 2, 2023, from https://www.researchgate.net/ publication/350443283_Preparing_our_Youth_for_an_Inclusive_and_Sustainable_ World_The_OECD_PISA_Global_Competence_Framework

Papa, M. J., Daniels, T. D., & Spiker, B. K. (2008). *Organizational communication: Perspectives and trends* (5th ed.). Thousand Oaks, CA: Sage.

Pitts, E. A., & Jameson, J. K. (2016). Promoting ontological insecurity to transform the governance of science. In P. Kellett & T. Matyok (Eds.), *Transforming conflict through communication in personal, family, and working relationships* (pp. 249–270). Lanham, MD: Lexington Books.

Soliz, J., & Giles, H. (2014). Relational and identity processes in communication: A contextual and meta-analytical review of communication accommodation theory. In E. Cohen (Ed.), *Communication Yearbook 38* (pp. 108–143). Thousand Oaks, CA: Sage.

Spencer-Oatey, H. (2020). Intercultural competence and harmonious intercultural relations: Interdisciplinary perspectives and insights. *China Media Research, 16*(2): 1–12. ISSN: 1556-889X.

Tannen, D. (1986). *That's not what i meant! How conversational style makes or breaks relationships*. New York: Morrow.

Taylor, P. J., & Thomas, S. (2008). Linguistic style matching and negotiation outcome. *Negotiation and Conflict Management Research, 1*: 263–281. https://doi.org/10.1111/j.1750-4716.2008.00016.x.

Trust. In *Merriam-Webster.com*. Retrieved January 2, 2023, from https://www.merriam-webster.com/dictionary/trust

Žegarac, V., Caley, J., & Bhatti, J. (2015). Communication and core conditions in rapport building: A case study. *International Review of Pragmatics, 7*(2): 216–243. http://dx.doi.org/10.1163/18773109-00702004.

9

Building an Organizational Culture of Forgiveness

Taking responsibility for oneself is by definition an act of kindness.

Sharon Salzberg (author)

If our rearview mirror were as big as our windshield, we'd never get anywhere.

Lucia Kanter St. Amour (attorney and mediator)

In this chapter I continue the focus on building and maintaining rapport with attention to the roles of apologies and forgiveness in workplace conflict and considering how organizational members can promote this behavior by constructing a culture of forgiveness. In Chapters 6 and 7, I focused on the importance of *acknowledging* others' contributions and experiences. We learned that when we give recognition it communicates empathy and understanding and often shifts the conflict dynamic from contentious to collaborative. Once we are able to understand the other's experience in a new way, we can more easily move from blaming them to taking responsibility for our own role in the conflict. In Chapter 5, I described mediation research that showed how taking responsibility can move parties from adversarial to cooperative communication (Jameson, Sohan, & Hodge, 2014; Poitras, 2007). However, the emotions that accompany workplace conflict, such as pride (which may prevent one from accepting or admitting one did anything wrong) and fear (for example, of losing status or the confidence of coworkers), can prevent parties from taking responsibility. If, however, we are focusing on the relationship and building or maintaining good rapport, it may enable us to, to paraphrase the words of Sharon Salzberg that opened this chapter, take responsibility as an act of kindness.

I'm not suggesting that we accept blame that is undeserved, but rather, that we accept whatever role we may have played in conflict escalation, such as avoiding

Communication for Constructive Workplace Conflict, First Edition. Jessica Katz Jameson.
© 2023 John Wiley & Sons, Inc. Published 2023 by John Wiley & Sons, Inc.

the conflict rather than confronting early on or saying something we wish we hadn't. As this book has endeavored to show, communication during conflict is complicated, and it is hard to imagine any protracted conflict in which both parties do not play some part in making it worse before it gets better. This is likely why Jean Poitras's (2007) study of taking responsibility in mediation found that it has the best results when both parties accept responsibility. Importantly, and as discussed in Chapter 8, when one party accepts responsibility, this may encourage the other party to also accept responsibility in an act of reciprocity or communication accommodation. One way we communicate that we accept our responsibility is through the act of apologizing, so this chapter will review research on the act of apology in the workplace. Of course, apology on its own may or may not be considered enough and may or may not be accepted. We, therefore, also look at the concept of forgiveness in the workplace.

Parties in conflict are often unwilling or unable to offer an apology or forgiveness. When we are angry at someone we believe has treated us unfairly, we often stay focused on the past. Third parties can change the conflict conversation by helping parties accept the past and move forward to a focus on future interaction. The second quote that opened this chapter describes how one experienced mediator reminds her clients to look ahead instead of behind (Kanter St. Amour, 2021). Because third parties are often needed to help parties move on from conflict, and because the organizational culture and employee communication are mutually reinforcing, this chapter also examines *restorative justice* and what it looks like when workplace interaction comes from this moral foundation (Paul & Putnam, 2017). Restorative justice is perhaps best defined by distinguishing it from retributive justice, which is the foundation of the US justice model and emphasizes punishment. Retributive justice requires parties who violate the law to pay retribution to the "state," for example paying a fine for speeding or losing freedom when convicted of a major crime. In contrast, the goal of restorative justice is to help the offender understand the harm they caused and make amends directly to the victim (if possible).

Restorative justice emphasizes the relationship among parties in a conflict rather than focusing only on the offender and restoration to a more abstract body such as the organization or state. In the words of the Restorative Justice Exchange, restorative justice starts with an invitation to participate in a facilitated session so that "all stakeholders impacted by the wrongdoing – victims, offenders, and community members – have a voice in the justice process" (Restorative Justice Exchange, 2023, n.p.). While restorative justice has often been discussed in the context of the legal system or community-based conflicts, scholars have proposed its potential application in organizational settings (see, for example, Goodstein & Aquino, 2010; Goodstein & Butterfield, 2010; Kidder, 2007), and a few studies have examined its use in the context of K-12 education (Paul & Riforgiate, 2015;

Paul, 2017). This chapter starts with a review of studies that examine the micro-level interactions of apology and forgiveness in the workplace and transitions to an examination of the norms and characteristics of organizations that are guided by restorative justice.

Apologies

Apologies are interesting conversational acts because they are used for a range of minor to major transgressions. One study that analyzed meeting interaction demonstrated how group members use an explicit "I'm sorry" to negotiate turn-taking (Park & Duey, 2018). Using conversation analysis, which analyzes the turn-by-turn speech acts of each group member, the authors demonstrated that the use of "I'm sorry" often supported rapport by acknowledging and taking responsibility for the interruption, while also showing politeness by reducing the face-threat to the other. This is important because interruption is often perceived as communicating power and dominance (Youngquist, 2009). Interruption is a common microaggression (see Chapter 6 and Sue et al., 2007), and if someone in a meeting is repeatedly interrupted it is likely to be felt by the person and seen by others as disrespectful and silencing. If the pattern persists, interruption will fuel a culture of oppression as opposed to one of constructive and collaborative interaction.[1]

On the other hand, Youngquist's study also demonstrated that when observers expected the interruption (i.e., the speaker was known to interrupt habitually), it was often viewed less as a sign of domineering. The relational context – and existence of rapport – is critical to whether a norm violation is considered acceptable. See Box 9.1 for another explanation of the acceptance of workplace transgressions.

Another study of communication in group meetings examined the difference in acceptance of a transgression when the explanation included an apology versus an excuse (Mroz & Allen, 2019). Being late is another common norm violation that may seem mundane, but can have significant impact on the individual's reputation and the organization – such as when it leads to disgruntled employees or perpetuates a culture of conflict avoidance. Mroz and Allen define an *apology* as a speech act that "includes expressing sorrow, acknowledging the wrongfulness of the act, and accepting responsibility for it, while promoting a sense of remorse,

---

[1] Interruption is not always a sign of dominance and may be a sign of good rapport between parties. An interruption may show enthusiasm for the speaker and invite them to continue. Scholars such as Cantrell (2013/2014) and Tannen (1986) have illustrated how interruption can help coordinate interaction and build rapport.

Box 9.1 Why Do We Excuse Some People More Easily Than Others?

One big difference in whether a coworker's norm violation is excused by others depends on the perception of their overall group contributions. The concept of *idiosyncrasy credit* was introduced by social psychologist Edward Hollander in 1958 to describe how individuals build up "credit" for good behavior. A group member who often shows up on time, makes helpful contributions, and supports all their teammates will likely be forgiven if one day they show up late (discussed further below) or violate some other expectation. The idea of idiosyncrasy credit is consistent with the relationship between trust and rapport described in Chapter 8. If history has shown that an organizational member acts with *benevolence, ability,* and *integrity,* an occasional rule violation will more easily be accepted and excused. This dynamic underscores that the more organizational members communicate in ways that focus on relationships and building rapport, the more they are constructing an organizational culture that supports collaborative conflict management.

For Reflection and Discussion:

Discuss with a partner or small group.

1) Many of us have had the experience of a supervisor or manager who appeared to have "favorite" employees. Reflect back on such a situation and consider whether the "favorite(s)" might have earned idiosyncrasy credit.

2) Theories of interpersonal attraction demonstrate that people often feel drawn to others who are most like them, in terms of characteristics including where we are from geographically, race, religion, sexual orientation, etc. Given this, discuss how you might identify the difference between instances where idiosyncrasy credit is earned and situations where certain employees receive unearned privilege. What can leaders do to monitor their own behavior to ensure that employees are only treated differently based on performance, not based on their membership in a given identity group?

---

repentance, and humility" (p. 187). The authors contrast this speech act with an *excuse*, which "lacks the moral component of an apology, and in the scientific literature, excuses are self-serving accounts of a behavior with the goal of reducing perceptions of personal responsibility for the event" (p. 188). Mroz and Allen used an experimental design to show participants videos of a meeting in which someone arrived late and offered an excuse, an apology, or no explanation. In this experiment, participants responded most positively to those who made an excuse for their lateness. Specifically, they rated the latecomer's future performance as likely to be higher and indicated they would be more likely to help the latecomer who offered an *excuse* as compared to someone who either *only apologized* or did nothing. However, a follow-up study in which participants described the behavior of a coworker who was actually late to a meeting (a real versus a hypothetical situation) found that excuses and apologies almost never occurred independently of each other. In fact, they found that in 71% of the cases reported, the latecomer offered an excuse which was followed by an apology. This finding makes it a bit more challenging to separate the value of an excuse without an accompanying apology.

There is one more variable of interest here, which is whether the lateness is habitual or rare. The study found that coworkers had higher expectations for future performance and were more willing to help those who were rarely late as opposed to habitual latecomers. In other words, an excuse may be acceptable if the audience is willing to accept a situational attribution for a socially acceptable reason (i.e., I was late to a meeting because my child was ill); yet if someone is late habitually, it may be perceived as a dispositional trait that someone could control and chooses not to. Ironically, while we may forgive the person who we know has a habit of interruption, we may be less forgiving of someone who is habitually late. The difference in how we respond will depend not only on our relationship with the person who violates the rule (and whether they have earned idiosyncrasy credit, see Box 9.1), but also on how strongly we feel about the rule and its impact when it is violated. Again, these examples show that the better rapport we have with our coworker, the more easily we will forgive and the more likely a conflict will either be mitigated or resolved.

Another important factor in whether an apology is accepted is how the apology is communicated. Bisel and Messersmith (2012) synthesized research on apology across organizational and interpersonal settings to develop a model for effective apologies in the workplace. The authors point out that recommendations are often contradictory, as scholars looking at the organizational level (such as in cases of crisis communication) often warn organizational leaders that an apology is an admission of guilt. Importantly, in a crisis situation, the organization's primary goal is to restore its image and reputation, which is different from the interpersonal goal of building rapport. In apologies between organizational members who may have (willfully or inadvertently) harmed or offended another, the goal is not only restoring confidence, but also relationship repair, which often includes some tangible (taking on extra work) or symbolic (taking someone to lunch) form of restoration to compensate for the breach.

Based on their review of the apology literature, Bisel and Messersmith (2012) suggested a four-component model of apology that includes (i) a narrative account of the offense that clearly acknowledges the infraction and how it was done, (ii) an explicit statement of regret, (iii) reassurance that it will not happen again, and (iv) the offer of reparations. They tested this model in situations where the offender is a collective (the organization) as opposed to an individual (a coworker or supervisor). The authors hypothesized that working adults would be less forgiving of an organization than an individual. They further examined whether working adults would be more forgiving in situations where the apology came from a friend, a supervisor, or an organization's spokesperson. A survey of 147 working adults was designed that presented different offense/apology scenarios that controlled for the severity of the offense and the content of the apology (all apologies included the four components described above, see Box 9.2 for examples).

Box 9.2   Apology Using The Four-Component Model

One example used in Bisel and Messersmith's (2012) study is provided here to illustrate an apology that persuaded participants in their study to give forgiveness. Notice how the apology includes the four components. In the study, the apology was identical whether coming from a friend, a coworker, or an organizational spokesperson, with the exception that the organizational apology used "we" instead of "I."

> I made a mistake. I owe you a $500 reimbursement. I am doing what I can to repay you as soon as possible; however, I can't repay you just yet. [1. *Narrative account of the offense that clearly acknowledges the infraction*] I sincerely apologize! [2. *An explicit statement of regret*] I promise to do everything I can to make sure this doesn't happen again [3. *Reassurance that it will not happen again*] and I promise to reimburse you soon. What can I do to make this up to you? [4. *The offer of reparations*]. (p. 442, appendix A)

Source: Bisel, R. S., & Messersmith, A. S. (2012) / SAGE Publications.

For Reflection and Discussion:

Discuss with a partner or small group.

1) Organizations are often advised not to offer an apology because it is seen as an admission of guilt and may open the organization to legal ramifications. What are some of the obstacles that might prevent an individual organizational member (either a coworker or a supervisor) from offering an apology? What would make it easier for someone to offer an apology (in terms of interpersonal relationships or organizational culture, for example)?

2) Come up with examples of workplace situations in which the organization, a supervisor, or a coworker committed an offense against one or more others that warrants an apology. Use the four-component model to write an apology and consider how the words used might be different coming from an organizational spokesperson, a supervisor, or a coworker. Discuss how the apologies differ based on who committed the offense as well as the severity of the offense and any potential existing relationship between the offender and offended party(ies).

Source: Bisel, R. S., & Messersmith, A. S. (2012) / SAGE Publications.

Bisel and Messersmith's (2102) experiment confirmed that participants were significantly less forgiving of the organization (compared to a friend or supervisor) prior to the apology. Results also revealed that participants were significantly more forgiving of the offense after the four-component apology was given – and this was true regardless of who provided the apology. Implications of this study reinforce the importance of rapport in that organizations as a whole are at a disadvantage because people cannot build rapport with an organization, per se. From a public relations perspective, the study supports the idea that organizations should attempt to foster interpersonal relationships with customers to create the potential for empathy and greater likelihood of forgiveness. Another interesting finding from a second study conducted by Bisel and Messersmith was that people trained in the four-component model more effectively constructed apologies. In other words, they were able to offer apologies that persuaded study participants to forgive them. This is important because, as described in this chapter and consistent with the communication as constitutive of organization framework, the authors conclude that "effective apology giving performs and enacts communication practice that embodies many similar virtues and reinforces positive organizational culturing" (Bisel & Messersmith, 2012, p. 441; see also Bisel, Messersmith, & Keyton, 2010).

Forgiveness

It is hard to talk about apology without attention to the corollary of forgiveness. Forgiveness is defined as the action that occurs when some who feels wronged removes negative thoughts and feelings toward the transgressor and refrains from seeking revenge (Aquino et al., 2003; Thompson & Audrey Korsgaard, 2019). This is clearly important for long-term relationships and fostering collaboration in the workplace.

A recent study of adolescents and forgiveness found that children are more likely to forgive when they are able to engage in perspective-taking and when they receive a sincere apology (Mulvey et al., 2022). Consistent with the idea of taking responsibility and Bisel and Messersmith's model, these authors found that a sincere apology makes it clear that the speaker understands why what they did was wrong. Adolescents in this study were also more likely to forgive someone who was perceived as in-group rather than out-group, which has significant implications for how we learn to forgive and for the importance of fostering forgiveness in the workplace. It also underscores the importance of establishing strong inter-group relationships and rapport.

Thompson and Audrey Korsgaard (2019) examined the relationship among relational identification, forgiveness, and relationship resilience in situations where a transgression took place in the workplace. Relational identification refers to how much one person considers the relationship an important extension of their own self-concept – in other words, any benefit to the other is also perceived as a benefit to oneself, which then predisposes the relational partner to consider their interests (Thompson & Audrey Korsgaard, 2019). It makes sense that an organizational member would be more likely to forgive someone with whom they have relational identification (similar to the in-group in Mulvey et al., 2022). Relationship resilience is defined as whether one party perceives the relationship as stronger following adversity. This study used an experimental design to explore the relationship between organizational identification and forgiveness, and forgiveness and relationship resilience, as well as whether these dynamics were different depending on whether the transgressor was a coworker or supervisor. Thompson and Audrey Korsgaard collected examples of situations in which survey participants (undergraduate students) perceived that a transgression had occurred in the workplace. They then compared forgiveness and relationship resilience across conditions of high and low relational identification and conditions in which the transgressor was a coworker or supervisor. They followed this with a field test of the findings with a second sample of working adults. The study confirmed the hypothesized relationships, suggesting that, indeed, relational identification predicts forgiveness and forgiveness predicts relationship resilience. This finding was the same whether the transgressor was a coworker or a supervisor.

This study supports the value of engaging in, rather than avoiding, conflict, because the process of addressing a workplace transgression that leads to forgiveness is likely to benefit both organizational members (through the strengthening of relationships and good rapport) and the organization as a whole, because its members will be more likely to care about each other's interests and collaborate. While this review highlights individual-level predictors of forgiveness – perspective-taking and relational identification (Mulvey et al., 2022; Thompson & Audrey Korsgaard, 2019) – there are actions that organizational leaders can take to support identification among members, such as holding orientation sessions for new employees, offering mentoring, supporting team building, and fostering a culture that emphasizes relationships. At the organizational level, scholars have identified characteristics of "forgiving organizations" (Fehr & Gelfand, 2012).

In their multilevel model of forgiveness climate, Fehr and Gelfand (2012) proposed core values of and actions taken by organizational leaders who promote prosocial responses to conflict. Specifically, Fehr and Gelfand's work supports many of the ideas incorporated into the LEARN framework as they describe leadership behaviors such as listening and responding with empathy to support employee professional success and overall well-being. Another important component of their model is self-restraint, defined as being mindful and thoughtful in one's response rather than responding in anger or making quick judgments (see the discussions of non-evaluative listening and suspension in Chapter 3). A final core value in Fehr and Gelfand's model is restorative justice, which promotes the importance of relationships and encourages parties in conflict to take responsibility for their actions through making apologies and forgiveness. Fehr and Gelfand argue that as leaders align their actions with these core values, they model expected behaviors which are then adopted by employees. Further, organizational leaders can promote a forgiveness climate through physical symbols of their commitment to these values, such as employee wellness programs, mindfulness training, and conflict management systems grounded in restorative justice. Fehr and Gelfand describe research illustrating not only that encouraging prosocial responses to conflict is good for individuals and relationships, but also that a forgiveness climate can lead to long-term organizational success by increasing employee commitment and retention. While conflict management systems will be discussed in Chapter 10, the final section of this chapter takes a closer look at restorative justice and the features of organizations that promote this value.

Restorative Justice

Restorative justice "is a theory of justice that emphasizes individual, relational, and communal growth and healing through facilitated dialogue among stakeholders" (Paul & Riforgiate, 2015, n.p.). While traditional, rights- and power-based forms of organizational conflict management emphasize rational behavior and whether a policy or expectation was violated, restorative justice requires a greater focus on interests and the emotions that accompany conflict. A major challenge to restorative justice is that Western-based organizational norms associated with being "professional" often suggest that emotion is not relevant in the workplace, where the emphasis is on task-related communication and getting the job done (Bodtker & Jameson, 2001; Paul & Putnam, 2017). This emphasis on rationality promotes a culture in which organizational members minimize or hide emotions at work unless they benefit the workplace, such as acting happy, pleasant, or enthusiastic even when one does not feel those emotions (Hochschild, 2012). As several aspects of the LEARN framework demonstrate, hiding our emotions and acting in ways that are inauthentic are likely to impose long-term harm on individuals, workplace relationships, and organizational culture.

If an organization is committed to fostering a collaborative culture, an alternative form of conflict management is required that values emotions and encourages employees to communicate about emotion to increase understanding and empathy and restore relationships. Box 9.3 describes an experimental study that compared the agreements that resulted from negotiated versus mediated conflicts and revealed that conflicts assisted by a third-party mediator were more likely to address emotions and include items in the final agreement that serve to restore and promote relationships (Jameson et al., 2009).

Box 9.3   Advantages of Addressing Emotion in Conflict Management

In 2009 I led a study that asked the question: Are parties in a workplace conflict more likely to address emotion in a mediated as opposed to a negotiated conflict? (Jameson et al., 2009). We also examined whether parties were more satisfied with the outcome of the conflict, and we analyzed the written agreements parties crafted at the end of their mediation or negotiation session. While this study was an experiment in which undergraduate and graduate students enrolled in communication courses were role-playing a workplace conflict scenario, experienced mediators were the third parties in the mediation condition. A survey of participants before and after the conflict simulation supported our hypothesis that emotion was more likely to be addressed in mediated rather than negotiated conflict. In addition, surveys revealed that parties reported more positive than negative emotion and improved perception of the other following the mediated simulations.

Parties in the negotiation condition reported increased negative affect, and there was no difference in their perception of the other following the simulation. This study provided some evidence that parties in a workplace conflict are more likely to talk about emotions when there is a third-party mediator.

The analysis of the resulting agreements indicated that parties were more likely to directly address their relationship in the mediated agreements. Sample mediation agreements included the following statements:

"Pat and Chris agree to respect each other's personal difficulties during this transition."

"Pat and Chris agree to meet for lunch every week and hope that they can develop a more social relationship to support their work together."
"Chris and Pat agreed that they understand they were both living difficult personal lives and they were not aware before."

Negotiated agreements, on the other hand, were more likely to emphasize specific behaviors that the parties would enact; they focused on the work tasks rather than the relationship, such as:

"Pat will help Chris with assignments in return for Chris's mentorship."
"Pat will not go to Chris with additional questions and Chris will give Pat a positive evaluation."

We concluded that conflict management that included a third-party mediator was more likely to focus on feelings, restore or manage relationships, and lead to the possibility of conflict transformation, whereas when parties were left to negotiate conflicts on their own, they emphasized reciprocal agreements or what each could do for the other. However, one interesting and unexpected finding was that participants in the negotiation condition reported greater *satisfaction with the outcome* than those in the mediation condition. We speculate that this is related to the stigma attached to getting third-party help in a Western culture that privileges independence, as well as the preference for managing problems on one's own rather than seeking assistance (see Jameson, 1999, 2001). This underscores the importance of having an organizational culture that values relationships and institutionalizes interest-based approaches to conflict management, consistent with promoting a forgiveness climate as described elsewhere in this chapter (Fehr & Gelfand, 2012). A focus on relationships – and both building and maintaining rapport – will help build a culture of prosocial response to conflict that supports collaborative conflict management.

For Reflection and Discussion:

Discuss with a partner or small group.

1) Consider a conflict you have had (or are currently having) with a classmate or colleague. What emotions are evoked when you reflect on this conflict? Have you spoken to the colleague about how you feel or asked them how they feel? What would prevent you from having this conversation? What would have to change to make this possible? Do you have the same concerns about talking about how you feel in conflicts with a friend, relational partner, or family member? (And yes, the answer might be different for each of these relationships!)

2) Are there differences in how you would approach emotion or relational concerns in conflict based on different places you have worked? Try to identify the characteristics of a workplace (or classroom) where you felt comfortable talking about emotions as compared to a workplace where you did not. Do these characteristics support Fehr and Gelfand's (2012) model of forgiveness climate? (You might also reflect on whether this organization has any of the characteristics described in Table 9.1.)

Table 9.1 Comparison of traditional and restorative organizations.

	Traditional	**Restorative**
Behavior governed by:	Rules and procedures	Relationships and context
Primary focus on:	Task accomplishment	Community solidarity
Good organizational members as:	Professional	Community citizen
Individuals as:	Independent	Interdependent
Manage conflict through:	Avoidance and hierarchy	Participation
Communication as:	Argumentative and task-focused	Dialogic and maintenance
Concerned with:	The working person	The whole person
Emotions viewed as:	Distraction	Valuable
Organization structured as:	Hierarchy	Democracy
Wrongdoing results in:	Consequences	Reparation and reintegration

Source: Paul, G. D., & Riforgiate, S. E. (2015) / Communication Institute for Online Scholarship, Inc.

Fehr and Gelfand's (2012) description of the forgiving organization and the case described in Box 9.3 provide some insight into what restorative justice might look like in an organization. Paul and Riforgiate (2015) illustrated the different characteristics of traditional organizations compared to those that embrace restorative justice (see Table 9.1).

Restorative characteristics promote an emphasis on people and relationships, not in opposition to tasks and effectiveness, but to create an environment that honors the "whole person" rather than seeing individuals only as instruments in the production of output. Restorative justice does not suggest that rules and procedures are unimportant, only that they should be in service to organizational members rather than the other way around. For example, if an organization prioritizes task accomplishment, this may promote a competitive climate in which employees are motivated to be *the most* productive or serve *the most* clients as opposed to being engaged organizational citizens who go out of their way to support their coworkers. Furthermore, an emphasis on efficiency or how much one can produce in a day may lead to sacrifices of quality, creativity, and innovation. A focus on task accomplishment similarly promotes conflict avoidance, because conflict is seen as an impediment to getting work done or as evidence that a person is problematic as opposed to being seen as a valuable trigger for collaborative problem solving (Paul & Riforgiate, 2015). Table 9.1 illustrates that the characteristics of organizations that embrace restorative justice are more likely to place an emphasis on promoting relationships, building rapport, and fostering collaborative conflict management.

However, restorative justice is not a panacea, and scholars have found challenges in implementing restorative justice practices due to our cultural and organizational emphasis on rights and legalistic frameworks (Paul, 2017). For example, organizations have many hiring and employment policies in place to protect employees and the organization, such as those that prohibit nepotism, sexual harassment, or discrimination based on ability, gender, race, sexual orientation, or other protected classes. These policies are important, yet as noted in Table 9.1, a focus on the traditional, legal issues puts the focus on identifying the wrongdoing and determining individual consequences, such as assigning appropriate punishment (examples include docking an employee's pay or requiring an employee to attend training). These traditional (rights-based) outcomes do not address the underlying relationships and often result in continued harm to the organization due to unresolved emotions, anger, and resentment. The need for and emphasis on legal protection thus makes it difficult to fully embrace restorative practices.

A paradox identified by Greg Paul (2017) is that of requiring restorative responses when conflict occurs. Interviews with teachers in a private school that emphasized the importance of relationships revealed a contradiction in that the employee handbook required employees to talk to each other before going to an administrator to help resolve a conflict. While the intent of the policy may have been to empower employees and encourage them to engage in dialogical practices that foster rapport and relationships, the paradox is in the hierarchical system that requires them to do so. Further, many employees do not have the communication or emotion regulation skills to engage in conflict constructively, which can result in conflict escalation that might have been prevented with the help of a skilled third party (such as a mediator). An organization that embraces a restorative justice model must therefore also model the desired behavior and provide appropriate training and support, such as described by Fehr and Gelfand (2012).

Chapter Summary

The goal of this chapter was to continue the discussion of the importance of building and maintaining rapport with coworkers through acknowledging our role and responsibility in conflict situations. One important way to take responsibility for our actions is to apologize for harm to another – whether intentional or accidental. The four-component model of apology (Bisel & Messersmith, 2012) was described as including (i) a *narrative account* of the offense that clearly acknowledges the infraction, (ii) an *explicit statement of regret*, (iii) *reassurance that it will not happen again*, and (iv) an *offer of reparations*. In order for an apology to facilitate rapport, coworkers must be willing to forgive the other. While there may be situational characteristics of the infraction that may make one more or less likely to forgive, organizational leaders can foster a forgiveness climate by emphasizing relationships and encouraging employees to feel and share relevant emotions to improve understanding and empathy. Four features of "forgiving organizations" described by Fehr and Gelfand (2012) include leaders who embrace servant leadership and show compassion for employees, model self-control and mindful responses, and embrace restorative justice. Specific practices that foster a forgiveness climate include offering employee support and well-being programs, providing mindfulness training, and building dispute system design based on restorative justice and interests as opposed to rights- and power-based orientations to conflict management. This brings us to the final section of the LEARN framework, nurturing relationships, which will go into greater depth about the design of conflict management systems that emphasize collaboration (Chapter 10) and how we increasingly nurture relationships and manage conflict through online communication (Chapter 11).

Activities

1) Read the following case of a conflict that emerged between Pat and Chris. As you read the case, choose one party and consider what emotions you would be feeling if you were in Chris or Pat's situation. After reading the case with this in mind, answer the questions that follow.

2) Work with a partner to role-play a conversation between Pat and Chris about their conflict. Pay attention to how the emotions each party is experiencing are impacting the conversation and whether discussing feelings comes naturally into the conversation. After the role-play, discuss how the conversation went and whether there were barriers to expressing emotion, taking responsibility, and/or apologizing.

Case for Activity: The Dependent Coworker*

Pat is a junior accountant who has become dependent on the senior accountant, Chris, for assistance in learning the new job. Chris was originally helpful but over time has become annoyed with a perception that Pat is overly dependent and a slow learner. Pat is facing an upcoming three-month review and is concerned about losing his or her job. The scenario describes various personal issues that have an impact on Pat and Chris but are unknown to the other party. For example, Pat is new to the area, a single parent, and has no support system to help with childcare. Chris has recently taken out a second mortgage so has financial concerns which are further driving her or his motivation to apply for and receive a promotion. These details supply additional cues to the participants about emotions they may be experiencing in this conflict, such as fear, frustration, and stress. Both Pat and Chris have a specific conflict they need to address: how they can each get their respective jobs done without harm to the other. Because they are in the same department and Chris may soon receive a promotion where she or he will more directly supervise Pat, it is important that they maintain a positive relationship while coming to an agreement about how to get their tasks completed.

*Note: This is the case used for the simulation in Jameson et al., 2009.

References

Aquino, K., Grover, S. L., Goldman, B., & Folger, R. (2003).When push doesn't come to shove: Interpersonal forgiveness in workplace relationships. *Journal of Management Inquiry, 12*: 209–216.

Bisel, R. S., & Messersmith, A. S. (2012). Organizational and supervisory apology effectiveness: Apology giving in work settings. *Business Communication Quarterly, 75*(4): 425–448.

Bisel, R. S., Messersmith, A. S., & Keyton, J. (2010). Understanding organizational culture and communication through a gyroscope metaphor. *Journal of Management Education, 34*: 342–366. https://doi.org/10.1177/1052562909340879.

Bodtker, A. B., & Jameson, J. K. (2001). Emotion in conflict formation and its transformation: Application to organizational conflict management. *The International Journal of Conflict Management, 12*(3): 259–275.

Cantrell, L. (2013/2014).The power of rapport: An analysis of the effects of interruptions and overlaps in casual conversation. *INNERVATE Leading Undergraduate Work in English, 6*: 74–85. Retrieved January 1, 2021, from https://www.nottingham.ac.uk/english/documents/innervate/13-14/06-lucy-cantrell-q33103-pp-74-85.pdf

Fehr, R., & Gelfand, M. J. (2012). The forgiving organization: A multilevel model of forgiveness at work. *Academy of Management Review, 37*: 664–688. https://doi.org/10.5465/amr.2010.0497.

Goodstein, J., & Aquino, K. (2010). And restorative justice for all: Redemption, forgiveness, and reintegration in organizations. *Journal of Organizational Behavior, 31*: 624–628. https://doi.org/10.1002/job.632.

Goodstein, J., & Butterfield, K. D. (2010). Extending the horizon of business ethics: Restorative justice and the aftermath of unethical behavior. *Business Ethics Quarterly, 20*(3): 453–480.

Hochschild, A. R. (2012). *The managed heart* (3rd ed.). Berkeley, CA: University of California Press.

Hollander E. P. (1958). Conformity, status, and idiosyncrasy credit. *Psychological Review, 65*(2): 117–127. https://doi.org/10.1037/h0042501.

Jameson, J. K. (1999). Toward a comprehensive model for the assessment and management of intraorganizational conflict. *International Journal of Conflict Management, 10*(3): 268–294.

Jameson, J. K. (2001). Employee perceptions of the availability and use of interests-, rights-, and power-based conflict management strategies. *Conflict Resolution Quarterly, 19*(2): 163–196.

Jameson, J. K., Bodtker, A. M., Porch, D., & Jordan, W. (2009). Exploring the role of emotion in conflict transformation. *Conflict Resolution Quarterly, 27*(2): 167–192.

Jameson, J. K., Sohan, D., & Hodge, J. (2014). Turning points and conflict transformation in mediation. *Negotiation Journal, 30*(2): 125–237.

Kanter St. Amour, L. (2021). The law of conformity – Conflict lessons from 2021. *Mediate.com*. Retrieved December 27, 2021, from https://www.mediate.com/the-law-of-conformity-conflict-lessons-from-2021/

Kidder, D. L. (2007). Restorative justice: Not "rights," but the right way to heal relationships at work. *International Journal of Conflict Management, 18*: 4–22.

Mroz, J. E., & Allen, J. A. (2019). To excuse or not to excuse: Effect of explanation type and provision on reactions to a workplace behavioral transgression. *Journal of Business and Psychology, 35*: 187–201.

Mulvey, K. L., Gönültaş, S., Herry, E., & Strelan, P. (2022). The role of theory of mind, group membership, and apology in intergroup forgiveness among children and adolescents. *Journal of Experimental Psychology: General, 151*(3): 613–627. https://doi.org/10.1037/xge0001094.

Park, I., & Duey, M. (2018). I'm sorry (to interrupt): The use of explicit apology in turn-taking. *Applied Linguistics Review, 11*: 377–401.

Paul, G. D. (2017). Paradoxes of restorative justice in the workplace. *Management Communication Quarterly, 31*(3): 380–408. https://doi.org/10.1177/0893318916681512.

Paul, G. D., & Putnam, L. L. (2017). Moral foundations of forgiving in the workplace. *Western Journal of Communication, 81*(1): 43–63. https://doi.org/10.1080/10570314.2016.1229499.

Paul, G. D., & Riforgiate, S. E. (2015). Putting on a happy face, "getting back to work," and "letting it go": Traditional and restorative justice understandings of emotions at work. *Electronic Journal of Communication, 25*(3/4).

Poitras, J. (2007). The paradox of accepting one's share of responsibility in mediation. *Negotiation Journal, 23*: 267–282.

Restorative Justice Exchange. (2023). Three core elements of restorative justice. Retrieved January 3, 2023, from https://restorativejustice.org/what-is-restorative-justice/three-core-elements-of-restorative-justice/

Sue, D. W., Capodilupo, C. M., Torino, G. C., Bucceri, J. M., Holder, A. M. B., Nadal, K. L., & Esquilin, M. (2007). Racial microaggressions in everyday life: Implications for clinical practice. *American Psychologist, 62*(4): 271–286. https://doi.org/10.1037/0003-066X.62.4.271.

Tannen, D. (1986). *That's not what I meant! How conversational style makes or breaks your relations with others.* New York: Morrow.

Thompson, B. S., & Audrey Korsgaard, M. (2019). Relational identification and forgiveness: Facilitating relationship resilience. *Journal of Business and Psychology, 34*: 153–167. https://doi.org/10.1007/s10869-018-9533-1.

Youngquist, J. (2009). The effect of interruptions and dyad gender combination on perceptions of interpersonal dominance. *Communication Studies, 60*(2): 147–163.

Unit Five

Nurture

10

Nurturing through Organizational Conflict Management Systems

Management is about arranging and telling. Leadership is about nurturing and enhancing.

Thomas J. Peters (Management and leadership author)

We have arrived at the last part of the LEARN framework, *Nurture*. Attention to nurturing is important because building *rapport* in relationships is necessary, but not sufficient, for maintaining and building a network that is grounded in trust and goodwill. In organizational settings, it is all too easy to fall back on routines that focus on task accomplishment, and if we only call on others when we need them for something, we are ignoring relational maintenance. I hesitate to use a gardening metaphor as I am famous for killing plants, but just as plants need to be watered or they will wither and die, relationships also need to be nourished and nurtured. This chapter will emphasize the role organizational leaders play in creating a nurturing workplace environment through the design, implementation, and institutionalization of conflict management systems to support employees and encourage collaborative engagement as opposed to conflict avoidance. Chapter 11 will examine the ways in which we nurture relationships in online environments, whether through email, social media, or other platforms that have become all the more relevant as our organizations are increasingly geographically dispersed and even more centrally located workplaces have embraced remote work in the wake of the COVID-19 pandemic.

The Emergence of Conflict Management System Design

During the industrial revolution in the early 1900s, a popular model of management was based on Frederick Taylor's book *Principles of Scientific Management* (1911). Taylor is mentioned in nearly all the organizational communication

Communication for Constructive Workplace Conflict, First Edition. Jessica Katz Jameson.
© 2023 John Wiley & Sons, Inc. Published 2023 by John Wiley & Sons, Inc.

textbooks due to his influence on management theory (see, for example, Mumby & Kuhn, 2019). One of the main principles he advocated was conducting time and motion studies to determine the *one best way* to complete a task. It was considered the role of management to learn the one best way and communicate these instructions to workers, who would then execute the tasks. Taylor also advocated paying workers by the "piece" (how many units they could produce in a day) so that they were paid for how much they performed rather than being paid by the hour. Taylor believed this would motivate workers to produce as much as possible, whereas paying by the hour would reinforce laziness. From a communication perspective, a criticism of Taylor's ideas is the treatment of humans as mere tools in a production machine. It is reported that Taylor went so far as to say that workers were there to do what they were told, and had no reason to "talk back" to their supervisors (Hounshell, 1988). This unidirectional model of communication from management to labor explains a lot about how union membership reached its peak in the mid-1950s, as workers needed advocates to fight for safe, fair working conditions (Mayer, 2009).

Importantly, around the same time that Taylor's ideas were popular, a different set of management principles was being offered by a less well-known consultant, Mary Parker Follett. Follett believed that managers should listen to workers and advocated for collaboration between management and employees. Follett encouraged managers to take a *power-with* rather than a power-*over* orientation (Mumby & Kuhn, 2019). A power-with approach suggests that rather than seeing communication as one-way, from supervisors to employees, there should be ongoing, collaborative interaction, which requires a workplace environment in which employees feel comfortable and safe sharing their work experiences with supervisors. Follett's ideas about workplace democracy were a bit ahead of their time and, as a woman, it is unlikely she was fully celebrated in her lifetime. Yet research developments from fields such as management and organizational psychology drew from Follett's ideas about workplace democracy as they emphasized human relations and human resource theories of management, which popularized the idea that employees respond well when they are paid attention to and asked for their opinions. Rather than seeing workers only in terms of how much they could produce, human resource management theories looked at the whole person, considering needs for esteem, belonging, and continuous personal growth (Mumby & Kuhn, 2019). Human resource management theory led to the development of management styles that encouraged employee participation, much like Follett had many years before. I share this brief (and selective) overview of management theory to underscore the point that, as times have changed and we have moved from a manufacturing to a service and information economy, organizational leaders have become more likely to balance concerns for output and production with the need to develop and nurture employee relationships.

As related to conflict, while Taylor's management style mandated that employees keep their concerns to themselves, management styles following the democratic ideas of Follett recognize that employees should express their concerns and bring conflicts to the surface for the best organizational outcomes. Yet despite how far management theory has come, today's employees still have difficulty engaging in conflict at work due to power differences and the fear of retaliation (as described in Chapter 4). This is why many organizations have invested in conflict management systems that make it safe and practical for employees to communicate their concerns and resolve differences. The subsequent section describes dispute system design research[1] and studies that outline conditions that support employee use of such systems.

Characteristics of Effective Conflict Management System Design

The goal of a conflict management system is to provide options to help organizational members resolve their conflicts at the lowest cost to the organization and the individual. The costs of conflict can be to finances, employee health and productivity, or relationships. The term dispute system design (DSD) was first coined by Ury, Brett, and Goldberg (1988), who studied and consulted with the coal mining industry to help manage a series of highly escalated power contests that resulted in adversarial relations between labor and management, including strikes and lockouts. The point of DSD is to bring alternative dispute resolution (ADR), sometimes called *appropriate* dispute resolution, to organizations. Ury et al.'s research revealed that organizations typically managed conflicts through a power-based orientation (a power struggle where those with the most power win or decide the conflict outcome), followed by a rights-based orientation, in which someone (or a panel of judges) examines the evidence and determines who is right or wrong, and, least often, through an interest-based orientation, a collaborative approach that considers the interests of all parties to develop a solution for mutual benefit. The high cost of power- and rights-based orientations may be obvious: these are both adversarial approaches that pit parties against each other and result in a conflict where there is a winner and a loser. As a result, one party is often dissatisfied and considers the outcome unfair. This can lead to reduced productivity and motivation, reduced organizational identification, and increased turnover. Another cost of rights-based

---

[1] While I often use the broader terminology of conflict management system, this body of research started with the term "dispute system design," and I use these terms interchangeably throughout this chapter.

approaches is that they take a long time, as parties must develop their case materials, present to a third party for review, and potentially go through a system of appeals that can include a legal case. Ury, Brett, and Goldberg therefore recommended that effective dispute systems be designed such that most conflicts are managed through interest-based processes (such as described by the ombuds in Box 10.1 on mediation), only resorting to rights- and power-orientations as a last resort or for those situations that demand them (such as human rights violations or emergencies where making a quick decision is paramount to safety).

Box 10.1   Conflict Management Systems in Education

You may be aware of examples of conflict management systems in your educational experience. For example, some K-12 schools have integrated peer mediation programs into the school. By training students as young as those in kindergarten basic principles of mediation – listening, asking questions to identify interests, and collaborative problem solving – peer mediation programs allow students to take conflicts with other students to a peer who helps them resolve the conflict without interference from teachers, administrators, or parents (Jones, 2004). At the college and university level, a variety of systems for student, faculty, or staff conflict may be available. For example, a common type of conflict in the university is between a student and instructor. While it is always the best first step to talk to the person you have a conflict with to see if there is a misunderstanding, a mistake, or a collaborative solution, this can present a challenge for the student because of the power difference and concerns that a complaint over a grade will harm the relationship with the instructor and result in a lower course grade. In the ideal situation, the instructor will have created a classroom environment that makes students feel safe to approach them with concerns, but that is not always the case.

For those situations when the student has approached the instructor and does not feel their complaint was adequately addressed, their college will most likely have a grievance process in place. This is a rights-based system that will likely start in the academic department, where a third party will look at the relevant information and make a decision regarding whether the instructor assigned a grade in accordance with what is stated in the syllabus and the written assignment. If the student remains unsatisfied with the decision, they have the right to appeal their grievance, and it will likely go to the college dean's office and can continue up to a formal grievance hearing in front of a university review panel if needed.

In order to provide more collaborative or interest-based options for students who have concerns about their interaction with instructors, some universities have an ombuds office (see Harrison & Morrill, 2004; Hopeck et al., 2014). The ombuds is someone who will listen to the student's concerns, keep the conversation anonymous, and provide advice on options the student has for moving forward. The ombuds may coach the student by role-playing a conversation with the instructor, suggesting that the student go to the department head, or recommending that they file a formal grievance. If the situation calls for it, an ombuds might even suggest that the student and the other party seek mediation. (This is probably most common when the conflict is with a classmate or roommate as opposed to an instructor). Some universities have created conflict management systems specifically for roommate conflicts, such as Temple University's Conflict Education Resource Team (CERT), which offers coaching, consultation, and mediation for students (see https://studentconduct. temple.edu/conflict-education-resource-team-cert for more information).

For Reflection and Discussion:

Discuss with a partner or small group.

1) Can you think of a time in your K-12 education when you had a conflict with a classmate or a teacher? How was it managed? Did your school have a peer mediation program and, if so, did you have any experience with it? Discuss why you might or might not use a peer mediation program if it existed.

2) Common conflicts among students and instructors at the university level are about the clarity of assignments or grading decisions. Reflect on a time when you had a disagreement with a college instructor and think about how you handled it. Did the rank of the instructor impact your decision (i.e., lecturer versus a professor with a PhD)? What other factors did you consider in determining how to manage the situation? Were there any third parties you could go to for assistance? Is there anything the university could have done to make the situation easier to manage?

Since Ury et al.'s groundbreaking work, many other scholars have investigated and described features of conflict management systems that are likely to be effective, used by organizational members, and perceived as fair. Based on Ury et al.'s work and that of others, Conbere (2001) describes the central principles of DSD: (i) conflict management should move from low- to high-cost options, (ii) employees should participate in the design process, (iii) there should be loopbacks to interest-based options, such as mediation, (iv) employees should be educated about conflict management and their options for addressing different types of conflicts, (5) there must be support from top management, including lack of retaliation, and (6) the system should be evaluated for continuous improvement.

Many public, or government, organizations have developed conflict management systems to protect employees from unfair practices and ensure organizational justice in situations when employee behavior must be addressed. The Office of State Human Resources of North Carolina provides one example of a grievance policy that follows the principles of DSD summarized by Conbere. According to their most recent policy (dated August 6, 2020), the objectives of the employee grievance policy are to "provide procedural consistency across the agencies of North Carolina State government, Ensure employees have access to grievance procedures to address grievable issues timely, fairly, and without fear of reprisal, and Resolve workplace issues efficiently and effectively" (State Human Resource Manual, Employee Grievance Policy, p. 2). When an employee has a grievance, the employee starts by requesting an informal discussion. It is important to note that if the grievance involves a denial of hiring or promotion, discrimination, or harassment, it is managed by Equal Employment Opportunity staff. In other cases, the informal discussion would be with either the employee's direct supervisor or another appropriate party. If the employee is not satisfied with the outcome of the informal discussion, they begin the formal grievance process, which includes the following steps:

1) Mediation between the grievant and respondent with State approved mediators. Note that mediators have been trained by an external organization contracted by the State. Most mediators are state agency employees who volunteered (or were recommended) for mediation training. The value of this model is that mediators are simultaneously internal (in that they are familiar with many of the policies of State agencies) but also external, because they only mediate cases that are not internal to their own agency. If parties cannot come to agreement and want to pursue the grievance further, they move to the next step. It is important to note that many grievances stop at this step, even without a formal agreement, because the employee is satisfied in knowing that they were heard and listened to (Jameson et al., 2017). It is also important to the goal of efficiency that the mediation should be scheduled within 35 days of the grievance filing, and the process should never exceed 90 days.

2) A hearing with a hearing officer or grievance panel. A grievant also has the right to challenge the appointment of the hearing officer or panel if they believe that an officer involved in this process cannot be impartial. This process should also be completed within 35 days, never to exceed 90 days.

This DSD reflects the principles outlined by Conbere, such as moving from low-cost, interest-based options, before moving to a more costly, rights-based hearing. The process also allows for two interest-based options (informal discussion and mediation). There is a clear statement from leadership that the goal of the process is to "ensure employees have access to grievance procedures to address grievable issues timely, fairly, and without fear of reprisal," which shows the commitment to a lack of retaliation. The time limits imposed on each stage of the grievance process align with the objective of a timely and fair process. Finally, as part of a team that evaluated a previous version of the grievance process, I am aware that the NC Office of State Human Resources follows the principle of constant evaluation and improvement of the process (Jameson et al., 2017).

In addition to creating a conflict management system, organizational leaders must communicate the process to employees in ways that encourage them to use the system. Blancero and Dyer's (1996) research on the relationship between fairness ratings and dispute system characteristics found that credibility of the procedure is the main factor in predicting employee use. (This is consistent with the discussion of trust and rapport in Chapter 8.) Focus group participants described in earlier parts of this book made it clear that employees were more trusting of human resources staff when they were not perceived as close friends with management (see Chapters 4 and 5). Having an ombuds who is completely separate from the chain of command, peer mediators, and conflict coaching are all examples of DSD features that can increase credibility (Jones, 2016). Blancero and Dyer further found that ADR systems receive higher fairness ratings when managers display their willingness to abdicate power through allowing other parties (such as review panels or arbitrators) control over the final decision. One of the interesting features of the Unity Hospital dispute system (described in Chapter 4) was that the employee (grievant) had the choice about whether to retain attorney representation during the process. If the employee chose not to retain an attorney, the hospital agreed not to retain an attorney as well. This was an important symbolic gesture that communicated management's willingness to abdicate power to the employee and make a good faith effort to resolve the conflict collaboratively.

These findings are consistent with a plethora of studies comparing fairness perceptions in dispute procedures where disputants retain outcome control (such as mediation) to practices in which a third party makes the final decision (such as a manager or arbitrator). These studies have been unanimous in their finding that perceptions of fairness and procedural justice are higher when parties retain outcome control (Brett, Barsness, & Goldberg, 1996; Karambayya & Brett, 1989; Keashly & Newberry, 1995). It should be noted that there are circumstances under which employees are likely to perceive third-party decisions as fair. These include when the third party provides explanations (Conlon & Ross, 1997) and when the conflict involves a specific task over which a manager is perceived to have jurisdiction (Keashly & Newberry, 1995). Others have found that employees are more likely to approach a third party with a conflict or grievance if they believe the manager will consider their position (Gordon & Fryxell, 1993) or they feel they have influence over the final outcome (Shapiro, 1993). Fairness perceptions therefore depend on the reputation of the process, trust in third parties, and the specific interaction that occurs (Bies & Moag, 1986; Karambayya & Brett, 1989).

A final feature of effective conflict systems includes training in conflict management (Jones, 2016). While training alone is insufficient for adoption of more productive conflict management, several examples from the focus groups described in Chapters 4 and 5 suggested that when managers and human resources professionals have communication skills training, organizational members are more likely to seek them out. At Unity Hospital (described in Chapter 4), we found that employees with managers who had participated in mediation and arbitration training were more likely to be aware that mediation was an option. I also found evidence that those managers who had been through the training handled conflict more effectively. This is consistent with other research that has found that participating in mediation may lead to improved future conflict management behavior (Burrell, Zirbel, & Allen, 2003; Nabatchi, Bingham, & Moon, 2010). Perhaps most importantly, employees are more likely to have positive experiences when third parties are trained in conflict management, and this will help the organization institutionalize conflict management practices by constructing a culture that encourages coworkers to seek third-party assistance.

Specific Conflict Management System Practices

There are many questions that organizational leaders must consider when deciding what specific processes and practices are available to support conflict management. There should be a sense of the big picture, such as the organization's culture and existing practices, so that the employees will be comfortable and see the processes as congruent with prevailing norms. Jones (2016) describes three guiding questions for conflict management system designers as: What is the goal of the conflict management system? Whose interests is the system designed to protect? and Who defines success of the system? The specific conflict management options available may be different if the primary goal is to prevent litigation versus to create a collaborative culture. In the former case, a popular approach is to have new employees sign an agreement that any employment issues will go to arbitration rather than be taken to court. While this may protect the organization from litigation, it creates an adversarial relationship between management and employees. It also suggests the answer to the second question is that the system is intended to protect the interests of the organization over those of the employee, and success of the conflict management system is likely defined as reduced litigation. If the goal is to create a more collaborative workplace environment, conflict management options should include more confidential third-party options and interest-based processes such as coaching or mediation. This approach suggests that the system is designed to protect *all* parties' interests and conflict management system success will be measured by a reduced number of grievances filed as well as the number of mediated agreements reached, higher employee satisfaction, and increased organizational commitment (often measured by decreased employee turnover).

In the case of Unity Hospital, the goal of their conflict management system design process was to increase the fairness of conflict management processes and protect all parties' interests. They described this in the language that introduced the new grievance and appeals policy:

> All employees have the right to participate in dispute resolution free from interference, coercion, restraint, discrimination, or reprisal. The [Unity] System is committed to fair and equitable treatment of its employees as embodied in The [Unity] Way. When concerns or problems arise, employees and their supervisors are strongly encouraged to resolve them by informal means such as mediation, compromise, and good faith. Talk over any workplace concerns, disagreements, or grievances with your supervisor. When possible, resolve work-related problems at the most immediate and effective level of authority. To assist you, [Unity] has established policies and procedures for fair, orderly, and prompt resolution of work-related problems.

While our initial assessment suggested that employees approached the new system with some suspicion, Unity Hospital's process of conflict management system design followed the principles of effective DSD and incorporated many important features that had the potential to improve employee relations over time. Importantly, long-term success requires ongoing commitment to, and nurturing of, the dispute system.

An example of a conflict management system that has received a lot of scholarly attention is the REDRESS program developed by the United States Postal Service (Bingham, 2012; Bingham & Pitts, 2002; Nabatchi et al., 2010). REDRESS stands for Resolve Employment Disputes, Reach Equitable Solutions Swiftly, and the program was developed in response to a class action lawsuit involving claims of racial discrimination. The program was specifically developed to manage equal employment opportunity (EEO) disputes, and, after a pilot test in 1994, the program was implemented nationally by 1999. An important design feature of the REDRESS conflict management program is that it not only integrated mediation into the organization, it was specifically based on transformative mediation which, as described in Chapter 6, is an approach that emphasizes relationships among the employees in conflict (Bush & Folger, 1994, 2005). Some of the specifics of the program's design illustrated concerns for employee interests and perceptions of organizational justice, including making mediation optional for the grievant but mandatory for the respondent; allowing parties to bring any representative they choose to the mediation; holding mediation during work hours; and the promise of confidentiality and timeliness (Bingham & Pitts, 2002). All these features are consistent with the best practices of DSD described above.

The decision to use mediators trained in transformative mediation is especially relevant to this chapter on the importance of nurturing relationships for organizations who wish to construct a collaborative conflict management environment. Remember that the goal of transformative mediation is not settlement (having the parties come to agreement) but, rather, to provide parties opportunities for empowerment and recognition (Bush & Folger, 1994, 2005). In one study evaluating the REDRESS program, Bingham and Pitts (2002) found that participants were highly satisfied with the process and perceived it as fair. The authors also provided evidence that the REDRESS program reduced the number of formal EEO complaints, further demonstrating that participants were satisfied by the process and did not take the grievance process any further. In addition to satisfaction and perceived fairness of the conflict management process, Nabatchi et al. (2010) also examined *interpersonal justice*, which is whether the mediating parties perceive they were treated fairly by the co-disputant. When comparing transformative mediation to a more traditional facilitative style, their study found that the transformative style was more likely to lead to perceptions of disputant–disputant interpersonal justice, which is an important outcome of mediation when the goal is to create an employee culture that includes nurturing and collaboration.

As discussed in Chapter 9, while many scholars are thinking and writing about the potential for restorative justice in the workplace, these ideas are still working their way into organizational conflict management systems. The most promising examples can be found in education, and I conclude this presentation of dispute system examples with an illustration of a restorative justice program at North Carolina State University called the Bias Impact Response Team, or BIRT.

As has been discussed throughout this book, interpersonal conflicts in the workplace may stem from cultural differences, and there are often differences in expectations about what is considered acceptable, respectful communication. In some cases this is relatively benign interaction that is corrected through feedback and informal negotiation (for example, coworkers learn through interaction whether topics of communication are limited to work or they also talk about their social lives; these interactions determine whether a friendship develops). In other cases, organizational members may offend others by engaging in microaggressions (see Chapter 6; Sue et al., 2007) or explicitly biased communication. Going away to college may be the first time that students have interacted with people who are different from themselves and the people in the communities where they grew up, and this is the perfect place to learn to reduce bias and gain skills in intercultural competence. The Bias Impact Response Team is situated in the Office for Institutional Equity and Diversity (OIED), and its goal is to "invite students, faculty, and staff to lean into restorative approaches and practices to build transformative communities of practice that are equipped to identify, name, interrogate, and repair the harm caused by implicit and explicit bias" (Adrienne M. B. Davis, quoted by OIED staff, 2019). In other words, when a student, staff, or faculty member communicates or acts in a way that has a negative impact on another, the BIRT program provides an opportunity for the offender to learn the impact of what they did, gain empathy (by acknowledging others' feelings, thoughts, or values), and repair the relationship. This is in contrast to other disciplinary responses to harmful communication which tend to shame and punish the offender and increase, rather than decrease, the distance between themselves and others. The benefits of restorative justice for the person who was harmed include being heard, feeling a sense of wholeness through closure with the other person and, when possible, having the relationship restored. As noted by the research on relational resilience (Thompson & Audrey Korsgaard, 2019), it is possible that having the opportunity to talk about hurtful interaction and come to apology and forgiveness will actually strengthen a relationship in the long run, and this has obvious benefits for students who must learn how to interact with future diverse coworkers, as well as faculty and staff who will likely work together for many years.

The process of working with the Bias Impact Response Team begins with submitting a bias impact report. This is available online and can be submitted anonymously. The person who submits the report is encouraged to share contact information so that a trained coordinator can follow up and determine the most appropriate response given the incident that occurred and the impact it caused. Bias impact is defined as "any physical, psychological, and/or emotional response to bias-related events, incidents, interactions, or practices" (OIED, 2019). When the bias impact response team member speaks to the person who was harmed, they will talk to them about what they need or hope to gain from the process. It may be that they want their feelings acknowledged, to increase the other's awareness of the impact of their words or actions, or to advocate for institutional change. In other cases the victim may want to hold the other party accountable and have a facilitated conversation with the offender. Importantly, the person who was impacted has a place to go where their concerns can be heard in a safe environment where they are protected from future harm. While this is similar to the ombuds model described in Box 10.1, bias incidents require a specific type of training that not all ombuds may have. The fact that NC State University has an ombuds for faculty and staff, a separate ombuds for students, the Bias Impact Response Team, and a mediation program for employees is an example of a multipronged approach to conflict management that includes a variety of resources for organizational members who may experience different types of conflict.

Low-Cost Conflict Management Practices

While the preceding discussion has described comprehensive conflict management systems that require resources including financial costs, time, and additional training or third parties, there are other conflict management practices that
can be intentionally integrated as a natural or routine part of organizational procedures. One example I have heard in my research is the integration of a monthly
debrief into staff meetings. One organization used this existing process to encourage staff members to speak up about problems they were experiencing and collaboratively develop solutions. This enabled staff members to take ownership of
concerns and address them proactively before conflicts escalated. Importantly, a
process like this only works when the staff are confident that others are open to
constructive criticism, no one feels like they are being attacked, and people state
their observations without placing blame.

In my research in an anesthesia department (described in Chapter 6), I witnessed an interesting variation of this process in what they called their weekly
clinic. This is a regularly scheduled meeting including all anesthesia providers
(doctors and nurses) during which they discuss a particularly challenging case
someone experienced that week. The purpose is not for the people involved to be
blamed or placed in the proverbial hot seat, but for everyone to learn from the
situation to prevent future harm. These two examples, the monthly staff meeting
and weekly medical clinic, illustrate how organizations can construct a norm of
engaging difficult issues that need to be addressed while showing care and concern for the parties involved and nurturing healthy relationships. The bottom line
is that there are a variety of ways that organizations can put processes in place to
make it easier for employees to share their concerns and get them addressed.
What we know for certain is that if organizational leaders do not talk about conflict and do not provide any resources, conflict will often be avoided, and this will
have negative implications for employees, managers, and the organization as
a whole.

Chapter Summary

The goal of Chapter 10 was to begin the discussion of the N in the LEARN
framework, *Nurture*, by demonstrating how organizational leaders can create
conflict management systems to encourage employees to constructively engage,
rather than avoid, conflict. Such systems will nurture employees and relationships
with coworkers as well as between employees and management. Applied scholarship on DSD has proposed several principles to support organizational leaders
looking to create conflict management practices that best meet the needs of their

employees. These principles include: (i) moving from low- to high-cost options, (ii) including employee participation in the design process, (iii) providing loop-backs to interest-based options, (iv) educating employees about conflict management options, (v) providing top management support and zero tolerance for retaliation, and (vi) evaluating the system for continuous improvement (Conbere, 2001). Examples of conflict management systems in a hospital setting, educational settings, state government, and the US postal service were used to illustrate the design of conflict management systems based on an organization's core values and the culture they wish to create and reinforce. Conflict management systems, also referred to as "dispute resolution systems" or "grievance procedures," typically start with interest-based approaches, either encouraging parties to work together informally or providing an ombuds who can help individuals consider their options as well as practice their conflict communication. More formal interest-based practices include mediation and restorative justice, where the goals are to encourage parties in conflict to learn more about each other, gain empathy and give recognition, accept responsibility, and work toward a collaborative agreement whenever possible. When interest-based approaches are unsuccessful, rights-based processes such as hearing panels or review boards are often a second (or third) step in trying to resolve organizational conflicts when someone has violated an expectation, policy, or law. Power-based options for managing conflict should be reserved for situations in which time or safety are paramount and a quick decision must be made, such as in a crisis. However, even when rights- and power-based strategies are needed, it is suggested that there are "loopbacks" to interest-based processes to nurture the relationship among parties in the conflict by increasing understanding, empathy, and a sense of organizational justice. Institutionalizing a conflict management system that provides options that match the needs of organizational members and the variety of conflicts that occur in the workplace sends a strong message that the organization values people and relationships and provides the resources to nurture them and promote a collaborative environment.

Activity

Work independently or with a group to design a conflict management process for a specific organization. Consider the following questions, adapted from those suggested by Tricia Jones (2016):

1) What are the goals of the conflict management system? What values are central to the organization that you want to convey through the design and options provided? (For example, is the primary goal: Cost savings? Preventing litigation? Promoting dialogue and collaboration?)

2) Who is the primary audience for the conflict management system? Are you focusing on certain types of employees or organizational members (such as managers and line staff) or conflict with external stakeholders (such as vendors, customers, or clients)? Consider who your audience members would be most comfortable going to for conflict management support and how you could provide incentives for them to use the conflict management system. What obstacles might get in the way and how can you reduce those barriers to adoption of the conflict management system?

3) What is the structure of your organization and how might you suggest conflict management options and procedures that are aligned with the existing structure? (For example, if employees work in teams, you might provide team facilitation options or a place team members can go to seek advice on how to manage conflicts within a team or between teams).

4) What resources are available to support the system? Can you appoint someone internal to the role of ombuds or coach, or can you hire someone to fill this role? Can you integrate conflict management and/or mediation training into leadership development or other employee training practices? (If organizational leaders say there are no resources, consider the costs of doing nothing in terms of employee morale, productivity, retention, and turnover.)

5) How will you know the conflict management system is successful? Consider here how you would evaluate whether the system was achieving your goals (defined in question 1). What metrics would you use to measure whether it is working or you need to revise the system?

References

Bies, R. J., & Moag, J. S. (1986). Interactional communication criteria of fairness. In R. J. Lewicki, B. H. Sheppard, & M. H. Bazerman (Eds.), *Research on negotiation in organizations, Vol. 1* (pp. 7–23). Greenwich, CT: JAI Press.

Bingham, L. B. (2012). Transformative mediation at the United States Postal Service. *Negotiation and Conflict Management Research*, 5: 354–366. https://doi.org/10.1111/j.1750-4716.2012.00112.x.

Bingham, L. B., & Pitts, D. W. (2002). Highlights of mediation at work: Studies of the national REDRESS® evaluation project. *Negotiation Journal, 18*: 135–146. https://doi.org/10.1111/j.1571-9979.2002.tb00256.x.

Blancero, D. & Dyer, L. (1996). Due process for non-union employees: The influence of system characteristics on fairness perceptions. *Human Resource Management, 35*(3): 343–359.

Brett, J. M., Barsness, Z. I., & Goldberg, S. B. (1996). The effectiveness of mediation: An independent analysis of cases handled by four major service providers. *Negotiation Journal, 12*(3): 259–269.

Burrell, N. A., Zirbel, C. S., & Allen, M. (2003). Evaluating peer mediation outcomes in educational settings: A meta-analytic review. *Conflict Resolution Quarterly, 21*: 7–26. https://doi.org/10.1002/crq.46.

Bush, R. A. B., & Folger, J. P. (1994). *The promise of mediation: Responding to conflict through empowerment and recognition.* San Francisco, CA: Jossey-Bass.

Bush, R. A. B., & Folger, J. P. (2005). *The promise of mediation: The transformative approach to conflict.* San Francisco, CA: Jossey-Bass.

Conbere, J. P. (2001). Theory building for conflict management system design. *Conflict Resolution Quarterly, 19*(2): 215–236.

Conlon, D. E., & Ross, W. H. (1997). Appearances do count: The effects of outcomes and explanations on disputant fairness judgments and supervisory evaluations. *The International Journal of Conflict Management, 8*(1): 5–31.

Gordon, M. E., & Fryxell, G. E. (1993). The role of interpersonal justice in organizational grievance systems. In R. Cropanzano (Ed.), *Justice in the workplace: Approaching fairness in human resource management* (pp. 231–255). Hillsdale, NJ: Lawrence Erlbaum.

Harrison, T. R., & Morrill, C. (2004). Ombuds processes and disputant reconciliation. *Journal of Applied Communication Research, 32*: 318–342.

Hopeck, P., Desrayaud, N., Harrison, T. R., & Hatten, K. (2014). Deciding to use organizational grievance processes: Does conflict style matter? *Management Communication Quarterly, 28*(4): 561–584.

Hounshell, D. A. (1988, November). The same old principles in the new manufacturing. *Harvard Business Review.* Retrieved January 30, 2021, from https://hbr.org/1988/11/the-same-old-principles-in-the-new-manufacturing

Jameson, J. K., Berry-James, R. M., Daley, D. M., & Coggburn, J. D. (2017). Effectiveness of mediation in the state agency grievance process. In A. Georgakopoulos (Ed.), *The handbook of mediation: Theory, research and practice* (pp. 164–169). London: Routledge.

Jones, T. S. (2004). Conflict resolution education: The field, the findings, and the future. *Conflict Resolution Quarterly, 22*: 233–267. https://doi.org/10.1002/crq.100.

Jones, T. S. (2016). Mediation and conflict coaching in organizational dispute systems. In K. Bollen, M. Euwema, & L. Munduate (Eds.), *Advancing workplace mediation through integration of theory and practice, industrial relations & conflict management, Vol. 3* (pp. 89–110). Cham, Switzerland: Springer International. https://link.springer.com/chapter/10.1007/978-3-319-42842-0_6.

Karambayya, R., & Brett, J. M. (1989). Managers handling disputes: Third-party roles and perceptions of fairness. *Academy of Management Journal, 32*(4): 687–704.

Keashly, L., & Newberry, J. (1995). Preference for and fairness of intervention: Influence of third-party control, third-party status and conflict setting. *Journal of Social and Personal Relationships, 12*(2): 277–293.

Mayer, B. (2009). Cross-movement coalition formation: Bridging the labor-environment divide. *Sociological Inquiry, 79*(2): 219–239. https://doi.org/10.1111/j.1475-682X.2009.00286.x.

Mumby, D. H., & Kuhn, T. R. (2019). *Organizational Communication: A Critical Introduction* (2nd ed.). Thousand Oaks, CA: Sage.

Nabatchi, T., Bingham, L. B., & Moon, Y. (2010). Evaluating transformative practice in the U.S. Postal Service REDRESS program. *Conflict Resolution Quarterly, 27*(3): 257–289. https://doi.org/10.1002/crq.259.

North Carolina State Human Resource Manual, Employee Grievance Policy. (2020). Retrieved March 16, 2022, from https://oshr.nc.gov/policies/discipline-appeals-grievances/employee-grievance-policy

OIED Staff. (2019, March 8). Restorative bias impact response: Answers you didn't know you needed. NC State's *Diversity Digest*. Retrieved March 16, 2022, from https://diversity.ncsu.edu/news/2019/03/08/restorative-bias-impact-response-answers-you-didnt-know-you-needed/

Shapiro, D. L. (1993). Reconciling theoretical differences among procedural justice researchers by re-evaluating what it means to have one's views "considered": Implications for third-party managers. In R. Cropanzano (Ed.), *Justice in the workplace: Approaching fairness in human resource management* (pp. 51–78). Hillsdale, NJ: Lawrence Erlbaum.

Sue, D. W., Capodilupo, C. M., Torino, G. C., Bucceri, J. M., Holder, A. M. B., Nadal, K. L., & Esquilin, M. (2007). Racial microaggressions in everyday life: Implications for clinical practice. *American Psychologist, 62*(4): 271–286. https://doi.org/10.1037/0003-066X.62.4.271.

Taylor, F. W. (1911). *The principles of scientific management*. New York: Harper and Brothers.

Thompson, B. S., & Audrey Korsgaard, M. (2019). Relational identification and forgiveness: Facilitating relationship resilience. *Journal of Business and Psychology, 34*: 153–167. https://doi.org/10.1007/s10869-018-9533-1.

Ury, W. L., Brett, J. M., & Goldberg, S. B. (1988). *Getting disputes resolved*. San Francisco, CA: Jossey-Bass.

11

Nurturing Relationships through Online Dispute Resolution, Information and Communication Technologies, and Social Media

However revolutionary it may be, the Internet still hasn't altered the basic law of human communication: Being nice to your interlocutors is a good way to start any negotiations, particularly, when being hostile is an open invitation for a cyber-fight.

Evgeny Morozov (writer and researcher)

No book on conflict management would be complete without specific attention to the myriad ways that conflict communication happens in online spaces. When we think about online conflict, it is easy to imagine highly polarized communication and "cyber-wars," as alluded to in the opening quote from Evgeny Morozov. Indeed, I have researched and written about some of the hate speech that occurs when Internet users seek out forums with like-minded others, reinforcing beliefs that can spiral into escalated, intractable conflict and hate for those labeled as "other" or out-group (Harel, Jameson, & Maoz, 2020). However, as Banschick and Banschick have noted, "[T]he Internet functions as an amplifier: It increases our potential for good and productive work as well as for inappropriate and immoral endeavors . . . Ultimately, a technology is only as useful as the intentions of its users" (2003, p. 161). Hence, this chapter emphasizes the use of communication technology and the Internet for nurturing relationships and describes how individuals, groups, and organizations can use all the lessons from the LEARN framework so that online communication practices mirror, and even transcend, our face-to-face efforts to construct productive and collaborative workplace environments.

The emphasis of this chapter is on the N of the LEARN framework, *Nurture*. There are a wide variety of ways that organizational members use technology to communicate, and these technologies have different *affordances* that may assist with – or create challenges to – nurturing relationships, conflict, and conflict management. The theory of affordances, originally attributed to ecological psychologist James Gibson (1986), describes the relationship between the properties of an object and how individuals may use the object in different ways or contexts. The theory has been adapted to communication technology, and scholars such as Treem and Leonardi (2012) describe the media affordance as constructed by the relationship between the features of the medium and the user's interpretation of how it can be used to meet their needs. In other words, users can consider the affordances offered by different technologies in order to select the most suitable medium for a given interaction or communication goal. For example, email has been described as having several affordances that support cooperation, including *revision*, which allows the user to rewrite many times; *reviewability*, providing time to reflect on word choices before sending; *exchange*, email can be used to send information and solicit a reply; and *inclusion*, information can be shared with many recipients at once (Bülow, Lee, & Panteli, 2019, p. 398). On the other hand, email has several limitations. The recipient(s) may misattribute the tone or intention of an email, may choose to delay or ignore an email, or may abdicate responsibility by forwarding an email to others. The asynchronous nature of email, therefore, has the potential to reduce efficiency and create opportunities for conflict and misunderstanding. Table 11.1 includes commonly used digital media, their affordances, and advantages and limitations for nurturing relationships, collaboration, and conflict management.

Table 11.1 Digital media affordances: advantages and limitations for nurturing relationships, collaboration, and conflict management.

Digital Media	Affordances	Advantages	Limitations
email	Asynchronous • Connection • Editability • Exchange • Persistence	No time coordination required; reach many people at once; time to carefully craft message; can record and store information	Miscommunication, misunderstanding, potential for conflict or conflict escalation
Instant messenger	Synchronous • Connection • Exchange	Immediate response and coordination can increase efficiency	Recipient must be available and use the technology; generally limited to brief communication
Teleconference (Zoom/ Microsoft Teams)	Synchronous • Connection • Exchange • Persistence	Immediate feedback, clarification, answers to questions; reproduce face-to-face remotely (if necessary); can record and store	Requires time coordination; online format reduces number of nonverbal cues (i.e., corporeal and proximal)

Table 11.1 (Continued)

Digital Media	Affordances	Advantages	Limitations
Slack (and other collaboration platforms)	Synchronous or asynchronous • Connection • Editability • Exchange • Persistence	Task coordination, information storage and retrieval, ability to co-author/edit texts	Team members must agree to use the space and have training on its affordances/ capabilities
Google Docs (and other shared document platforms)	Synchronous or asynchronous • Editability • Exchange • Persistence	Information storage and retrieval, ability to co-author/edit and/or share texts	Requires training, and team members must agree to use the space; document retrieval can be challenging
Social media (Facebook, Instagram, Twitter, YouTube)	Asynchronous • Connection • Persistence	Excellent tool for connecting, nurturing, staying in touch; posts are permanent and can be referenced in future	Not immediate; different levels of user attention; potential for public disagreement and conflict escalation; persistence can have negative repercussions

Source: Adapted from Treem & Leonardi (2012).

This list demonstrates that online tools can range from fairly informal, such as instant messenger or email, to more formal venues such as integrating a teleconference into an online dispute resolution (ODR) system. In order to build on the discussion of conflict management systems in Chapter 10, this chapter continues by describing how formal ODR systems might be used, whether for Internet-based organizations (such as Amazon, eBay, or Squaretrade), or as an option for organizations with distributed employees and/or remote workers. With this as background, I then move to a discussion of how individuals and groups in organizations can use technology to nurture relationships, resolve conflict, and collaborate as well as how organizations as entities use technology to communicate with consumers and other external audiences (and vice versa). This final focus examines organizational communication from a more public perspective, considering how consumers use digital media to air grievances and hold organizations accountable and how organizational leaders use digital media to manage conflict and nurture relationships with consumers and the public.

Online Dispute Resolution (ODR)

In Chapter 10, I described how organizational leaders can create and institutionalize conflict management systems to help employees more easily engage in conflicts that happen at work. Having such a system in place sends the message that leaders want to create an organizational environment where employees feel safe expressing their concerns or dissent internally (recall the discussion of organizational dissent in Chapter 5). Offering multiple options for employees is likely to increase the perception of fairness and organizational justice by making it easier for employees to start the conflict management process. In today's world of e-commerce, an international workforce, and increased remote work, online options are necessary for connecting organizational members when face-to-face meetings are not practical. While many ODR processes have most of the same features as their face-to-face counterparts, such as e-mediation, the addition of the technology as the "fourth party" provides unique opportunities and challenges as the technology itself influences the process (Rifkin, 2010). New ODR platforms are constantly being developed as we learn how to use artificial intelligence to automate more parts of the process and develop the most optimal agreements most efficiently. Of course, these platforms also have their limitations. The remainder of this section summarizes some of the key principles of e-mediation and then describes emerging trends in the field of ODR.

E-mediation

While traditionally mediation is done face-to-face, there have long been mediation programs that use technology, including the telephone, when bringing parties together in person is not cost-effective or otherwise practical. As in an example of a successful Medicare mediation program in the state of North Carolina, telephone works well for mediations in which the primary goal is efficiency (resolving a large number of claims quickly) and parties are less concerned with nurturing their relationship. According to the Carolina Dispute Settlement Services website, the Medicare mediation program began in 2002, mediates over 8,000 cases per year, saved the state 26 million dollars in its first nine months of operation, and boasts a 90% success rate (see https://www.notrials.com/medicaid-mediation.html). Results such as this demonstrate that being co-located is not a prerequisite for a successful mediation.

Any organization that used mediation services was required to shift to e-mediation in 2020 when the workforce was forced to go remote during the COVID-19 pandemic. While at first this was met with skepticism – even from mediation trainers (see Hartmann-Piraudeau, 2022) – studies have demonstrated the effectiveness of e-mediation when certain principles are followed to optimize success (Parlamis, Ebner, & Mitchell, 2016). These principles include (i) establishing trust, (ii) making sure everyone is comfortable with the technology, (iii) keeping the parties together as much as possible, and (iv) being adaptable to new technologies and the needs of participants. Each of these are elaborated below.

Trust

The affordance of persistence, described above, means that it is easier for any member of an e-mediation to record and get a transcript of the session. While arguably any party could illegally record an in-person mediation, the fact that this is a feature of most teleconferencing platforms could make it more tempting. An agreement as to whether the mediation should be recorded would need to include all parties, as there must be confidence that anything divulged in mediation will not be used as evidence should the grievance move to a more adversarial step such as litigation. Another affordance that e-mediation allows is that each party can control their location and what is seen on camera. This means a party could have others in the room with them that the mediator and other party are unaware of. Mediation programs have different rules about who a party may be able to have with them during a mediation (for example, a lawyer, a family member, or friend). These rules must be clear and agreed upon by all parties, and there must be trust that no one is violating these rules in order for e-mediation to be successful.

Comfort with the Technology

Many of us had to learn how to use teleconferencing software very quickly in 2020 when teaching and many kinds of work were forced to move online. In that situation, teachers and students, for example, did not have time to get trained on the technology, and the results were quite challenging, as documented in many news reports and research studies (see for example, Greenan, 2022). Parties should be provided with instructions for logging on to the technology, including testing their video and microphone in advance. If feasible, organizations might even provide a space with technology ready-to-go for employees who do not have good broadband connection or video cameras in their homes. Mediators also need to be comfortable with the technology to create an atmosphere for collaboration. For example, mediators may use a caucus during mediation – a time when one party moves to a separate room or waiting area while the mediator speaks with the other party privately. In a teleconference, such as zoom, a mediator must know how to easily move one party into a waiting room to ensure the privacy of the other party. They must also make sure that the party is not left in the waiting room too long and that they are available to come back into the main mediation room when the mediator is ready. While the technology may provide the affordances to allow for all this, something as simple as a caucus can be more challenging when mediators do not have as much control over where the parties are located.

Keeping Parties Together

The affordances of teleconferencing (such as waiting or breakout rooms in Zoom, described above) may tempt mediators to act more like intermediaries who shuttle back and forth between parties with their offers or terms for agreement. This is especially likely in mediation settings where the parties are adversarial and/or reticent to share much information in the joint session. However, mediation is arguably the best third-party approach for managing conflict among coworkers because of the emphasis on coming to collaborative agreement, long-term relationship management, and fostering a collaborative organizational environment. Even when using e-mediation, mediators should work with parties jointly as much as possible to encourage listening, engaging, acknowledgment, and rapport, as described in other parts of the LEARN framework.

Adaptability to New Technologies and Disputant Needs

New digital communication tools and platforms are constantly being introduced to the marketplace, and this is equally true for conflict management software. While the telephone may be adequate for some kinds of disputes (such as the Medicare mediations described above), it does not have the affordance of the waiting room. Emerging, innovative ODR technologies use artificial intelligence to assist in negotiating the most optimal agreement, such as by conducting research to access information and answer questions to assist parties in coming to agreement more efficiently. Given the variety and potential complexity of conflicts (such as negotiating multi-million-dollar contracts or settlements), mediators should have an understanding of the various technological tools and their affordances to help parties take advantage of ODR systems that may be most useful for their needs. Again, such systems may be more useful for disputes where mediation is not the ideal third-party approach, as the next section briefly describes.

Artificial Intelligence and Automated ODR

Automated systems are part of our daily lives, from calling customer service ("press 1 for your account balance, press 2 for an appointment") to asking Alexa for the weather forecast. It makes sense to take advantage of the affordances of technology to make our lives easier and more efficient. Of course, we have all experienced frustration with automated systems, and sometimes we just yell into the phone to find us a human to talk to. This is an important point, because when we have a conflict, we want to get it resolved as painlessly as possible, and organizations designing ODR systems should take this into consideration so that the system designed to nurture relationships and manage conflict is not frustrating its users and escalating conflict instead. With that consideration, it is worth noting some of the important ways that technology has been or could be used to manage conflict online. John Zeleznikow (2022) has taken a user-centered approach to examine existing and potential systems to discuss how artificial intelligence could provide the most ideal support for ODR users (see Table 11.2).

If you engage in online or e-commerce, such as eBay, Amazon shopping, or PayPal, you can likely see the appeal of these automated ODR processes. For example, I recently decided to try one of the many pre-made meal programs that ship meals to your home. Due to some confusion, I ended up creating two separate accounts, and I needed to figure out how to solve the problem. I went to the customer service link on their website and interacted with an agent through the online text chat feature. While I cannot be certain whether I was communicating with a human or a bot, my complaint was understood and corrected within minutes (including a canceled order and a refund). I also received a clear explanation of why the error occurred and what I could do on my end to prevent future problems. This was a rather simple conflict, but the fact that I was able to resolve it online and after typical business hours left me feeling good about their customer service and enabled the company to keep me as a customer. E-commerce businesses such as eBay, PayPal, and Amazon are all examples of organizations that use one or more of the tools outlined above. It is worth noting that apps have been developed specifically to support ODR. Three noteworthy examples help explain the tools Zeleznikow describes and provide more insight to future trends in ODR: *Canada's Civil Resolution Tribunal*, *OurFamilyWizard*, and *Smartsettle*.

Table 11.2 Ideal features of intelligent ODR design.

Tool	Function
Case management	Collects user information, description of the dispute; suggests remedy
Triage	Assigns the dispute to appropriate person/venue (i.e., customer service, human resources, legal, Office for Equal Opportunity)
Communication	Allows the parties to communicate with each other and/or a third party. Chat (using human or chatbot), appointment scheduling, email, or video conference
Decision support	Provide proposals for optimal agreement
Advisory	Provide advice to one or both parties to reality test the agreement
Drafting	Draft the agreement for the parties

Source: Zeleznikow (2022) / De Gruyter.

Civil Resolution Tribunal (https://civilresolutionbc.ca/)

This ODR system is part of the legal system and allows users to manage conflicts such as car accidents, small claims, and property disputes on their own, saving money on legal fees. The user starts by providing information about themselves and their dispute (case management, triage), is asked questions to help them determine the desired outcome, and then is provided appropriate forms. The process includes a "solution-explorer" (decision support) as well as resources for reviewing past decisions (advisory). There is a space for conducting a negotiation, getting help from a facilitator, and even getting a decision from an independent tribunal member if parties cannot resolve the dispute on their own (communication/drafting). The website promotes the tribunal as a fair, impartial, and collaborative approach to conflict resolution.

OurFamilyWizard (https://www.ourfamilywizard.com/)

While family conflict is outside the scope of the workplace, it is worth mentioning this app because of unique features that may become more commonplace in the future. The app was created for separating couples who have children and must continue to co-parent, which is a challenging and ubiquitous form of conflict that can have a devastating impact on children. OurFamilyWizard provides a location for shared information such as doctor's appointments, visitation schedules, and after-school activities as well as financial information such as child support payments. While this is mainly a communication tool, it also allows for money transfers and other practical tasks and allows users to connect directly with other parties such as attorneys, child support services, and even grandparents to ensure that all parties share critical information.

Smartsettle (https://www.smartsettle.com/)

This is one example of an e-negotiation program that can be integrated into an organization's website. Like the Civil Resolution Tribunal described above, the program collects information and provides forms and templates for resolution, providing the decision support and advising tools described in Table 11.1. Smartsettle also provides facilitators if needed and drafts a possible agreement for disputants.

The purpose of this opening section about ODR was to illustrate the many ways organizations can enlist the help of technology to manage conflicts among employees and with customers and the public. These few examples provide a glimpse of what the future of automation and artificial intelligence will look like as advancements are made. There may be a lot of promise for collaborative conflict management here as long as organizations do not completely lose sight of the human element and the goal of maintaining and nurturing relationships during the process. The ensuing section addresses some of the main communication and information technology tools used in the workplace and shows how choices about how we use them serve to either escalate conflict or nurture relationships.

Information and Communication Technologies

Communication technology has been a ubiquitous part of organizational life at least since the 1990s, and the number of digital media platforms and tools has multiplied 100-fold since then. Despite the wide variety of options for communicating with others remotely, email appears to remain the most common form of workplace communication (Bülow et al., 2019). Of course, this depends on the nature of one's work, access to technology, and the organizational norms or culture, and I should acknowledge that there are many types of labor in which daily communication is primarily or exclusively face-to-face (construction, retail, maintenance, landscaping, farming, just to name a few). Yet even in face-to-face dominated work environments, technology is used to share schedules, manage hourly work, order supplies, and perform other important tasks. The point I focus on here is that the decisions we make about which media to use to communicate should consider the message content, the communication goal, workplace norms, the context of the relationship, and the target's preferences.

Media Richness Theory

As highlighted in Table 11.1, we have several choices for communicating with coworkers in order to accomplish daily tasks and workplace goals. One way to choose the most optimal medium for a given communication is based on media richness theory (Daft & Lengel, 1984, 1986). Differences in media richness are based on the number of cues made available and the potential for immediate feedback (Daft & Lengel, 1986). For example, face-to-face communication is highest in *media richness*, because it allows for a variety of verbal and nonverbal cues to help the receiver interpret the message being communicated (i.e., facial cues, hand gestures, body language, tone of voice). Simultaneously, receivers can use verbal and nonverbal cues to send immediate feedback to indicate they understand or do not understand the message (this may be indirect, through a look of confusion, or by asking a direct question). This is in contrast with a medium low in richness, such as email, which includes fewer cues and does not allow for immediate feedback. Figure 11.1 presents a comparison of communication media in terms of their richness based on original theorizing of Daft and Lengel and more current research applying media richness theory to social media (Kaplan & Haenlein, 2010).

While research testing media richness theory over the years has found mixed results regarding the efficiency and perceived productivity of various media

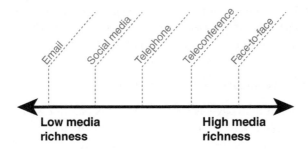

Figure 11.1 Communication media richness (adapted from Daft & Lengel, 1984; Kaplan & Haenlein, 2010).

choices (Moghavvemi, 2014), when considering the potential for conflict, the more ambiguous or complex a message is, the richer the medium that should be used. And, given that the topic of this chapter is about nurturing relationships, it is relevant that richer media may be more important for relational development. Having said that, organizations and relationships are unique, so there are other variables to consider. For example, imagine that you are writing a report that is due tomorrow, and there is information you need from a coworker to complete the project. Assuming you and your coworker work in the same building, do you (i) walk to their office, (ii) call on the phone, (iii) send an instant message, (iv) send a text, or (v) send an email? I'm sure you are thinking "it depends." How far away is the coworker's workstation or office? How urgently do I need the information? How easy is it for me to explain what I need? Is this request going to be warmly received or will it be seen as an imposition? Another way to consider that last question is: how face-threatening is this request? As discussed in Chapter 6, our communication choices are often influenced by the desire to save face for self or others. Recall the idea of politeness theory (Brown & Levinson, 1987), which states that we use politeness strategies to protect our own need for autonomy and to minimize the imposition on others. By selecting email, an unobtrusive (asynchronous) mode of communication, we allow the recipient to choose when they will read their email and how quickly they respond to our request. In contrast to going to their office or calling, which may send an implicit message that we are making demands on our coworker's time, email allows us to protect our own as well as our coworker's face.

This brief example demonstrates why we often rely on email even when there are far more efficient ways to get the information we need to get our work done. Other predictors of which media we choose include the organizational culture or norms. In organizations where workers are typically at their computer and there is an expectation of turning on a public notification when one is "away," sending an instant message may be the more efficient and acceptable way to ask for the information you need. If the coworker is someone you have a good relationship with, you may call or even send a text message. Again, this decision will largely depend on the norms and, importantly, your knowledge of the coworker's habits and preferences. At my university, for example, administrators often use Google Chat if they need a quick question answered. (They may use the phone, although I have noticed that my telephone almost never rings in the workplace, and I expect this is true for many organizations.) Since faculty do not keep traditional nine-to-five hours, an instant messaging service might not reach them, so email is the norm. Yet in situations where efficiency is needed and the request is complicated, I may call or text someone, depending on my relationship with them and my knowledge of their media use.

You may be thinking that this all seems terribly obvious, but it is important because I have observed an over-reliance on email that was exacerbated during the lockdown period of COVID-19, which sent faculty and students home and working remotely in the United States from approximately March of 2020 through August of 2021.[1] Remote work required us to forego face-to-face channels, and many of us began doing all our work through Zoom (or other video teleconference) meetings and email. As my ability to manage the level of email correspondence waned, I rediscovered the value of the telephone. Calling a coworker rather than sending email had a variety of benefits: I was able to reach them quickly (or leave a message or text), I was able to explain what I needed and why, and, in a critically important side benefit, I was able to connect with faculty or staff that I was not routinely seeing in the hallway. In the pursuit of getting our work done, we often overlook the importance of corridor conversations (Long, Iedema, & Lee, 2007) and casual collisions (Morgan, 2017), which not only allow us to connect with our coworkers socially (building trust and rapport; see Chapter 8), but also spark spontaneous conversations, information sharing, and new ideas (Methot et al., 2021). As more and more work is done in remote settings, a main point here is that we should be using a multitude of media channels to communicate with our coworkers in order to connect, share information, and coordinate our activities.

At the risk of belaboring the point, it is important to note there are times when email is the best, and possibly the only, choice, such as in the case of global organizations where employees are distributed and distanced by time, space, and language. One study of email use in international organizations found that two reasons employees relied heavily on email included the desire for self-presentation and relationship maintenance (Bülow et al., 2019). For example, one interviewee in this

---

[1] Some campuses and workplaces started and ended their mandated remote work policies based on state or federal guidelines and requirements or other health regulations depending on the nature of the work.

study described that they did not have high confidence in their knowledge of the dominant language used in the organization, and the affordances of asynchronicity and editability of email allowed the employee to carefully construct the message and ensure the language was used correctly. In a second example, an interviewee described the preference for email in a situation where there was already conflict with a coworker and this employee believed they might lose their temper if they engaged in a synchronous conversation (Bülow et al., 2019). Again we see that face saving and nurturing relationships are important factors in determining our choice of media for workplace communication. Despite its many benefits, a more in-depth look at some of the potential limitations of email and other asynchronous or lean media due to the potential for miscommunication is provided in Box 11.1.

Many work teams do their work virtually. This may be due to globalization, increased remote work, and/or the use of interdisciplinary and inter-agency

---

Box 11.1   What Did You Mean by That?

One of the biggest challenges of asynchronous media channels, which are also those lowest in media richness, such as email, chat, and text, is the increased possibility of miscommunication. As described by media richness theory, the loss of nonverbal cues such as facial and body cues and paralinguistics (pace of speech, volume, and tone) all impact the way a message is read and interpreted. Consider the following examples of emails one might receive from a coworker:

- I heard you will not be able to complete that report by tomorrow, is that true?
- What is going on with the Lucas account?
- Can't get an answer on the budget, is no one around?

As you read each of these emails, reflect on *how* you read them. In other words, what tone of voice or inflection did you hear in your mind as you read the words? Of course, there is important context that is missing since these emails would be just one piece of a larger interaction, but the point is that even without that context, you read the words in a certain way. Taking the first bullet point – "I heard you will not be able to complete that report by tomorrow, is that true?" – think about that last part of the sentence specifically. Do you hear frustration in the sender's voice, as if they are angry at you? Or perhaps you hear it as incredulous, like the sender does not really believe you won't get it done because they know you are always dependable. The person who receives this email is going to attribute the speaker's intent, and this will impact how they respond, which may create a conflict. Whenever we receive an email (or chat or text), we should consider earlier lessons from this book including:

- *Don't assume* the other's intent (see Chapter 4 on obstacles to engaging conflict).
- *Ask questions* such as "why do you ask?" (see Chapter 5 on rules for engaging).
- Consider *acknowledging* your interdependence to focus on face saving for yourself and the sender in your response (see Chapter 6).

For Reflection and Discussion:

Discuss with a partner or small group.

1) Consider how you might interpret each of the above questions differently depending on whether the sender is your supervisor (or someone else with higher status in the organization) versus a peer. How would that impact your reply in terms of what you say but also which medium you choose to respond?
2) If you were sending one of the above messages, what might you add to help ensure the receiver interprets your meaning as you intended? In other words, what are some strategies we have developed to make *lean* media more *rich*?
3) Share an example of a time you misinterpreted an email or text that led to or escalated a conflict. What would you do now if you could have that interaction over again?
4) Discuss some ideas for when it makes more sense to call someone or schedule a face-to-face meeting (or video teleconference) instead of relying on email.

partnerships to work on solutions to a plethora of challenges, such as water and energy use and conservation, global health, and international security (to name just a few of the complex problems facing our world today). Many organizations were working remotely long before the COVID-19 pandemic sent much of the workforce home, yet there is still a lot to learn about online collaboration and informal conflict management. This section will discuss two of the challenges of virtual team collaboration: the selection of communication tools and managing virtual meetings, and tips for nurturing team member engagement and team cohesion while minimizing frustration and destructive conflict.

Selecting Virtual Collaboration Tools

Have you ever tried to schedule a large meeting via email? It is quite cumbersome to try to keep track of multiple messages to come up with an ideal date, and by the time you hear from everyone, several attendees will have accepted other meeting invitations. With today's scheduling tools, such as Doodle, When2meet, or Google Calendar, you may be wondering why anyone would ever do that . . . but we did! There was also a time when, if you were co-authoring a paper or report, you shared attachments through email. This resulted in multiple versions of the same document, difficulty keeping track of which was the most current version, and everyone storing the document in a different place (probably with a unique file-name). The good news is that there are a plethora of tools available that make group work much more efficient. The bad news is that there are so many tools to choose from. One of the major challenges interorganizational groups face is that members may be used to different technological tools, customs, and norms. Box 11.2 describes an example of how this created a challenge for one interorganizational team.

Box 11.2 Team Participation in a Proprietary Conferencing Platform

A team of about seven members was tasked with the design of a tool to predict group behavior based on social media activity. Part of the task was to test the tool for its usability among the professionals who would be the end-users of the product. The team consisted of members from a technology company, academic faculty, and representatives of the end-user group. The team lead was from the tech company, and therefore opted to use the proprietary video conferencing technology that was used for meetings on a regular basis. Information was sent to all members in advance about how to log on to the meeting. At the first meeting, several members who were not employees of the tech company received error messages when we tried to log on. We emailed the team lead and eventually received a response with more information about the username and password to use. About 10 minutes past the meeting's stated start time, we all got into the meeting. Due to the delay, we did not have time for introductions of all members and had to get into the task at hand. The primary speaker shared their screen and provided a lengthy presentation about the work they were doing on the project. Unfortunately, the speaker did not know the backgrounds of other team members and appeared frustrated when members asked a lot of questions that required the speaker to backtrack and find new ways to explain the information. At the end of the time allotted for the meeting, the group tried to figure out the purpose of the meeting, what the team's goal should be, and what they needed to do to prepare for the next meeting. Several team members left the meeting frustrated and unsure why we were there and what our role should be. When the team met the next week, members once again had difficulty logging on to the meeting. Some were successful and some were not, and there was a glitch in the screen sharing so that we could not all see the screen and we could not all see who was present in the meeting. The team lead tried to enlist help from others in the company to figure out how to solve the problem, and it took a full 45 minutes before everyone who was supposed to participate in the meeting was in the virtual space. At that point a little bit of work was done, but the team members were again frustrated and most of the discussion was about how to divide the tasks so that the team had something to show for their efforts at the next meeting. Ultimately, rather than the initial goal of working collaboratively to integrate the perspectives and ideas of all members throughout the process, the team members worked in parallel, such that the developers created the product, and it was subsequently tested by the end-user group and studied by the researchers. This division of labor defeated the original purpose of team collaboration.

For Reflection and Discussion:

Discuss with a partner or small group.

1) What are some considerations for deciding what video conferencing platform should be used by a new virtual team?
2) What are some things this team could have done to prepare for each meeting to better utilize and respect everyone's time?
3) How could different types of technology be used to nurture relationships among the various members of this team?

When leading a virtual team, one of the most important decisions is what tool to use and making sure that everyone on the team has access to the tool and knows how to use it. The most successful teams will provide training and allow team members to get some practice. When preparing for virtual collaboration, make sure everyone is on board and knows where team communication and documents are stored and how to use them, and set some ground rules so that there are shared expectations regarding everyone's role in the group and how technology will be used to support the group's work. You want to avoid the "provide and pray approach," described as *providing* a collaboration technology and *praying* something good comes of it (Weinberg et al., 2013). As further noted by Weinberg et al., "The most common barrier to success is the lack of a compelling purpose for using a collaboration tool" (p. 300).

The anecdote in Box 11.2 highlights the additional preparation and negotiation needed for online teams to be productive and successful. Based on my research on interdisciplinary and cross-sector teams (see Jameson et al., 2020), we developed several recommendations to improve collaboration and satisfaction in virtual teams. The first task is to discuss how meetings will take place. What affordances does the team need? While a proprietary video teleconference (VTC) platform might work well when team members are all from the same organization, the situation described in Box 11.2 illustrates that this works less well when there are external members on the team. Due to the COVID-19 pandemic, many people adopted platforms such as Zoom (especially in the university context) and Microsoft Teams (often used for business). Some of the affordances of Zoom include the ability to see everyone in the meeting; the ability to participate from a phone or without a camera if needed; screen sharing; the ability to participate via chat (text); the flexibility to chat with individuals, the host, or everyone in the meeting; and the availability of breakout rooms for subgroup discussions if needed. While these are all useful features, many of us have experienced meetings that were frustrating, either because the technology did not work as expected, or because not everyone knew how to use the tools effectively, or because members were unclear on the rules or expectations for participating.

So far we have only discussed tools for meetings. As described above, virtual teams also need to share, store, create, and retrieve information and documents. These tasks require a different type of technology, with examples including Google Docs, Dropbox, Microsoft Teams, and SharePoint, and enterprise social networks (such as Yammer). There are also open source tools (not specific to Apple, Google, or Microsoft, for example) specifically created to help teams with project management, such as Slack. While these tools can improve our ability to coordinate tasks, schedule meetings, and share information, many organizations make use of multiple tools, which can create confusion and inefficiencies for members trying to locate a specific document. Therefore, in addition to choosing the best meeting technology, time and space should be dedicated to training all team members on the technology, negotiating how documents will be shared, and even agreeing on naming conventions for files. The time spent discussing these details will be more than worthwhile in preventing unnecessary conflict and frustration. Some teams find it useful to develop a team charter that includes all this information in one place, such as the team goals, deliverables, and deadlines, team member names and contact information, individual contributions and goals, where and how information and documents will be stored, what software will be used to co-author documents, when and where meetings will take place, and when and where the agendas and relevant meeting information will be available (Joines & Jameson, 2020). Team leaders bear the responsibility of facilitating this communication among team members and modeling the desired online customs (Gibbs, Rozaidi, & Eisenberg, 2013). While this is true for all teams and not only those that meet virtually, virtual meetings and teams have unique challenges (many of which were noted in Box 11.2). The next section specifically describes promising practices for managing virtual meetings to improve collaboration and nurture relationships.

Managing Virtual Meetings

Most would agree that the ability to hold remote meetings via VTC is a vast improvement over the days of conference calls where it was hard to know who was in the meeting and nearly impossible to provide any turn-taking cues.[2] Many of us have become familiar with VTC platforms such as Zoom, as many face-to-face college classrooms in the United States were shifted to zoom overnight in March of 2020 due to the COVID-19 pandemic. The trial and error of that mass migration of classes and meetings to the online platform provided a lot of lessons about how to engage participants and try to replicate the features of face-to face meetings. With good meeting preparation, training on the tools, and clear communication about meeting etiquette, it is possible to hold effective meetings and create space for collaboration, and members can take advantage of the unique affordances of the technology to nurture workplace relationships in ways that are not available in more conventional meeting spaces. Three specific affordances of virtual meetings that support listening, engagement, acknowledging, building rapport, and nurturing include (i) video, (ii) shared screens and polls, and (iii) chat. While there may be occasions when not all these features can be used, because a meeting is so large and/or bandwidth limitations do not allow for them, these three main ideas can promote all the aspects of the LEARN framework even in a remote work environment and, therefore, should be considered best practices.

Video

There are several advantages the video part of VTC provides that were missing from teleconferences. The most obvious is the ability to see other team members, which makes the medium more rich, as described above. Obviously there are some limitations here, as the larger the meeting, the more difficult it is to be aware of who is in the meeting, but for a small team meeting, this absolutely provides for greater connection and the potential for team members to be more engaged because others can see them. In my experience in both the virtual classroom and group meetings, the experience is best when everyone has their camera turned on and members are truly engaged in the meeting as opposed to multitasking. Aside from access to reliable technology (having a location with strong and consistent Internet connection and a computer with a camera), the biggest limitation of virtual meetings of any kind is the ability for participants to be

---

[2] For a humorous look at what this experience feels like for many, check out "A Conference Call in Real Life" by Trip and Tyler: https://www.youtube.com/watch?v=DYu_bGbZiiQ. They have a more updated version for the VTC experience called "A Video Conference Call in Real Life": https://www.youtube.com/watch?v=JMOOG7rWTPg. Full disclosure: this video is sponsored by Zoom.

distracted by other work (i.e., checking email during the meeting) or the environment (pets, family members, someone at the front door, laundry, etc.). I would suggest that part of the ground rules agreed upon for team meetings include full engagement during the meeting time. Even in face-to-face meetings, people are guilty of checking email or doing other work due to the prevalence of having laptops, tablets, and smartphones everywhere we go, so this is worth an explicit agreement for *any* group meeting, especially where collaboration is desired. Fortunately, VTC platforms have other affordances that can help engage members. One that is related to video and the ability to see others in the virtual meeting is the use of emoticons and hand raising tools. In online teleconferences, VTCs enable participants to signal when they want to talk, either through facial cues, or by raising a literal hand in front of the camera or using the hand-raising icon. Additionally, participants can show their support for another's comment through selecting the happy face, thumbs up, or celebration emoticons that are available in platforms such as Zoom. Many VTC platforms have additional tools that meeting leaders can use to engage participants through the ability to visually share information.

Shared Screens, Polls, and Breakout Rooms
In addition to being able to see other participants through their videos, the ability of all members to look at the same material on the screen, participate in polls that share instant results, co-author documents (through virtual whiteboards or Google Docs, for example), and work in breakout rooms are additional ways VTCs can mimic face-to-face meetings. These tools are important because, when used well, team leaders can keep members engaged and encourage participation, brainstorming, and even the generation of reports and other written documents. VTC platforms such as Zoom also allow for group members to work in smaller breakout rooms, which provides an opportunity for geographically distributed team members to get to know each other, encourages increased participation and engagement, and builds team cohesiveness. Finally, I have witnessed facilitators who do an excellent job of preparing documents in advance so that, in addition to all team members looking at shared information on their screens, they can actually contribute to a whiteboard or document simultaneously.

As discussed above, however, it is important that leaders know how to use these tools effectively and that participants know how to use them as well. I will share my own virtual meeting facilitation "fail" as a simple example. In some faculty meetings when we needed to vote, we did not have a clear process in place, and some members raised their hands physically while others used the "thumbs up" icon and others used the "yes" button. Some of these icons only stay on screen for a limited time, and members would lower their hands too early. This comedy of errors could easily have been part of a Trip and Tyler satire. It was a humbling experience and, on a practical level, made it quite challenging to count the votes. A simple solution would have been to create a meeting rule for voting, such as asking everyone to use the green check mark for "yes" or the red x for "no." While this seems obvious in retrospect, it gets complicated when you are trying to run a meeting and team members do not have a shared understanding of the tools. The many possibilities provided by VTCs underscore the value of investing time to have team leaders and participants trained on the features of the VTC platform you plan to use for virtual meetings. A final feature of VTCs that I want to highlight for its ability to reinforce engagement, inclusiveness, and nurturing relationships is the chat.

Chat

The chat is one affordance of VTCs that has the potential to offer an improvement over face-to-face meetings. The chat is a space where any meeting participant can type in text, such as a question or comment. Based on the size and goals of a given virtual meeting, facilitators can control who has access to the chat. At one extreme, in meetings where leaders want to have more control, participants may not be able to use chat at all, or they may only be able to send messages to meeting facilitators or panelists (in the case of a panel presentation or workshop). At the other extreme, all participants have access to send messages to the whole group or a private message to any other individual in the group. In terms of fostering inclusiveness, the chat may be under-appreciated for its ability to engage participants who may otherwise be silent. In Chapter 2, I described several reasons why group members may not participate during meetings – they may feel intimidated by others they perceive as having greater expertise or status, for example, or they may need more time to process the conversation and reflect on what they want to say. The chat provides a space where members may feel more comfortable expressing their thoughts or ideas. In the classes I taught on Zoom during the COVID-19 pandemic, some of the most insightful student comments came from the chat. I was fortunate to have had a teaching assistant (TA) who could monitor the chat so that when a question or comment was raised while I was talking, the TA could keep track of the comments and raise them – even interrupting me at times for an especially good point – which I welcomed. It can be very tricky for meeting facilitators to pay attention to items on the agenda and participants with raised hands while managing a shared screen and the chat simultaneously. When chat questions and comments are ignored, the problem of privileging certain members and silencing others is reinforced just as in face-to-face settings. In order to take full advantage of the chat and the affordance of engagement and inclusivity, the chat should be monitored, even if a team member must be assigned to make sure everyone's contributions are acknowledged and addressed. Finally, chat offers the affordance of connection that once again separates the VTC from in-person meetings. When group members have "sidebar" conversations in a face-to-face meeting, it is typically considered disrespectful and disruptive. The chat feature enables the sidebar conversation in a way that does not disrupt the meeting and enables participants to engage in sensemaking as well as nurturing relationships. For example, it is common for me to find myself in a Zoom meeting with a colleague that I have not seen in a while, and I may send a private message to make a connection. While there is a line between connecting and multitasking (which would be distracting and the opposite of being engaged in the meeting), taking a moment to say hello is a good way to activate one's network, even suggesting a follow-up meeting at a later date. Participants may also use the chat if they missed something a speaker said or to get clarification from another group member, which keeps the larger meeting on track rather than interrupting the speaker. There are obvious advantages and limitations of the chat feature, but it is important to consider its potential value to building rapport and nurturing relationships in ways that may not exist in more traditional, face-to-face meetings.

My research on interdisciplinary teams that often involved completely virtual or hybrid meetings (in which some members were physically in the same space and others were remote) revealed several additional promising practices that helped team members have the best, most collaborative experiences. These ideas are included in Table 11.3.

Table 11.3 Tips for engaging and inclusive virtual and hybrid meetings.

Distribute agendas and important materials at least one week in advance

Build in meeting time to account for late arrivals and technical difficulties

Introduce all meeting attendees (especially if members do not already know each other)

Announce when a new participant has joined the meeting so everyone knows who is present

Presenters should pause at routine intervals for questions, clarifications, and comments

Display relevant visual content on a shared screen

Invite participants to ask questions or make comments in the chat

Assign someone to monitor the chat to raise important questions or statements that may have been missed in the spoken interaction

In hybrid meetings, those in the shared space should minimize sidebar conversations that exclude remote participants

Suggest that team members arrive early to have time for social interaction, or build social interaction into the meeting through breakout room or shared activities (depending on the size of the group)

Social Media Use in the Workplace

Thus far I have not discussed the use of social media in the workplace. In this final section of the chapter I want to discuss how organizational members can use social media to nurture relationships and support a collaborative workplace environment. This includes attention to how coworkers use social media to nurture their networks as well as how organizations might best use social media to nurture relationships with their publics, such as customers, consumers, or members. This section calls attention to how the use of social media can easily lead to conflict escalation and the need to reflect on the goals of social media posts and consider the potential impacts of posts and comments in public forums.

Nurturing Employee Relationships through Social Media

The COVID-19 lockdown that lasted about one full year in the United States created challenges of isolation as people were no longer able to interact with others in the usual spaces such as school, work, church, or activities such as sporting events. In response, we had to find alternative ways to make connections, whether through video teleconferencing, telephone, or social media. A major advantage of social media platforms is their ability to connect us with friends, family, and our professional network. In the "old days" when I spoke to students about the importance of networking, I would suggest the use of handwritten notes to thank someone for their time (after an interview, for example). I also suggested that it was good practice to clip relevant news articles or cartoons and send them to others as a way to stay "present" in their minds. These small gestures generate goodwill and nurture relationships so that we can activate our network when needed (such as when you are seeking a new job and want to reach out to someone working in your dream organization!). While some people still send the occasional handwritten thank you note (and I believe it is still appreciated), many people use email, text, or social media for communication these days. Obvious benefits include time and cost efficiencies (no need to buy special paper or find a stamp). In my opinion, this is the number one benefit of social media, especially since platforms like Facebook and LinkedIn allow you to send a private message or otherwise limit your post to a smaller group. One of the biggest risks of social media use, however, is the tendency to share information with a very diverse network at once: family, friends, neighbors, and coworkers, just to name a few. While people in our closest circles may share similar social and political views and values, this is rarely the case for everyone in our social media network. It is therefore worth a moment of reflection before making any social media post. I recognize this is another obvious statement, but all too often we see conflict arise or escalate because an employee aired a grievance or annoyance on a social media platform seen by coworkers or even a supervisor. As described in Chapter 5, this kind of *displaced dissent* may give us momentary satisfaction, but might also create ill feelings that disrupt future collaboration.

In a related example, it may be important to consider what social and political posts one wants to share. While we all have a right to our views and values, and social media can be a useful way to advocate for policy change, there is a lot of misinformation that can be spread, and we can unintentionally damage relationships with others we might need to ask for help in the future. The key point here is we should all take advantage of the ways social media platforms can be used to nurture relationships and connect with others, while doing our best to minimize the use of social media to divide and polarize. While it is outside the scope of this book, there is excellent research on how to increase social media literacy to reduce misinformation (Damasceno, 2021) and how social media can be used to invite and encourage dialogue (Kent & Taylor, 2021), even on contentious issues such as conflict between Israeli Jews and Arabs (Ron, Suleiman, & Maoz, 2020) and supporting the voices and views of Black women in the United States (Edrington, 2022). As employees and coworkers, there are more positive and productive ways to articulate our concerns, as described in Chapter 5 and throughout this book, than through social media outlets. For customers however, social media may seem like the ideal place to share our dissatisfaction as a warning or notice to others. For this reason, organizational leaders should think carefully and strategically about how they use social media, with special consideration to how it can be used to nurture organization–public relationships.

Nurturing Organization–Public Relationships through Social Media

Organizations must attend to both internal and external communication, and scholars have noted the need for consistent messaging across stakeholder groups to reinforce organizational values, such as corporate social responsibility and collaboration (Christensen & Cornelissen, 2011). Public relations scholars also emphasize the importance of organization–public relationships (Ledingham & Brunning, 1998) and call for two-way symmetrical communication as an ideal for organizations communicating with their stakeholders (Grunig & Hunt, 1984). Social media is an important location for organizational public relationship maintenance, whether for responding to customer questions and complaints (Gearhart & Maben, 2021; Weinberg, et al., 2013) or in the context of crisis management, as Amtrak recently discovered when customers engaged in escalatory comments on YouTube in response to mask and safety messages (Spradley & Spradley, 2022; see Box 11.3). However, it has been noted that organizations have remained more likely to use social media to transmit one-way messages than to take full advantage of the opportunities for two-way communication social media offer. The final section of this chapter looks at a few examples of organizations that have done

Box 11.3   Responses to Amtrak's Mask Policy[3]

In 2020 and 2021 Amtrak (the US transportation company) found itself in the midst of a political conflict among divergent publics: those who supported and those who resisted its mask mandate. Amtrak used YouTube videos to communicate their mask-requirement policy, and readers left several comments on the video(s), including those who showed appreciation for the policy, such as "thank you Amtrak ..." but more often communicating resistance of the policy, such as "Love Amtrak, Hate Masks ...Won't be taking Amtrak until they act American ..." (Spradley & Spradley, 2022, pp. 150–151). Amtrak's posting of the videos thus resulted in escalatory comments among members of the public. This case raised the question of Amtrak's role in this conflict. Organizations that get caught in the middle of a public conflict (especially one with political undertones) find themselves in a potential public relations crisis. The recommendations for organizational conflict management on social media provided by case authors Spradley and Spradley mirror many of the best practices described by public relations practitioners and the studies included in this chapter, such as:

- Respond to stakeholder concerns (this will show the organization is listening and engaging in two-way symmetrical communication).
- Anticipate the conflict, address the tensions, and emphasize the public safety message by partnering with public health and promoting health literacy (or appropriate partners and public policy, depending on the content of the conflict).
- De-escalate the conflict among stakeholders by acknowledging everyone's interests and communicating concerns for all, including those who disagree with the organization's policy.

For Reflection and Discussion:

Discuss with a partner or small group.

1) Can you think of other examples in which an organization took a stance in a social or political issue that created conflict? Discuss what the organization did and its effectiveness. How did they (or could they have) communicated with the public on social media to de-escalate any conflict that resulted?
2) Take a moment to imagine you are one of the people who watched the Amtrak video and decided to post a comment either in support of or against the mask policy. What do you think your primary goal for posting a comment would be? Is the comment targeting Amtrak and are you expecting to influence their policy? Are you expecting a response from Amtrak? Is the comment targeting other Amtrak customers to see if they provide support for your comment?

Source: De Gruyter.

---

[3] The case in this box is more fully described in Spradley, T., & Spradley, E. (2022).

especially well in connecting with consumers through social media (Weinberg, et al., 2013) and summarizes two studies that examined customer perceptions of response effectiveness based on active listening (Gearhart & Maben, 2021) and the use of humor (Shin & Larson, 2020).

Connecting with Stakeholders

Given the public nature of comments posted on social media, including organizations' Facebook pages or YouTube channels, organizations need to monitor their social media as messages can persuade others not to use their product or service and messages have the potential to be viewed by multiple audiences (Shin & Larson, 2020). As mentioned earlier, social media platforms provide a relatively easy way for organizations to engage in meaningful and authentic communication with their stakeholders. Weinberg et al. (2013) describe how Frank Eliason, of Comcast at the time, became the leader in using social media through creating the twitter handle @ComcastCares and using this to respond to specific customer questions and complaints. Of note, Eliason also made his social media posts personal through stories about his family, which humanized the organization. (You can read more about how he did this here: https://technical.ly/startups/frank-eliason-comcast/.) As Weinberg et al. explain, expressing individuality leads to engagement, trust, rapport, and relationship building that support collaboration. (Do these ideas sound familiar?) The authors further detail how the leadership of Dell Computers created an organizational culture of "collaborative community" both within the organization, where everyone understood their interdependence and desire to make a contribution, and with external stakeholders, whose insights and creativity were tapped as their feedback led to continuous improvement of Dell's products and customer service. Some of the necessary actions to reinforce collaborative community included: (i) creating a shared purpose of promoting customer loyalty (including creating metrics that were part of the employee-evaluation process), (ii) having multiple accounts on all major social media, such as Facebook, Twitter, YouTube, (iii) taking a customer-centric approach and focusing effort on providing technology-related solutions to customers, and (iv) "increasing conversations and deepening relationships with customers and employees" (p. 304) to promote engagement. One of the ideas that comes up in the Dell example multiple times is the value of using social media to listen to their customers. As discussed below, it is not enough to listen or even listen and acknowledge; the organizational response also matters.

Responding to Customer Questions and Complaints

The first point in the LEARN framework for collaborative conflict management is *Listen*, and it is no surprise that public relations scholars note that "Quality listening creates a dialogic space for understanding, engagement, and connection" (Gearhart & Maben 2021, p. 166). These authors also note that while the number of social media posts one organization receives in a day may make it impossible to engage with all of them, organizations need to show they are listening, and it is important to know what kind of response stakeholders are expecting. Gearhart and Maben conducted a study that asked this very question, specifically examining whether stakeholders expected organizational messages to communicate active-empathic listening (the kind of listening described in Chapter 3). An experimental study that asked participants to view several different types of responses to customer posts found that the highest ratings were for those responses that were active and showed empathy, such that the recipient felt that they were valued as an individual and that the relationship was valued by the organization. As suggested above, this means a canned robot or "bot" response may not provide the kind of customer engagement and nurturing that will promote goodwill among stakeholders. Qualitative responses to the question of what types of organizational social media responses were the most satisfying determined that messages should be timely, offer a solution, and make a personal connection with the stakeholder. Note that these findings are consistent with the recommendations of Weinberg et al. (2013), described above. Because social media responses are seen by viewers who were not part of the initial question or complaint, it is also important for organizational members to consider how their responses impact the organization's public image. Interesting insights on this question were generated from a study that investigated the impact of humor in social media responses (Shin & Larson, 2020).

Shin and Larson (2020) describe the goals of an organizational response as regaining customer trust, offering repair, and maintaining or restoring their image with observers of the interaction. They wanted to know how the use of humor in a social media response would impact the perception of the organization. In their research they found two types of humor: *affiliative humor* is directed at the person who posted the comment, but is either benign or benevolent, while *aggressive humor* shows little regard for the feelings of the person who made the comment. Shin and Larson found several potential advantages and disadvantages of the use of humor in response to an online complaint. Advantages include the possibility for enhancing positive affect toward the organization; reinforcing a company's image as cool, innovative, or exciting; building rapport; and it is especially appropriate if the original complaint incorporated humor. (Shin and Larson provide an example of a customer comment that a chicken sandwich tasted like it had been "beaten to death by Hulk Hogan," to which the store replied that they would "replace Mr. Hogan with the Ultimate Warrior on the production line immediately" [p. 2013].) On the other hand, risks of using humor in responses include reducing credibility and trust in the organization, reducing the perception of the sincerity of the response, offending the customer (and potentially escalating the conflict), harming relationships, and leading to avoidance of future interaction with the company. The bottom line here is that the aspects of the LEARN framework seem to apply equally to face-to-face and online communication as organizational members should communicate they are listening through direct engagement and acknowledgment of the customer's concerns as well as building rapport and nurturing the relationship. Decisions about how to respond should consider timeliness, reciprocity of tone (i.e., humor), providing a solution or repair, and making the response personal to consider the individual needs of the person who wrote the post or comment.

Chapter Summary

This chapter covered a lot of ground as the goal was to examine the variety of ways that conflict and collaboration occur online. The chapter started by discussing the *affordances* of various information and communication technologies and picked up where Chapter 10 ended by discussing several types and characteristics of ODR tools. ODR is often integrated into organizational dispute design to account for organizational conflicts that must be managed among geographically dispersed employees, and it is often the only way to manage disputes for online businesses such as Amazon or Ebay.

This chapter also introduced media richness theory as a tool to help organizational members select the most optimal communication medium for a given interaction and communication goal. This is relevant to a book on collaboration and conflict management because sometimes conflict occurs or is escalated due to miscommunication that can be attributed to the medium, such as when someone misinterprets an email or when a telephone call would be far more efficient for coordinating activities. The need for virtual collaboration has resulted in a wide variety of platforms ranging from shared calendars and documents to video teleconferencing and social media. This chapter described many ways those tools can be used, the challenges they present, and a variety of recommendations for using online tools to support the LEARN framework, both within organizations and in organizational communication with stakeholders.

Activity

Reflect on a group project you have been assigned in the past or are working on currently. This could be in a school or workplace context. Write down all the different people you needed to complete this project; consider drawing a diagram to show how the people in this group are or were connected. Add notes next to each person to indicate the best way to communicate with them. Do they respond best to emails, text, phone calls, video teleconferences? How is this different depending on the purpose of the communication (such as sharing information versus coordinating a meeting)? Based on this reflection, develop a group protocol that outlines the shared expectations for virtual communication for this group in order to complete this project. Consider laying out expectations for the following:

- The objectives of the project and what form the final product(s) will take (e.g., a report, a video, a PowerPoint presentation, a training guide, etc.)
- Where information such as articles or other resources documents will be stored
- How the group leader or facilitator will schedule meetings or other important events and how those will be communicated to the group (and whether RSVPs are required)
- Who will be responsible for facilitating meetings, preparing the agenda, monitoring the chat (if applicable), taking notes or minutes during meetings, and where the agenda and notes will be stored
- Which online medium should be used to communicate with group members in between meetings (e.g., email, instant messenger, Slack, enterprise social media, text, phone) and if the rules are different depending on the urgency or other goals of the interaction.

References

Banschick, M. R., & Banschick, J. S. (2003). Children in cyberspace. In L. Shyles (Ed.), *Deciphering cyberspace: Making the most of digital communication technology.* Thousand Oaks, CA: Sage.

Brown, P., & Levinson, S. C. (1987). *Politeness: Some universals in language usage.* Cambridge: Cambridge University Press.

Bülow, A. M., Lee, J. Y. H., & Panteli, N. (2019). Distant relations: The affordances of email in interorganizational conflict. *International Journal of Business Communication, 56*(3): 393–413. https://doi.org/10.1177/2329488416633847.

Christensen L. T., & Cornelissen, J. (2011). Bridging corporate and organizational communication: Review, development and a look to the future. *Management Communication Quarterly, 25*(3): 383–414. https://doi.org/10.1177/0893318910390194.

Daft, R. L., & Lengel, R. H. (1984). Information richness: A new approach to managerial behavior and organizational design. In L. L. Cummings & B. M. Staw (Eds.), *Research in Organizational Behavior, Vol. 6* (pp. 191–233). Homewood, IL: JAI Press.

Daft, R. L., & Lengel, R. H. (1986). Organizational information requirements, media richness and structural design. *Management Science, 32*: 554–571.

Damasceno, C. (2021). Multiliteracies for combating fake news and fostering civic engagement. *Social Media + Society*. https://doi.org/10.1177/2056305120984444.

Edrington, C. (2022). Chapter 6 can you hear me now? How #ShareTheMicNow used dialogue and collaboration to amplify the voices of black women. In J. Katz Jameson & M. Hannah (Eds.), *Contemporary trends in conflict and communication: Technology and social media* (pp. 91–108). Berlin, Boston: De Gruyter. https://doi.org/10.1515/9783110687262-007.

Gearhart, C. C., & Maben, S. K. (2021). Active and empathic listening in social media: What do stakeholders really expect? *International Journal of Listening, 35*: 166–187. https://doi.org/10.1080/10904018.2019.1602046.

Gibbs, J. L., Rozaidi, N. A., & Eisenberg, J. (2013). Overcoming the "ideology of openness": Probing the affordances of social media for organizational knowledge sharing. *Journal of Computer-Mediated Communication, 19*: 102–120. https://doi.org/10.1111/jcc4.12034.

Gibson, J. (1986). *The ecological approach to visual perception*. Hillsdale, NJ: Lawrence Erlbaum.

Greenan, K. (2022). Student engagement in the virtual classroom: Implications for overcoming conflict between instructors and students and creating collaborative virtual workspaces. In J. K. Jameson & M. Hannah (Eds.), *Contemporary trends in conflict and communication: Technology and social media* (pp. 209–222). Berlin, Boston: De Gruyter. https://doi.org/10.1515/9783110687262.

Grunig, J. E., & Hunt, T. T. (1984). *Managing public relations*. New York: Holt, Rinehart and Winston.

Harel, T. O., Jameson, J. K., & Maoz, I. (2020). The normalization of hatred: Identity, affective polarization, and dehumanization on Facebook in the context of intractable political conflict. *Social Media + Society*. https://doi.org/10.1177/2056305120913983.

Hartmann-Piraudeau, A. (2022). Surprises and new paths on the journey to developing online mediation training. In J. K. Jameson & M. Hannah (Eds.), *Contemporary trends in conflict and communication: Technology and social media* (pp. 239–248). Berlin, Boston: De Gruyter. https://doi.org/10.1515/9783110687262.

Jameson, J. K., Tyler, B., Vogel, K., & Joines, S. (Eds.). (2020). *Facilitating interdisciplinary collaboration among the intelligence community, academy, and industry*. Newcastle upon Tyne, UK: Cambridge Scholars.

Joines, S., & Jameson, J. K. (2020). Promoting collaboration. In J. K. Jameson, B. B. Tyler, K. M. Vogel, & S. M. B. Joines (Eds.), *Facilitating interdisciplinary collaboration among the intelligence community, academy, and industry* (pp. 138–172). Newcastle upon Tyne, UK: Cambridge Scholars.

Kaplan, A. M., & Haenlein, M. (2010). Users of the world, unite! The challenges and opportunities of social media. *Business Horizons, 53*(1): 59–68. https://doi.org/10.1016/j.bushor.2009.09.003.

Kent, M. L., & Taylor, M. (2021). Fostering dialogic engagement: Toward an architecture of social media for social change. *Social Media + Society*. https://doi.org/10.1177/2056305120984462.

Ledingham, J. A., & Bruning, S. D. (1998). Relationship management in public relations: Dimensions of an organization-public relationship. *Public Relations Review, 24*(1): 55–65.

Long, D., Iedema, R., & Lee, B. (2007). Corridor conversations: Clinical communication in casual spaces. In R. Iedema (Ed.), *The discourse of hospital communication: Tracing complexities in contemporary health care organizations* (pp. 182–199). Basingstoke and New York: Palgrave.

Methot, J. R., Rosado-Solomon, E., Downes, P., & Gabriel, A. S. (2021). Office chit-chat as a social ritual: The uplifting yet distracting effects of daily small talk at work. *Academy of Management Journal, 64*(5): 1445–1471. https://doi.org/10.5465/amj.2018.1474.

Moghavvemi, S. (2014). Media richness theory for social media: Research, opportunities and challenges. In A. Sulaiman & M. Muzamil Nagshbandi (Eds.), *Social media, dynamism, issues, and challenges* (pp.122–149). Bloomington, IN: Partridge.

Morgan, J. (2017). *The employee experience advantage*. Hoboken, NJ: Wiley.

Parlamis, J., Ebner, N., & Mitchell, L. D. (2016). Looking back to leap forward: The potential for e-mediation at work. In K. Bollen, M. Euwema, & L. Munduate (Eds.), *Advancing workplace mediation through integration of theory and practice, industrial relations & conflict management, Vol. 3* (pp. 233–249). Cham: Switzerland: Springer International. https://doi.org/10.1007/978-3-319-42842-0_13.

Rifkin, J. (2010). Online dispute resolution: Theory and practice of the fourth party. *Conflict Resolution Quarterly, 19*(1): 117–124. https://doi.org/10.1002/crq.3890190109.

Ron, Y., Suleiman, C., & Maoz, I. (2020). Women for peace: Promoting dialogue and peace through Facebook? *Social Media + Society*. https://doi.org/10.1177/2056305120984461.

Shin, H., & Larson, L. R. L. (2020). The bright and dark sides of humorous response to online customer complaint. *European Journal of Marketing, 54*(8): 2013–2047. https://doi.org/10.1108/EJM-08-2018-0522.

Spradley, T., & Spradley, E. (2022). Best practices for navigating escalatory messages in YouTube comments: Synthesizing conflict and crisis communication to address resistance to risk messages. In J. K. Jameson and M. Hannah (Eds.), *Contemporary trends in conflict and communication: Technology and social media* (pp. 139–166). Berlin, Boston: De Gruyter.

Treem, J. W., & Leonardi, P. M. (2012). Social media use in organizations: Exploring the affordances of visibility, editability, persistence, and association. *Communication Yearbook, 36*: 143–189. https://doi.org/10.2139/ssrn.2129853.

Weinberg, B. D., de Ruyter, K., Dellarocas, C., Buck, M., & Keeling, D. I. (2013). Destination social business: Exploring an organization's journey with social media, collaborative community and expressive individuality. *Journal of Interactive Marketing, 27*: 299–310.

Zeleznikow, J. (2022). Developing user centric intelligent online dispute resolution systems. In J. K. Jameson and M. Hannah (Eds.), *Contemporary trends in conflict and communication: Technology and social media* (pp. 259–274). Berlin, Boston: De Gruyter.

12

LEARNing to Communicate for Constructive Workplace Conflict

Do the best you can until you know better. Then when you know better, do better.
Maya Angelou (1928–2014, author and civil rights activist)

The LEARN framework I have presented in this book sounds deceptively simple. Yet the inspiration for writing a book was my own experience and observation of the many obstacles to putting effective conflict communication into practice in the workplace. I hope I have done a good job describing those obstacles while also providing practical suggestions for overcoming them. In addition to spelling out a useful set of principles: listening, engaging, acknowledging, rapport-building, and nurturing, the LEARN acronym can be used to reframe how we think about conflict. When we think about conflict as a fight, the idea of engaging the other party fills us with dread and fear. But what if we were to approach a conflict as an opportunity to learn something new? When we travel to a new place, especially one far from home, we know we are going to see new things and we are going to have to navigate new territory. We won't have our favorite restaurants and stores to fall back on, we will have to find our way through unknown streets, and we may even have to practice a new language. While the uncertainty is a little scary, it is also part of the fun and excitement of travel. Situations of workplace conflict often occur because of the unknown: we don't know why our supervisor has embraced a policy that feels unfair; we don't understand a colleague's conclusion about the best way to move forward on a project; we say something to a coworker that we did not realize was offensive. All of these situations are uncomfortable, but they also give us an opportunity to engage in conflict from a place of curiosity and a chance to learn something new. And just as Maya Angelou said, once we know better, we can do better. If we all approach conflict management from a place of learning, we will co-construct a workplace environment that is safe, engaging, and collaborative.

Communication for Constructive Workplace Conflict, First Edition. Jessica Katz Jameson.
© 2023 John Wiley & Sons, Inc. Published 2023 by John Wiley & Sons, Inc.

I'm still making it sound too easy. As a scholar and professor of conflict, I am all too aware that others expect me to be an expert on conflict. Yet when faced with that critical moment when I have had to choose whether to engage in conflict, I have often found myself paralyzed and uncertain how to proceed. I want to share three specific examples of times when I (i) failed to engage, (ii) corrected my inaction after the fact, and (iii) learned something new when I said something offensive. My hope is that by sharing these examples, I further illustrate the value of the LEARN framework and also remind you that conflict is hard for all of us. We will often "step in it" and get it wrong, yet in organizations where we will work with others over the long haul, we can follow up, get it right, and commit to doing better.

Failure to Engage

In Chapter 6, which presented the importance of acknowledging others, I described microaggressions as language that is offensive and hurtful to others, usually because it is racist, sexist, or ableist (or some other -ist that occurs when a speaker assumes the person they are speaking with shares the views, values, and experience of the dominant identity group; see Sue et al., 2007 for more on microaggressions). A microaggression is especially difficult to navigate because the speaker is often unaware of the error they are making and, for the recipient, correcting the speaker is a face-threatening act. I have had several experiences in which I heard a microaggression and I failed to say something. In one situation I was having a casual conversation with a friend, who used the word "nappy" to describe something that appeared disheveled and unpleasant. The problem here is that the use of nappy as an adjective is a reference to the hair of many people who are Black, often of African descent, and its use is derogatory. In that moment, I could not think of a face-saving way to interrupt the flow of the conversation to explain the origin of the word and prevent my friend from a future awkward interaction. That interaction was many, many years ago, yet it remains with me to this day and is a great example of how hard it can be to correct someone. If this were to happen today, I would apply the LEARN framework by acknowledging that my friend likely did not know the origin of the word and intend to offend, and I would build on the trust and rapport I have with this friend and use this as an opportunity to further nurture our relationship. Here is what I could have said when I heard the word "nappy": "Hey I'll bet you do not know this, and I feel a bit awkward bringing it up, but the word nappy actually refers to the nap of a Black person's hair, and using it as an adjective for something is offensive. I wanted to let you know since I know you would not want to offend anyone by accident in the future."

Better Late than Never

In a second example, I was witness to a homophobic joke that was said by a student in a classroom. In this situation I was the instructor and I was responsible for creating and nurturing an inclusive classroom climate where all students feel safe. It is, therefore, especially embarrassing that I did not say something to the class as soon as it happened. In this example, one student made an offensive joke and other students laughed. This was a small, cohesive summer class, and we had enjoyed good rapport to this point. I was frozen in the moment because, just as in the situation with my friend, I could not figure out how to say something without disrupting the climate of rapport we had created. After class, and throughout the night, I could not stop thinking about the joke and how it might have impacted other students in the class, whether from the LGBTQIA community or an ally (someone who is not a member of an identity group, but aligns with and supports that group). As someone who purports to be an ally myself, I was especially upset with myself and reflective of how I could correct my inaction. When I returned to class the next day, the first thing I said was that I needed to address something that happened in class the day before. I reminded everyone of the joke that was told, and said I was disappointed that students would engage in humor that was offensive and hurtful to members of any minority group. I pointed out that this was especially problematic in a college class on communication and leadership, and tried to turn the incident and my own leadership failure into a learning opportunity for all of us. In doing so, I modeled listening (I was paying attention to what students were saying in class as well as listening to myself and the emotions that were aroused), engaging (I said something directly to the class), acknowledging (I acknowledged people who could have been negatively impacted by the joke), rapport-building (I built on the trust and rapport we had created together), and nurturing (my actions nurtured the positive climate and, hopefully, repaired my relationship with anyone in the class who might have been hurt by the joke and my initial inaction). While I still wish I had said something the moment the joke was told, I was reminded in a recent diversity, equity, and inclusion workshop that it is okay if we need some time to reflect on what we want to say and how to say it – as long as we speak up.

Now I Know Better

My final example recounts a time I was volunteering to sell bagels to raise money for my congregation's Sunday school. After handing a customer his bagel I asked him to bring it back to me because I felt I had "gypped" him of cream cheese. After the man walked away, a woman who overheard us approached me when no one was nearby. She told me that she was sure I did not know this, but the term "gypped" was offensive to her because her family was Romany (a nomadic people who are believed to have originated in northern India, but live predominantly throughout central Europe). As I later confirmed from an NPR story, the word Gypsy was a common term for the Romany people (NPR, 2013). Gypped is a derivative of the word Gypsy and refers to being swindled or deceived. When I was confronted about my use of the term, I was embarrassed and my face was threatened. Yet the way the woman engaged with me followed the LEARN framework. She acknowledged that I probably did not know the origin of the word and she emphasized the desire for good rapport with me. Rather than feeling offended or becoming defensive, I thanked the woman for educating me about this so that I would not make the mistake in the future. And following Maya Angelou's words, since then I have tried to do better by removing the word "gypped" from my vocabulary. While I confess the word still slips out from time to time, I correct myself, both internally and out loud to anyone who heard me say it, as a constant reminder and to educate others not to use this word. Again, an important point here is that we will make mistakes. Our ability to be self-aware, acknowledge our mistakes, and forgive ourselves and others will help us engage in difficult conversations in constructive and collaborative ways.

Implications for Current and Future Employees, Leaders, and Third Parties

As discussed throughout this book, there are many obstacles to engaging in productive conflict management. Some managers believe that their employees should do what they say because they have power. They don't think they have the need or time to explain their decisions, yet they wonder why their employees do not like them, are not engaged, have low morale, or leave the organization. Many employees fear that asking for information or better working conditions will risk their relationships, reputation, or employment. Yet with effective and engaging communication, relationships can improve, respect can be earned, and problems can be solved. My goal in these final sections is to reinforce how the LEARN framework can be used to construct a collaborative workplace environment and why this matters to specific audiences including: (i) all organizational members; (ii) managers, supervisors, and team leaders; and (iii) senior leadership and organizational third parties.

All Organizational Members

As reviewed in Chapter 1, the communication of all organizational members constitutes, or constructs, the organization and, therefore, influences whether the prevailing communication climate is adversarial or collaborative. Every organization is also a social network and includes members who serve as critical bridge links and liaisons between and among subgroups. These liaisons are often *opinion leaders*, people who have earned respect and status from their peers and who are critical to spreading new information and ideas. These organizational members may or may not have formal positions or titles, yet they are still leaders with a strong influence on how people communicate and thus the organizational climate and culture that is constructed. The ideas in this first subsection speak to all organizational members, regardless of official status or title.

Individuals are frequently confronted with situations that create the perception of incompatible goals. The CEO announces a wage freeze that is incompatible with an employee's desire to send his or her child to private school. A supervisor wants to be more involved in an employee's work while the employee wants to be more independent. Two coworkers want to be assigned as team lead for the same new project. And so on it goes. Every day people are faced with decisions about which of these potential conflicts really matter, which should be confronted, and which might be ignored. This is the first vital decision encountered when considering whether to engage. The LEARN framework suggests that the first step is *listening* to oneself by reflecting on our emotions, assumptions, and biases that may be influencing our reaction. If upon reflection we decide not to engage the other, we should commit to that decision or we will end up ruminating on it or venting to others, which will increase, rather than decrease, our stress and threaten the workplace climate (Brett, 2014; Boren, 2014; Friedman et al., 2000).

Should we decide that a conflict should not or cannot be avoided, we should engage with a sense of inquiry and listen to understand the other party. Yet we should also prepare for engagement. Consider why this issue is so important. What is at stake, or what are the underlying interests? In the scenario that opened this book about the assistant director (AD), there was a need to complete a time-sensitive task – setting up a movie scene – in order to get the job done. There are other interests at stake in this scenario, however, as the AD wants to make a good impression on the director and other coworkers, nurture those work relationships, and be recommended for future work. These interests also provide guidance for our communication in conflict. We want to consider the other party's interests, and while we will need to ask questions to be certain, we can reflect on some of the common interests that are likely at play, such as security, belonging, and self-esteem. Through our reflective process, we can consider more carefully the other party's intention and whether we are making dispositional attributions that may be unfair. By considering situational attributions and the other party's interests, we may be able to engage the conflict with a collaborative rather than competitive or adversarial conflict style.

Some people may find this level of introspection and reflection difficult to do on their own. In such cases, there are other people one can turn to for assistance in preparing to engage. If your organization has an ombuds (described in Chapter 5), that is the ideal place to go for help and coaching from a neutral third party. In other organizations, the ideal third party may be someone in the employee relations or human resources department, a mentor, or a trusted colleague. Importantly, the third party should be someone who will listen with openness and empathy, ask good questions, and keep the conversation confidential so that the conflict does not become fodder for gossip that poisons the workplace climate.

Once parties have agreed to the time and place, the conversation must get started. There are several features of engaging communication that have been articulated throughout this book. The "A" in the LEARN acronym is for *acknowledge*. Communication that acknowledges the other party's needs, interests, arguments, and emotions is going to promote a more open and engaging climate that feels more like dialogue than a debate. Importantly, in order to acknowledge what another has said, one must be listening actively. This is a reminder that the LEARN framework of conflict communication is not linear, but cumulative, as these communication components must be happening simultaneously. Furthermore, when these features are present in most workplace communication, it will create a climate conducive to voice and participation, which should decrease the overall amount of conflict experienced. It is also important that people are listening not only to acknowledge others, but also to learn new information, especially to better understand the other's interests. As described in Chapter 2, people often listen just enough to determine how to refute the speaker and make their own next argument. When people are being attentive to interests, they demonstrate better understanding of the other and lay the groundwork for collaborative brainstorming of solutions that meet both or all parties' needs.

Active listening and acknowledgment also suggest being non-evaluative, a key feature of supportive, face-saving communication. This is the opposite of the adversarial, defensive communication that characterizes conflict interaction when motives for others' actions are assumed. The LEARN framework suggests that parties in more engaging conflict will build rapport, creating and sustaining a more collaborative interaction. Building rapport may look different depending on the organizational culture and the parties involved. In some cultures, starting with small talk such as inquiring about one's day or family is expected – to jump right into the business is considered disrespectful. Other professional or organizational cultures might have norms that keep family and work separate, in which case building rapport may be limited to communicating with a sense of inquiry and respect. The opening anecdote illustrated how the AD, Larry, built rapport with a group of people he did not know. He did this by acknowledging his needs as well as the tourists' interest in being in a Hollywood movie. He went on to build rapport by asking personal questions such as how long they had been in LA and where they were from. Such inquiry was appropriate to that context. In the research on communication among anesthesiologists and nurse anesthetists (described in Chapter 6), I found diverse strategies used to build rapport. In one hospital, doctors and nurses shared a break room, ate lunch together, and socialized together. They found that building relationships outside of work enhanced their collegiality and respect. In another hospital, the doctors and nurses did not socialize, yet they built rapport by acknowledging each other's expertise, giving deference when appropriate, and discussing any problems or disagreements in private rather than in front of patients and other medical staff. Those doctors and nurses who took the time to build rapport experienced less conflict and stress. Nurses felt respected and were given more autonomy while also feeling comfortable calling on doctors for support when needed. While the specifics of rapport-building are unique to the parties and the communication environment, it is always central to creating an environment for collaborative workplace interaction and conflict management.

This brings the discussion to *nurturing*, which must be done for individual relationships as well as the conflict environment. Conflicts are much harder to engage when there is not a positive relational history to build on. When there is little or no history, there is high uncertainty about how others will respond, and people are more likely to avoid the conflict out of fear or a sense of futility. In some cases there is a negative history, where a coworker or supervisor has not communicated in productive ways, and there is an expectation that they will not listen or will be adversarial. These are perhaps the most challenging conflict situations. As described in Chapters 5 and 6, proactive dissent strategies, reframing, inquiry, and confirming and acknowledging might be used to nurture these difficult relationships by changing the rules of engagement. In their book *Getting to Yes*, Fisher, Ury, and Patton (1991) advise that negotiators should "not deduce another's intentions based upon one's own fears" (p. 25). In other words, do not go into the situation with assumptions and attribution bias, but instead, enter the conversation with a sense of inquiry. Asking questions about the other's needs, listening to their responses, and acknowledging their interests may very well change the nature of the unfolding interaction and simultaneously nurture the relationship in a transformative way. Of course, if it always worked that way, there would be no need for this book. The point here is that one can communicate in ways that are more likely to lead to defensive and adversarial interaction or more supportive and collaborative interaction. The latter should be more effective most of the time and, even if not successful, should contribute to the nurturing of a more supportive and collaborative climate. While the LEARN framework provides guidance for engaging conflict, there will often be interpersonal or structural barriers to this kind of communication. Leaders can also pave the way for listening, engaging, acknowledging, rapport-building, and nurturing through conflict management system design and offering several face-to-face and online options to support conflict management, as described in Chapters 10 and 11.

Managers, Supervisors, and Team Leaders

It should go without saying that everything discussed in the previous section holds for managers and others in supervisory or team leader positions. However, official organizational leaders must also be aware of the added responsibility they have for setting communication expectations in the workplace. As described especially in Chapters 2 and 4, employees and group members are often reluctant to express disagreement or new ideas due to the fear of rejection, retaliation, or simply because they don't believe anyone will listen. Managers, supervisors, and team leaders are responsible for modeling open, supportive communication that will create a climate that welcomes employee voice and leads to more collaborative conflict.

Having said this, it is worth noting the challenging communication situation in which all managers and leaders operate. While in the previous section the focus was on individual employees attempting to get their own needs met or concerns expressed, those who have supervisory responsibility are accountable to multiple stakeholders. The most vivid example I can provide is in higher education, where department heads and deans are accountable to faculty, staff, and students on the one hand and scores of higher-level administrators (deans, provosts, presidents) on the other. In addition to the internal system, there are a host of external stakeholders, including the government (in public universities), board of trustees, alumni, parents, and the local community (to name a few). Managers in every organizational context experience this to some degree, although the specific cast of characters will differ. In nonprofit organizations, the executive director must serve patrons or clients while also being responsible to staff, volunteers, the board of directors, and funders. In private corporations, leaders are accountable to their employees, vendors, suppliers, clients or customers, and the board of trustees. The important point here is that understanding all parties' interests and developing solutions that will satisfy everyone's needs can be quite a monumental task for those serving in management and other supervisory roles. While there is no magic communication phrase that will solve this challenge, the LEARN framework again offers insights.

Here I focus primarily on communication between supervisors or team leaders and their direct reports or team members, since these interactions are most germane to the conflicts discussed in this book. Because the underlying theme is encouraging organizational members to productively engage conflict when possible, how leaders respond and communicate during these interactions is critical. In Chapter 5, I discussed the literature on organizational dissent, and this is a good place to reflect on how supervisors respond as the targets of upward dissent. As an administrator myself, I know it is easy to hear expressions of dissent as complaints that interrupt one's day. When employee concerns are heard in this way, the supervisors' goal is typically to make the problem go away as quickly as possible so they can get back to the "important" work they were in the middle of. Unfortunately, when supervisors respond this way, it does not send the message that the door is really "open" or that the employee's concerns are considered important.

In Chapter 4, I presented research from Morrison and Rothman (2009) that described how people in positions of higher status and power often send such signals to subordinates. While the message that complaints are unimportant or unwelcome may be sent unintentionally, it will still have a big impact on the climate that is created as employees share their experiences and expectations with coworkers. Herein lies the importance of listening. The preceding discussion of employee tendencies to avoid conflict due to fear or sense of futility should make it clear that when employees do express dissent, it is likely something that the employee feels very strongly about. Sometimes the problem that triggers the dissent is not actually the underlying interest, however, so, what to the target of dissent might sound like a small or inconsequential matter may be hiding the real issue for the employee. Supervisors must, therefore, develop the ability to listen for underlying interests. In keeping with the LEARN framework, this requires engaging with the employee by asking questions that help determine the real source of the problem. In the previous section, I discussed the issue of timing and the fact that sometimes it is best not to engage the conflict. The same holds true for supervisors. If a supervisor cannot commit themselves to listening and engaging with someone who needs to express dissent, they should postpone the conversation to another time. This may be inconsistent with the idea of an "open-door policy," but, as described above, such policies quickly become meaningless if employees repeatedly get the message that the supervisor is not listening and the door is not really open. The lesson here is to know one's own temperament and flexibility. The ideal situation may be one in which a leader can change gears rapidly and set one task aside to listen to and really engage with an employee's concerns. But when this is not possible, it is better for everyone to explicitly communicate this and set up an appropriate place and time for the conversation. Similarly, if a supervisor decides to listen to an employee's concerns and that employee is emotionally charged or cannot follow acceptable rules of engagement, it is okay to communicate that the conversation should be postponed until a time when the conversation can be more engaging. The important message to employees is that their concerns are important and the supervisor wants to have a constructive conversation about them.

This is of course related to the third part of the LEARN framework, *acknowledge*. If supervisors acknowledge their employees' need to share their concerns and commit to a time for discussion, they cannot be accused of not being open. Along with acknowledging, however, supervisors are responsible for providing information that is unknown to employees and helping them understand why certain policies or practices are in place. Employees are often unaware of larger, systemic constraints such as budgets, precedent-setting decisions, or demands coming from senior leadership. As described in the section on supportive communication, providing such explanations communicates that the employee is respected and important and is being treated as an equal. In the haste to end a conversation quickly and move on to the next task at hand, supervisors may inadvertently overlook the fact that providing information has the potential to transform a conflict situation. Supportive communication that treats employees as valuable members of the team both acknowledges and builds rapport with employees. That kind of communication should help construct a climate that is open and engaging.

Finally, providing explanations and new information helps to balance multiple stakeholder needs by making those interests clear to everyone involved. Sometimes helping employees understand the complexity of the system allows them to see the bigger picture and view their own concerns differently. Relationships among managers and employees should be nurtured through constant communication and interaction. This is not micromanaging but keeping channels of communication open to make it easier for employees to approach a supervisor when needed. The difference between a supervisor who nurtures an open climate and good rapport with employees and one who does not is parallel to the distinction between "management by walking around" and "management by exception." Management by exception is defined as only providing feedback when an employee does something wrong. When employees receive only negative feedback, it puts a strain on the relationship with the supervisor, making it harder to approach them in times of dissent. Given the multiple tasks managers juggle, it may be easy to see how management by exception occurs. If everything is going along smoothly, there is little need to say anything, and managers can tend to other tasks. In management by walking around, however, managers build rapport through constant communication with employees. They check in, compliment employees on a job well done, and, perhaps most relevant here, troubleshoot problems as they arise, before they turn into conflicts. The extra effort put into nurturing ongoing relationships and the overall climate thus creates an atmosphere in which employees are more likely to resolve problems early, approach their supervisor before conflicts escalate, and perceive less workplace conflict and stress.

This section would not be complete without talking about one of the most challenging features of supervisor communication: employee evaluation. Providing feedback to employees about their performance is one of the most important roles of the supervisor, yet it is not often done very well (Aguinis, Gottfredson, & Joo, 2012). It is easy to understand why this is, as evaluation is an inherently face-threatening communication act. Employees want to be seen as valuable, knowledgeable, and capable organizational members who can be empowered to act independently; yet they also want to be seen as part of the team. Performance evaluation feedback should acknowledge the strengths of the employee, while making expectations clear and identifying areas of needed improvement.

When negative feedback is delivered, it should be tied to specific knowledge and skills that can be developed; in this way the focus is on employee learning rather than a shortcoming of the individual (or dispositional attribution). Aguinis et al. also point out that the supervisor should help employees understand the impact of their performance for the larger organization, which highlights interdependence and nurtures relationships among organizational members. I would argue that one of the biggest challenges of performance evaluations is that they often only occur once a year. When conversations about performance are ongoing, they become part of the routine and are less likely to foster a defensive climate. While the discomfort associated with providing feedback can compel supervisors to avoid these interactions, this is another perfect example of how supervisors can take the advice in this book and use the LEARN framework to construct a constructive workplace conflict environment.

The LEARN framework also has implications for team leaders. While many of the ideas described so far are relevant, team leaders may not be official supervisors, and they may not be the targets of employee dissent nor be responsible for annual performance feedback. Nonetheless, team leaders are ultimately responsible for the communication climate of their team, and their leadership will set the tone for whether the team is more exclusive and adversarial or more inclusive and collaborative.

In Chapter 7, I discussed common obstacles to effective communication in groups. Groups include multiple members who each have individual needs, goals, and interests, although ideally the shared goal is clear and everyone is committed to it. Teams, therefore, struggle with the need to balance autonomy and connection. While high-performing teams have been found to gather information and ideas from heterogeneous members and external sources, this is only effective if those teams actually share information and are accepting and supportive of diversity (Ayub & Jehn, 2014). This is a tricky balancing act as groups benefit from diverse ideas but tend to privilege shared information and put pressure on those who think differently to conform. In order to overcome common group dynamics, there needs to be extra attention to listening, engaging, and acknowledging. Here again, the group leader is responsible for setting the expectation, which may involve resisting the urge to push the group through an agenda or move too quickly to solutions and implementation of the task.

Transcripts of board meeting interaction illuminate features of communication that were conducive to member engagement and generating new ideas. The major implications of effective group communication are consistent with the LEARN framework developed here and include:

• Members acknowledge new information or perspectives and engage in collective sensemaking, often through storytelling (listening, engaging, and acknowledging).

- Disagreement is characterized by supportive communication that is respectful and acknowledges others' expertise (acknowledging, rapport, and nurturing).
- Communication is inclusive of diverse perspectives, as shown through framing and reframing (acknowledging).
- Communication includes discussion of information from sources external to the group members (listening).
- Substantial communication is focused on understanding the problem or issue under discussion (listening, engaging).
- Communication focuses on inquiry and asking open questions, including a commitment to getting answers from outside the group (listening, engaging, acknowledging).

While none of these ideas may be surprising, it is important to note that implementing these norms requires balancing group tensions, such as devoting time to disagreement and forming connections and to brainstorming as well as decision making. Competing tensions will always create the potential for conflict, which effective teams will embrace and engage. Team leaders must be aware of and manage these tensions by modeling communication that fosters collaboration and constructive conflict management.

Senior Leadership and Organizational Third Parties

Once again, everything that has been discussed in previous sections is relevant for senior organizational leaders and organizational third parties. Yet senior leadership includes organizational members who are most responsible for creating or approving the organizational systems and policies that provide venues for employee dissent or conflict management. This section specifically summarizes implications of the LEARN framework for the design of effective conflict management systems.

Common dispute resolution practices such as grievance and appeals processes have limited utility for helping employees effectively engage conflict. The main shortcomings identified in my research include:

- Limited range of conflicts that can be addressed. Many workplace conflicts, such as those between coworkers, do not fall into the category of "grievance" and, thus, are outside the scope of these programs.
- Limited availability of conflict experts. If employees do not perceive that there is anyone knowledgeable who can help them in human resources or employee relations, they are most likely to vent to coworkers or engage in displaced (external) dissent.
- Limited distribution of power between employee relations officers and management. The problem here is twofold: concerns about confidentiality and about

organizational justice. When employee relations is perceived as operating on behalf of the organization, employees will not trust the process and are much more likely to avoid directly engaging the conflict.

One of the conclusions of my research and others is that employees are more likely to go to a trusted adviser than a formal conflict process. Yet when mediation programs exist, employees who have used them report they are very satisfied with the process and outcome. Mediation falls somewhere in between the use of an informal adviser and a formal grievance process, and while I am a big proponent of its benefits, it also has its limitations. Specifically, while mediation can help disputing parties engage in perspective-taking, learn more about each other, and construct mutually beneficial agreements, it falls short of implementing systemic change. For example, if two parties go to mediation regarding a charge of inappropriate behavior, a mediated agreement does not prevent the behavior from happening again with another employee or in another part of the organization. Put simply, the confidentiality and privacy that help make mediation effective also limit its ability to set a precedent for future organizational expectations. The addition of an ombuds, described in Chapter 5, provides a process for identifying systemic conflicts, such as those rooted in issues of diversity, that need to be addressed (Donnellon & Kolb, 1994; Gadlin, 2000).

Chapter 5 presented ideas from my focus group participants about characteristics of organizations and human resources departments that handled conflict well. The most important features included:

- Making sure third parties have skills in conflict management
- Investigating claims but also bringing parties together to problem solve whenever possible
- Keeping employee information confidential
- Providing an impartial third party that is separate from senior management.

This last point is the most challenging, given that in any organization third parties are ultimately accountable to senior leaders. One way organizations can manage this is by hiring external third parties, whether that means mediators and arbitrators or even contracting with external agencies to provide ombuds services. Whether the ombuds' office is internal or external, measures can be taken to demonstrate limited influence of senior management and the office. This can include physically separating the ombuds' office from senior management to keep visitors' identities anonymous and not having ombuds and senior officials eating lunch together. The ombuds plays an important systems role in providing feedback to senior leaders. This has the organizational benefit of preventing or limiting legal problems, such as discrimination or harassment, and simultaneously protects employees from a hostile work environment by recognizing conflict trends.

Depending on the resources allocated to the program, ombuds' offices have the advantage of being able to offer multiple conflict-management options. At a minimum, the ombuds can serve in an advisory role, listening to the employee's concerns and indicating whether they have a grievance, a legal case, or a dispute that would be appropriate for mediation. In the ideal scenario, the ombuds' office may be able to offer conflict coaching or more specific advice to help the employee resolve this and future conflicts on their own. There are differences of opinion regarding the level to which the ombuds should investigate complaints and provide official recommendations or decisions (Gadlin, 2000). In the most comprehensive conflict management system, one might expect an ombuds' office to offer employees options including advice, coaching, mediation, arbitration, group facilitation, and investigation in response to a formal grievance. Such a system might include training employees as mediators or contracting with third parties, as described above. Having a comprehensive conflict management system has several benefits for the organization and its employees.

- It sends an important symbolic message about the organization's commitment to ensuring employee voice, procedural justice, and a collaborative climate; in short, it shows that the senior leaders want to *listen* to employee concerns.
- It provides an appropriate and sanctioned venue for employees to *engage* relational or interpersonal conflicts with coworkers that would not be eligible for typical grievance procedures.
- It *acknowledges* the needs of employees so they have a place to go for assistance rather than engaging in lateral and displaced dissent.
- It provides a venue for building *rapport* between a disgruntled or unhappy employee and an organizational representative.
- It *nurtures* an open and supportive climate by addressing employee concerns and documenting recurring problems that need to be taken care of at a systems level to prevent recurrence.

Not only does having a conflict management system send an important symbolic message, having third parties available to help employees manage their conflicts can institutionalize constructive conflict management by diffusing the message and modeling the LEARN principles for employees, who can transfer these lessons into their future communication. However, the benefits of creating any conflict management system will only accrue to the extent that third parties support engaging conflict. During my focus group interviews, I heard several stories of third-party actions that discouraged future participation. A female manager described her experience when invited to participate in mediation with one of her direct reports. The mediator (an employee relations officer) asked the direct report to explain her concerns first, and as the supervisor described it, she sat quietly and listened to the charges against her. When it was the manager's turn, the mediator looked at her and said, "How do you defend yourself?" The manager was shocked that the mediator had accepted the employee's version of events and violated the expectation of neutrality and dialogue. The manager indicated she would never participate in mediation again, and she warned her peers not to participate either. This is an unfortunate example of how an organization might sabotage its own efforts despite the best intentions. One story like this will prevent people from using the program and resources will have been wasted. It is imperative that those who are in third-party roles have the skills to support and nurture a collaborative, engaging conflict climate.

Chapters 5 and 6 emphasized communication tools and techniques that third parties, mainly mediators, use to help parties move from adversarial to collaborative communication. There are implications from this research for organizational members who act as informal or formal third parties. Below is a review of how the LEARN framework applies to third-party communication.

Listen

This is the most important function of third parties, regardless of whether they are acting as an ombuds, adviser, mentor, coach, or mediator. Third parties should be listening with a non-evaluative posture to understand the underlying issues and interests. The third party's role is to ask questions to help themselves and the employee understand the problem. Asking the right questions can help the disputant explore perceptions of the other, identify attributions and assumptions, and generate options for engaging in productive conflict with the other party. If the third party is working with both disputants (as in mediation), they play an important role in helping the parties listen to each other without evaluation. This often involves reframing what one party says to remove any judgment of the other party. For example, if a disputant in mediation says, "She is micromanaging and is always finding fault with my work," the supervisor's immediate reaction will be defensiveness. Yet the mediator might paraphrase by saying, "It sounds like you get frustrated when you perceive she is checking up on you because you want to feel trusted." This statement removes the attack on the supervisor, making it easier for the supervisor to hear and more difficult to disagree with since most people want to be trusted. The ability to reframe in this way requires careful listening and ability to hear what lies beneath the words being said, that is, the underlying emotion and interests.

Engage

The third party needs to model engaging communication. This is done by listening, asking questions, and demonstrating authentic concern for the others involved. Remaining neutral and recognizing the emotions disputants are experiencing is vital here, as is being self-aware, so that the third party can protect themselves from emotional contagion or absorbing the emotions disputants are feeling. The third party's role may also be to empower parties to engage directly with each other by giving them good communication tools or referring the parties to a third-party facilitator or mediator.

Acknowledge

Third parties should acknowledge the interests and concerns of parties who come to them for help. This does not mean they agree with them, and it is possible that the third party's line of inquiry will help employees recognize that they overreacted to a coworker, misinterpreted a company policy, or attributed negative intent to benign supervisor communication. While a third party is less helpful when they overly empathize with or emotionally support the person venting, acknowledging recognizes the other has been hurt or angered in some way and helps them engage in perspective-taking and reframing. In the case of mediation, mediators are most likely to help parties achieve transformation when they foster interaction in which parties acknowledge each other's interests and provide recognition.

Rapport (building)

It probably goes without saying at this point that a third party must develop good rapport with parties. As described earlier, if a third party is not listening, is judgmental, or does not demonstrate concern for the employee seeking assistance, word will travel quickly and employees will not make use of the third-party process. Asking questions, communicating about the issues rather than characteristics of the individual, and attending to the emotions and fears of the employee will build trust in the third party and the conflict management process that will encourage employees to continue to engage. It may also be the job of the third party to help disputants build rapport with each other. By the time parties get to mediation, they have typically been involved in adversarial and defensive interaction. As described in Chapters 4 and 5, these patterns can be hard to overcome or alter. In my research, specific mediator strategies that moved parties from adversarial to collaborative communication included:

- Non-evaluative listening
- Reframing attacks on other as statements of interests and new information
- Identifying and validating emotions of all parties
- Encouraging emotional perspective-taking
- Encouraging disputant statements of acknowledgment for the other.

When mediators engaged in these activities rather than focusing only on the problem and providing possible solutions, parties actively engaged, learned more about each other, and often provided statements of apology and recognition that led to conflict transformation and restored relationships.

Nurture

Organizational members who act as third parties play a critical role as ambassadors who nurture an environment that reduces the sense of fear and futility that often discourages employee confidence. Third parties who follow the LEARN principles described here act as opinion leaders whose communication constitutes an organization that develops alternative norms for conflict management that challenge ingrained processes, fosters collaborative conflict management, and, in the words of Rummel (1976; see Chapter 1), changes the structure of expectations. Effective third-party practices will thus nurture an open-voice climate and change the way organizational members think and talk about conflict. The way people communicate about conflict both enables and constrains the options they believe are available for engaging conflict and thus creates and reinforces either a collaborative or an adversarial conflict environment.

Concluding Thoughts

Conflict is an inherent and necessary part of organizational life, but the ways in which it is talked about by individuals and portrayed in the media construct it as adversarial, uncomfortable, and unpleasant. Throughout this book I have provided theoretical and empirical support for an alternative view of conflict – one that is characterized by collaboration and mutual respect, openness, and engaging interaction. Hundreds of books and articles published over at least the past 50 years have made a similar argument, and many conclude with tips for addressing conflict in more productive ways through effective communication. Yet people often find it difficult to put these ideas into practice because of their fear of the power structures or sense that their concerns and ideas will not be seriously heard or considered. The contribution of this book is its synthesis of diverse bodies of conflict studies literature and a 25-year research program to demonstrate the construction of conflict and how organizational members simultaneously reinforce and challenge those assumptions through everyday communication and interaction. Understanding these possibilities for change presents a vision, using the LEARN framework, for how organizational members can construct a climate that is more open and inviting, allowing people to engage conflict in ways that are mutually beneficial and possibly transformational for relationships, groups, and organizations.

This book parallels other calls for increased engagement in areas such as business, healthcare, nonprofit governance, public policy, and academic research. As such, it is my hope that the ideas contributed here will be meaningful to organizational members and leaders across institutions and inspire individuals to take an active role in transforming relationships, routines, and results by LEARNing to create constructive organizational and workplace environments.

References

Aguinis, H., Gottfredson, R. K., & Joo, H. (2012). Delivering effective performance feedback: The strengths-based approach. *Business Horizons, 55*(2): 105–111. https://doi.org/10.1016/j.bushor.2011.10.004.

Ayub, N., & Jehn, K. (2014). When diversity helps performance: Effects of diversity on conflict and performance in workgroups. *International Journal of Conflict Management, 25*(2): 189–212. https://doi.org/10.1108/IJCMA-04-2013-0023.

Boren, J. P. (2014). The relationships between co-rumination, social support, stress, and burnout among working adults. *Management Communication Quarterly, 28*(1): 3–25. https://doi.org/10.1177/0893318913509283.

Brett, J. M. (2014, June). When and how to let a conflict go. *Harvard Business Review Blog Network*. Retrieved January 3, 2023, from http://blogs.hbr.org/2014/06/when-and-how-to-let-a-conflict-go/

Donnellon, A., & Kolb, D. M. (1994). Constructive for whom? The fate of diversity disputes in organizations. *Journal of Social Issues, 50*(1): 139–155.

Fisher, R., Ury, W., & Patton, B. (1991). *Getting to yes: Negotiating agreement without giving in* (2nd ed.). New York: Penguin Books.

Friedman, R. A., Tidd, S. A., Currall, S. C., & Tsai, J. C. (2000). What goes around comes around: The impact of personal conflict style on work conflict and stress. *The International Journal of Conflict Management, 11*: 32–55. https://doi.org/10.1108/eb022834.

Gadlin, H. (2000). The ombudsmen: What's in a name? *Negotiation Journal, 16*(1): 37–48. https://doi.org/10.1111/j.1571-9979.2000.tb00201.x.

Morrison, E. W., & Rothman, N. B. (2009). Silence and the dynamics of power. In J. Greenberg & M. S. Edwards (Eds.), *Voice and silence in organizations* (pp. 111–133). Bingley, UK: Emerald Group Publishing.

NPR. (2013, December 30). Why being gypped hurts the Roma more than it hurts you. Retrieved January 3, 2023, from http://www.npr.org/blogs/codeswitch/2013/12/30/242429836/why-being-gypped-hurts-the-roma-more-than-it-hurts-you

Rummel, R. J. (1976). *Understanding conflict and war, Volume 2: The conflict helix.* New York: John Wiley and Sons.

Sue, D. W., Capodilupo, C. M., Torino, G. C., Bucceri, J. M., Holder, A. M. B., Nadal, K. L., & Esquilin, M. (2007). Racial microaggressions in everyday life: Implications for clinical practice. *American Psychologist, 62*(4): 271–286. https://doi.org/10.1037/0003-066X.62.4.271.

Index

Page numbers in *italics* refer to Figures
Page numbers in **bold** refer to Tables
Page numbers in ***bold italics*** refer to Boxes

Communication for Constructive Workplace Conflict, First Edition. Jessica Katz Jameson.
© 2023 John Wiley & Sons, Inc. Published 2023 by John Wiley & Sons, Inc.